GIS professionals from a diversity of disciplines, as well as GIS educators and students, created the selections in *Esri Map Book Volume 32*. These outstanding maps demonstrate the broad reach of GIS in meeting significant global challenges and issues such as climate change, food production, loss of biodiversity, natural disasters, and civic engagement. Many of these maps are part of intuitive, interactive, and engaging apps that help organizations integrate their data and streamline their processes.

Esri is committed to supporting GIS practitioners with useful technology that expands their capabilities. More and more users rely on shared data and present their work through captivating story maps and 3D imagery. Maps and apps in this book illustrate how geospatial technology has evolved into a complete Web GIS platform that offers real-time data analysis and mobile device accessibility.

We are also committed to K–12 GIS education, and I am delighted that this book includes maps by high school students addressing environmental issues. I congratulate all the *Map Book* contributors whose heroic work is about planning, designing, and creating a more sustainable future for a smarter world.

Warm regards,

Jack Dangermond

A LETTER FROM JACK DANGERMOND

CONTENTS

BUSINESS

4 Goodwill Retail Store Expansion Analysis

6 The 3D View of Land Prices

8 New Location Feasibility Study for the Columbus, Ohio, Area

CARTOGRAPHY

10 Surficial Geology of Morris County, Kansas

12 Swiss National Map 1:10,000

14 Horizontal Hachures Map of Diamond Peak, Oregon

16 Colorado State, Regional, and Local Maps

18 Hydrographic Mapping of the Matanuska-Susitna Basin in South Central Alaska

20 Red Relief Image Map of Mount Usu Volcano

22 Visualization Tool: Scenario Planning Enhanced with 3D GIS

24 Global Tree Density

26 Lake Whatcom Watershed

28 Solar Potential in Kenton County

CONSERVATION AND SUSTAINABLE DEVELOPMENT

30 Multicriteria Evaluation to Determine Forest Bird Habitat during Spring Migration

32 Sandpoint Greenprint Priorities

34 Creating a Conservation Blueprint for Cuba

36 Natura 2000 at Iroise Marine Natural Park

EDUCATION

38 University of Minnesota Twin Cities Interactive Campus Map

40 Creating Safe Routes to School with Survey123

42 University of Maryland Facilities Management

EDUCATION: THE GEOSPATIAL SEMESTER

44 Rerouting the Iditarod

46 Risk Assessment of Climate-Induced Sea Level Rise in Virginia Beach by 2100

48 The Effects of Deforestation on the Amazon Rain Forest

ENVIRONMENTAL MANAGEMENT

50 Russian River Salmon and Steelhead Monitoring Map

52 The Environmental Burden Index

54 Marine Munitions Survey

GOVERNMENT-LAW ENFORCEMENT

56 Las Vegas Metropolitan Police Disorder Calls

GOVERNMENT-PUBLIC SAFETY

58 City of Phoenix Enhanced Flood Risk Analysis

60 Tsunami Vulnerability: Crescent City, California

62 Bike Aware

64 Landslide Susceptibility and Element at Risk Assessment

66 First Creek, Wolverine, and Chelan Complex Wildfire Map

68 Current Weather and Forecasts Web App

70 Arlington Expressway Mobility Corridor

72 Sidewalk Hazard Data Collection in City of West Jordan

74 Building Data for Climate Change Adaptation

GOVERNMENT-STATE AND LOCAL

76 GIS at the Office of the Assessor

78 St. Johns County Residential Building Permits

80 Tree Canopy Coverage and Change Detection for the City of Avondale Estates

82 Oxnard Zoning Map

84 Island of Maui, Hawai'i, Parcel Value

86 Automation of Lithuanian Geodata

88 European Union Referendum Results (Brexit)

HEALTH AND HUMAN SERVICES

90 North Carolina Low Birth Weight Analysis

92 County Performance Outcomes by Mental Health Provider Agencies

94 Built Environment and Asthma in Southern California

96 Twin Cities Urban Heat Islands and Social Vulnerability

98 Where Did Our Consumers Go for Vocational Rehabilitation Services?

100 Health Insurance Coverage

102 Measuring Area-Based Vulnerability to Gambling-Related Harm

HISTORICAL AND CULTURAL

104 Geostatistical Analysis, Kriging, and Weighted Statistical Modeling for Archaeological Sensitivity

HUMANITARIAN AFFAIRS

106 UNICEF: Unless We Act Now

NATURAL RESOURCES–AGRICULTURE

108 Crop Migration and Change for Corn, Soybeans, and Spring Wheat

110 Assessment of a Killer Freeze on Winter Corn in Mexico

NATURAL RESOURCES–FORESTRY

112 Hoover Wilderness Map

NATURAL RESOURCES–MINING AND EARTH SCIENCES

114 Displaying Electronic Navigational Chart Data in the MACHC

116 Using GIS for Hydrotechnical Assessment of Riverine Dynamics and Floodplain Hazards

118 Environmental Sampling at Palmer Station, Antarctica

120 2016 Kumamoto Earthquake: Measuring Uplift and Depression Using Synthetic Aperture Radar

NATURAL RESOURCES–PETROLEUM

122 10-Year Posting Trend for Petroleum and Natural Gas Rights in Northern British Columbia

NATURAL RESOURCES–WATER

124 Significant Sand Resource Areas in State and Federal Waters Offshore Monmouth County

PLANNING AND ENGINEERING

126 City of West Linn Street Tree Map

128 Overhead to Underground: A 3-0 GIS Utility Relocation Rendering

130 Climate-Smart Cities: New York City

132 Multiple Products, One Solution: Ancient Seas to Modem Charts

134 Air Operations Planning Map Series

136 3D Building Massing Model for New York City

138 LASAN: Protecting Public Health and the Environment

140 City of Scottsdale Hydrant Map

142 ADWEA Executive Dashboard

144 Sound Transit 3 Package and Climate Change

146 Sino-Singapore Tianjin Eco-City

148 Prague Institute of Planning and Development Maps

TELECOMMUNICATION

150 COVAGE Networks Maps

TOURISM AND RECREATION

152 Oregon and Washington Coast Large Print Map

154 Columbus Metro Bike Map

156 Desolation Wilderness Trip Planning

158 Wrangell Forest Visitor Map

160 City of Bellingham Bike Map

162 Palestine Tourist City Maps

TRANSPORTATION

164 Visualization of Origin-Destination Flow

166 Roads of Texas Basemap

168 Aviation in the United States

170 GIS-Based Investment Management Systems

172 VTrans Bicycle Corridor Priority

174 San Francisco International Airport Basemap

UTILITIES–ELECTRIC AND GAS

176 Digitized Power Networks and the Road Ahead

178 Project NOKOGI: A New Conception of GIS

UTILITIES–WATER AND WASTEWATER

180 Modeling Overland Flow in a Landscape with Forest Roads

182 El Segundo Scalable Water Atlas Project

184 Using GIS to Assist Sewer Authority Infrastructure Management

186 Major Water, Sewer, and Reclaim Water Facilities for St. Johns County Utilities

188 Wellhead Protection in Mesa

190 Joint Outfall System Sewer Analysis

Goodwill Retail Store Expansion Analysis

Austin Community College
Austin, Texas, USA
By Gillian Roos

Goodwill Industries is an international nonprofit organization that provides education, job training, and placement services for individuals facing employment challenges. However, Goodwill is most well-known for operating a large network of thrift stores, which also hold 503(c)(3) status. Over thirty stores are already open in Central Texas, but as population increases, so will demand.

This map was developed with a dual purpose: first, it shows the ideal blend of residential population demographics that create a high-performing Goodwill Store. Second, it exhibits where these demographics and rising populations coincide, thereby predicting potential sites for new retail locations.

Contacts
Sally Holl
sally.holl@austincc.edu

Sean Moran
smoran@austincc.edu

Software
ArcGIS® for Desktop 10.0

Data Sources
Goodwill Industries, Capital Area Council of Governments, Esri, Capital Area Metropolitan Planning Organization

Courtesy of Austin Community College.

Up and Coming Families and Midland Crowd: An affluent, family-oriented group creates a strong donor base, while the DIY, self-sufficient Midlanders make up the buyer population.

Young and Restless, Enterprising Professionals, Aspiring Young Families, Milk and Cookies, Exurbanites, Prosperous Empty Nesters: The one-mile radius surrounding the proposed Round Rock store provides a diverse client base. The Young and Restless are always on the move, buying and donating goods as they go, Aspiring Young Families buy used goods for children, while the Mik and Cookies families donate items as their children outgrow them, Wealthy and active, the Exurbanites and Prosperous Empty Nesters cycle through household goods as they improve their homes. Lastly, the Enterprising Professionals often show up in the one-mile radius of top-performing stores, proving to be strong donors.

Enterprising Professionals, Aspiring Young Families, Milk and Cookies: with demographics similar to the area proposed for the Round Rock store, the North Austin location has the same potential for success.

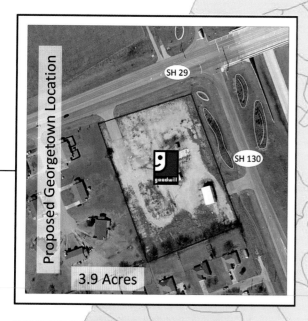

Proposed Georgetown Location

SH 29

SH 130

3.9 Acres

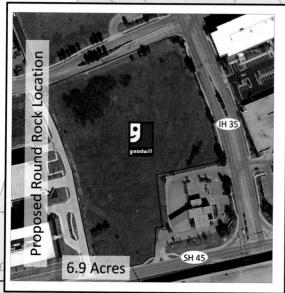

Proposed Round Rock Location

IH 35

SH 45

6.9 Acres

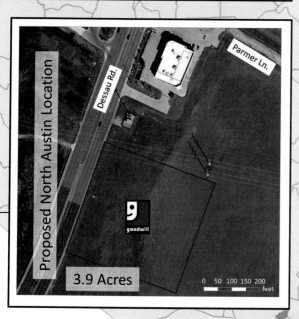

Proposed North Austin Location

Dessau Rd.

Parmer Ln.

3.9 Acres

0 50 100 150 200
feet

I-35

**2035 Population
Persons/Acre**

- 0 - 2
- 3 - 5
- 6 - 10
- 11 - 20
- 21 - 90

Proposed Store
Location

Existing Store
Location

Top Performing
Store

5

The 3D View of Land Prices

Kokusai Kogyo Co., Ltd.
Fuchu-shi, Japan
By Saya Ota, Shinichi Homma, Sakae Mukoyama, and
Yutaka Matsubayashi

This map is a shaded relief image of land prices around Tokyo. In Japan, the Ministry of Land, Infrastructure, Transport, and Tourism publishes market values per square meter of standard sites on January 1 every year on the basis of the real estate appraisal value.

ELSAMAP is a map representation method that uses lidar data to show the detailed terrain. ELSAMAP is created from digital elevation data by the transparent combination of a HSV (hue, saturation, and value) calculated from elevation and a grayscale value calculated from hillshade. It is possible to get an easier and intuitive representation of terrain by the value and range of colors indicating the altitude and slope that can be adjusted in accordance with the terrain to be represented.

This map uses the data of land prices instead of elevation value and helps visually capture the determining factor of land prices. For this reason, maps such as these have many uses including real estate appraisal, risk assessment of assets by the comparison of simulation results of earthquake disasters, and reference information for investors.

Contact
Saya Ota
saya_ota@kk-grp.jp

Software
ArcGIS for Desktop 10.2.2

Data Source
Japan Ministry of Land, Infrastructure, Transport, and Tourism

Courtesy of Kokusai Kogyo Co., Ltd.

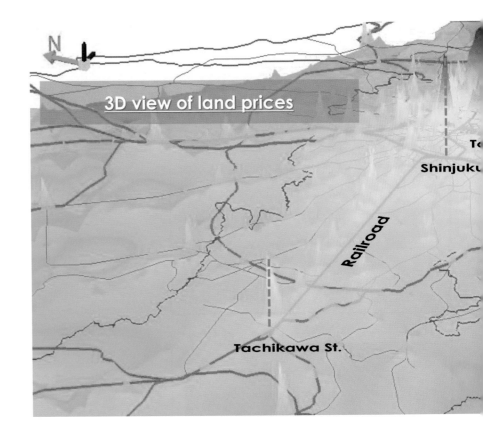

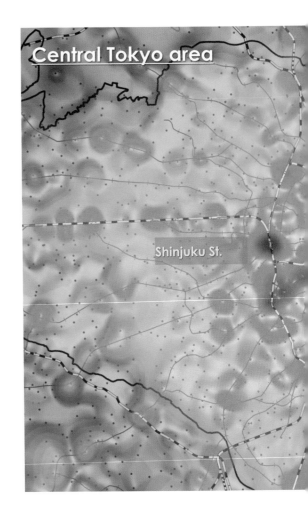

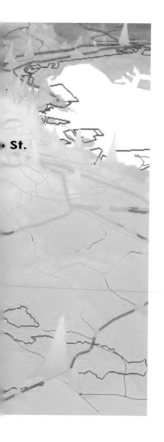

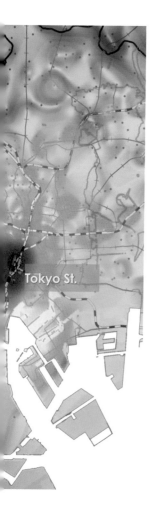

Land prices in Tokyo area

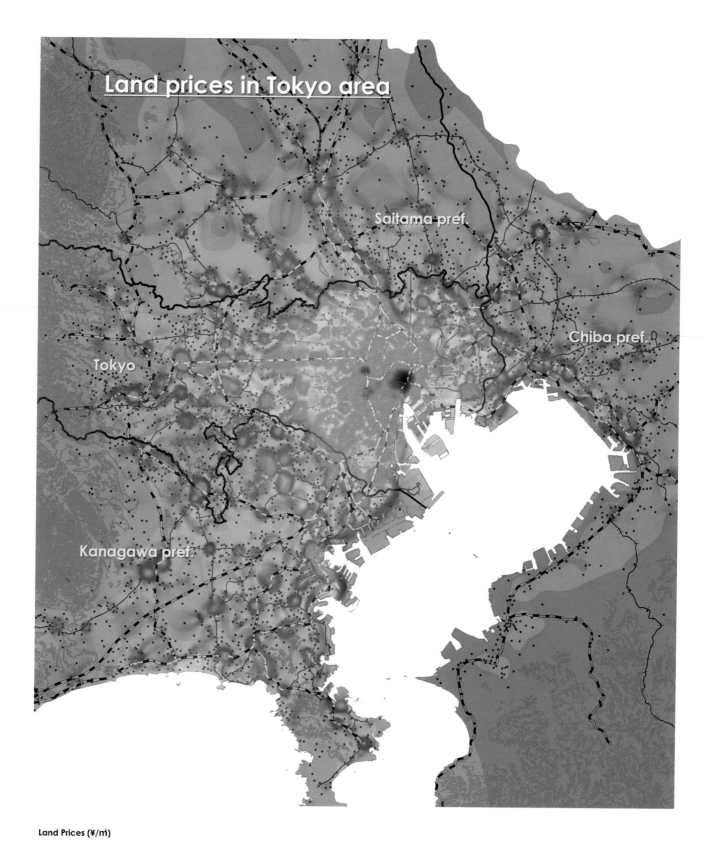

Saitama pref.

Chiba pref.

Tokyo

Kanagawa pref.

St.

Tokyo St.

Land Prices (¥/m̓)

High: 22,570,000

Low: 8,000

Survey points of land prices

———— Contour (100m)

━━━ Boundary of prefecture

┼┼┼┼ Private Railroad

▬ ▪ ▬ ▪ Public Railroad

New Location Feasibility Study for the Columbus, Ohio, Area

GeoTech Center
Gaston, Oregon, USA
By Mike Holscher

This map uses customer data to propose a new store location for Flyers Pizza and Subs in Columbus, Ohio. Customer data spanning three years was imported into ArcGIS software. Heat maps were produced from the point data to show the distribution of a store's customers (using frequency and amount spent per order). The service area tool was used to show that most customers are located within five miles of a store. Potential new store locations were digitized on the map and the ArcGIS® Network Analyst tool was applied.

Contact

Mike Holscher
mwholscher@gmail.com

Software

ArcGIS for Desktop 10.3

Data Sources

US Census Bureau, Flyers Pizza, City of Columbus streets data

Courtesy of GeoTech Center.

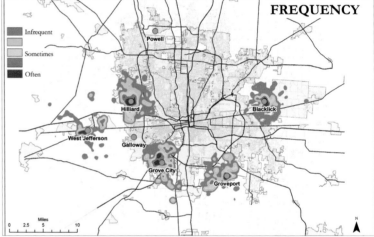

Heat maps were created using the Kenel Desity tool to find out where the frequent users and big spenders are located in the point density cloud of map 2. This heat maps is measuring the number of orders per customer in the last three years. It appears that the closer you live to Flyers the more you frequent their restaurant. There is an interesting anomaly to this west of the Groveport store and east of West Jefferson.

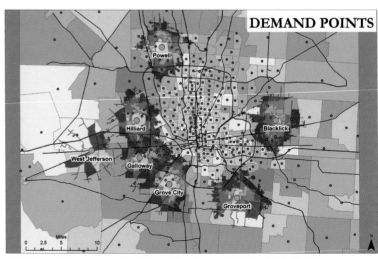

U.S. Census Bureau census tracts shapefile and population density tabular data were obtained and spatially joined. From that layer a conversion from polygon to point was done to create demand points for the final analysis.

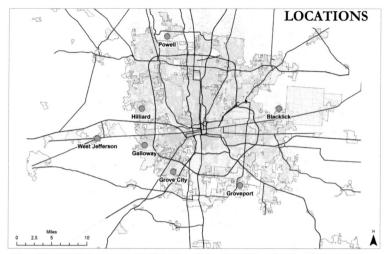

LOCATIONS

Flyers Pizza and Subs is located in Columbus, Ohio. As a final project for GIS Analysis, I would obtain customer data in order to determine the best location to open a new store. This map illustrates the distribution of their current store locations. By converting graphics to features, a layer was created for use with the "clip" tool. This was applied to all other layers to make data reasonable to manage.

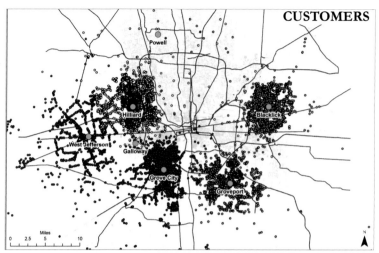

CUSTOMERS

Three years of customer data was obtained in the tabular form of .XLS files. After clean-up 72,380 customer lines of data were used to plot this map. About 50 percent of those points were geocoded with the US Census Bureau and Texas A&M Geocoder. The other 50 percent had a Lat/Long associated with it. Galloway and Powell data was not available.

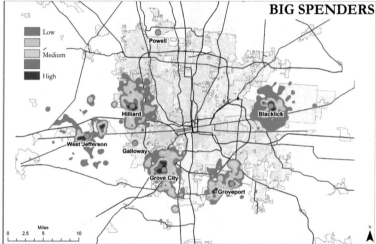

BIG SPENDERS

This heat map is based upon the average order price paid by the customers. It appears that the closer you are to a store the more you spend per order. One theory is that nearby businesses use the resuarant to treat employees for lunch or work parties which is naturally a bigger tab.

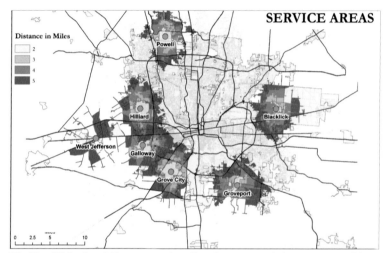

SERVICE AREAS

The City of Columbus did have a street shapefile and a new network dataset was created for further analysis. The shapefile had basic data so only distance could be used to define the service areas; no other impedances could be applied. Service area was calculated for 2, 3, 4 and 5 miles from each store. The 5 mile service area is remarkably similar to heat maps.

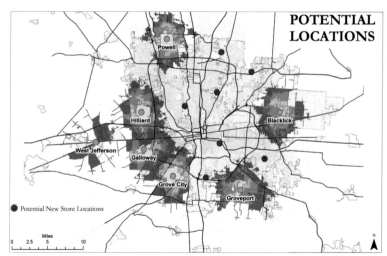

POTENTIAL LOCATIONS

7 potential store locations were digitized on the map in a distribution similar to the current stores spacing. Zoning data was available for the City of Columbus, but not for the surroundin cities that make up the metropolitan area. If there was consistent data, locations would have been selectively chosen based on commercial zoning and nearby high density residential.

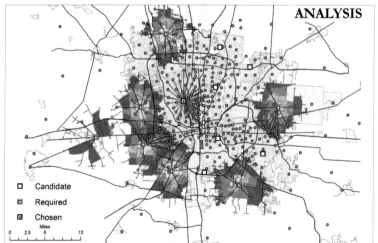

ANALYSIS

Ran Network Analysis Location Allocation with the following settings: Impedance set to feet with a cutoff at 26,400 (5 miles), demand to facility, maximize attendance, u-turns allowed, one-way restriction, applied "restricted" to the existing 7 stores, set the 7 potential stores to "candidate" status, facilities to choose set to 8. Best site chosen is coincidentally adjacent to Ohio State University.

Surficial Geology of Morris County, Kansas

Kansas Geological Survey
Lawrence, Kansas, USA
By John Dunham, Robert Sawin, Ronald West, Richard Jarvis, and R. Zane Price

Morris County, in the Flint Hills physiographic region of east-central Kansas, is an area of rolling prairie uplands and wooded stream valleys. This surficial geology map shows bedrock layers at the surface or immediately under vegetation and soil and was the first detailed geologic map of Morris County. This map helps users make informed land-use and resource-management decisions. Over half the county is still covered with native grassland used mainly for grazing livestock. The county's limestone resources are used as building stone, road material, riprap, and in concrete and agricultural lime.

The map shows the distribution, rock type, and age of bedrock. It can be used to identify surface and subsurface lithologic units and their stratigraphic relationships. The map also shows geologic structures, delineates thick surficial materials such as alluvium, and determines the features' spatial orientation. The map includes a stratigraphic column depicting the vertical sequence, thickness, and lithologies of the geologic units, and generalized descriptions of the units. An east-west cross section shows the vertical relationship of the rock units.

Contact
John Dunham
dunham@kgs.ku.edu

Software
ArcGIS for Desktop10.3.1, ArcGIS® Spatial Analyst, Profile Tool 1.2.1

Data Sources
Kansas Department of Transportation, US Geological Survey, Kansas Data Access and Support Center

Courtesy of Kansas Geological Survey.

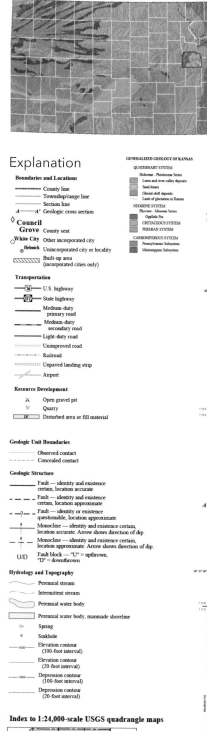

Index shows the names and locations of the 17 USGS 7.5-min 1:24,000-scale quadrangles used in the digital compilation of the Morris County map. The geology was mapped in the field using these topographic maps.

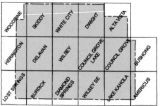

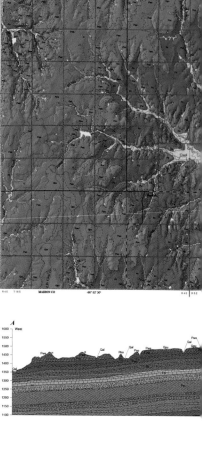

Swiss National Map: 1:10000

Federal Office of Topography (swisstopo)
Wabern, Switzerland
By Cartography Division, swisstopo

There is an increasing need for highly accurate and up-to-date geodata. A new map of Switzerland is created fully automatically each year and published with the most up-to-date data available from swisstopo's topographic landscape model. In high cartographic quality, this product is the ideal basis for applications used by administrations, businesses, science, and the general public.

The 1:10000 scale national map is a milestone in the history of Swiss cartography and was the highlight of swisstopo's involvement in the International Map Year supported by the United Nations in 2016. It combines the unique quality of traditional maps with innovative processes. What began two centuries ago with copperplate engraving is now done exclusively on computers and is fully automated. With this development, swisstopo gives due consideration to the growing importance of geoinformation for a changing society.

Contact
Urs Isenegger
urs.isenegger@swisstopo.ch

Software
ArcGIS Desktop

Data Source
swisstopo

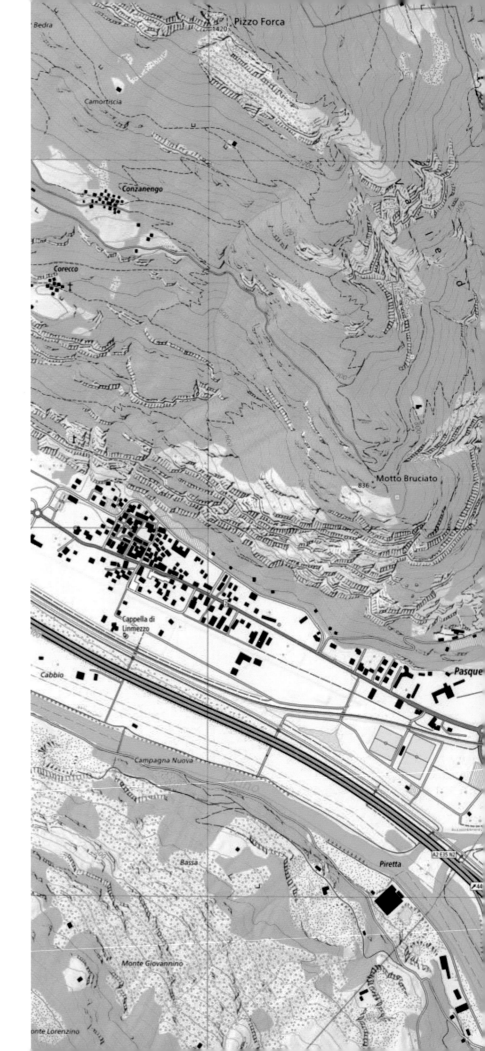

Horizontal Hachures Map of Diamond Peak, Oregon

Long Island University
Brookville, New York, USA
By Patrick J. Kennelly

Horizontal hachures form lines of equal elevation. They are differentiated from contours by being more compactly and evenly arranged, with exact elevation values not generally indicated on individual lines. Additionally, when rendered effectively, horizontal hachures can produce a hillshading effect that also adds a texture to terrain maps.

The methodology illustrated on this Diamond Peak map uses points derived from digital elevation models to first create short seed lines and then to grow horizontal hachures, with a lesser density of lines on the illuminated side of the terrain. Results are a fine stroke pattern that can provide a textured hillshading effect for nonilluminated areas, create more continuous horizontal hachures for both illuminated and nonilluminated terrain, or be used to supplement contours for highlighting both the form and shading of terrain.

Contact
Patrick J. Kennelly
Patrick.Kennelly@liu.edu

Software
ArcGIS Desktop

Data Source
US Geological Survey

Courtesy of Patrick J. Kennelly.

Colorado State, Regional, and Local Maps

GM Johnson & Associates, Ltd.
Vancouver, British Columbia, Canada
By GM Johnson & Associates, Ltd.

The Colorado large-print state map is a good example of map generalization. Building a state map from street-level data (large-scale detail) requires an efficient way to generalize. The process starts at street level mapping, such as the Denver street map (scale 1:32,000). The map will not be used just for a street map, but also for a medium-scale regional map and a small-scale state map (scale 1:640,000). The way the data is attributed must take in all these considerations.

The Denver regional map (scale 1: 200,000) example shows the transition to a state map. The Colorado map has insets derived from the both the street and regional maps so other products can be referenced into the state map as needed, making the process cost-effective and quick to design and produce.

Contact
Guy Johnson
gjohnson@gmjohnsonmaps.com

Software
ArcGIS for Desktop 10.1 ,Adobe Illustrator, Dbase, FME, Label-ez, Microstation

Data Sources
Colorado Department of Transportation, Colorado Department of Natural Resources, US Geological Survey, US Census Bureau, Larimer County, Weld County, Boulder County, Broomfield County, Denver City and County, Adams County, Arapahoe County, Jefferson County, Douglas County, Pueblo

Copyright © GM Johnson & Associates, Ltd.

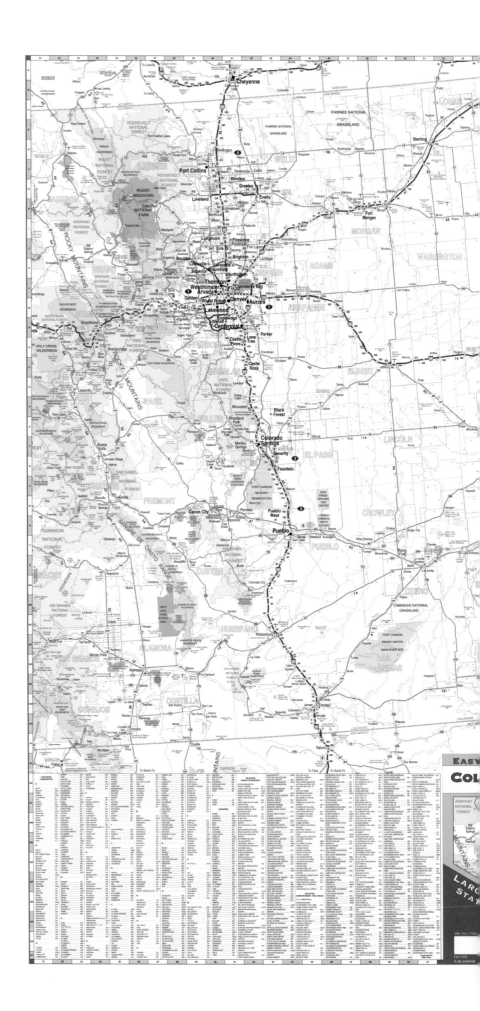

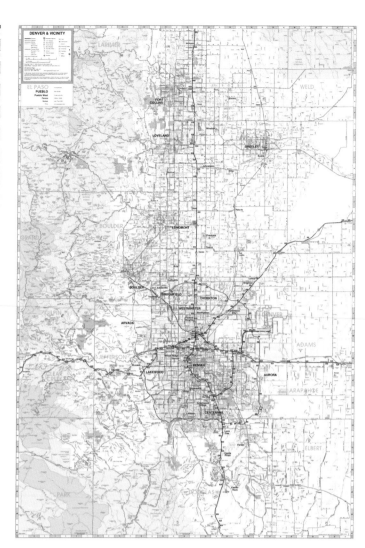

DENVER & VICINITY

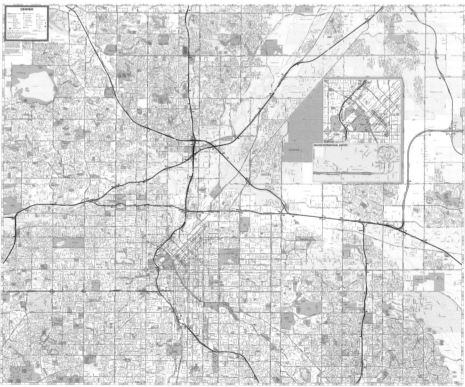

DENVER

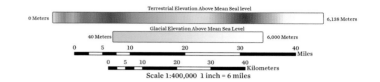

Hydrographic Mapping of the Matanuska-Susitna Basin in South Central Alaska

The Nature Conservancy (TNC)
Anchorage, Alaska, USA
By James DePasquale, GISP

Encompassing over 25,000 square miles, the Matanuska-Susitna (Mat-Su) basin is rich in aquatic resources and freshwater habitat critical to healthy, wild salmon. The Mat-Su is also home to Alaska's second-largest and rapidly growing human population. TNC believes this vast watershed can be one of the first places where people and salmon sustainably share habitat and thrive together. To achieve this goal, a holistic, science-based understanding of the freshwater environment salmon require is crucial, including mapping and identifying characteristics of the streams and lakes they use throughout their lifecycle.

This map depicts a hydrographic mapping and analysis program led by the TNC in Alaska using newly available, high-resolution elevation data to map all Mat-Su lakes, rivers, and streams. Through this work, over 27,000 miles of previously unmapped streams were discovered in the Mat-Su basin. The new stream maps are being used by agencies, local governments, nonprofits, and private firms for habitat and water quality assessments, regulatory needs, community planning, storm water management, climate studies, and decision support to balance conservation and resource development.

Contact
James DePasquale
jdepasquale@tnc.org

Software
ArcGIS for Desktop 10.2.3

Data Sources
Mat-Su LiDAR and Orthoimagery Project, Alaska Statewide Digital Mapping Initiative, US Geological Survey (USGS) National Elevation Dataset, Matanuska-Susitna Borough, Municipality of Anchorage, US Census, ArcGIS Online, USGS National Hydrographic Database, National Oceanic and Atmospheric Administration Electronic Navigational Charts

Courtesy of TNC in Alaska.

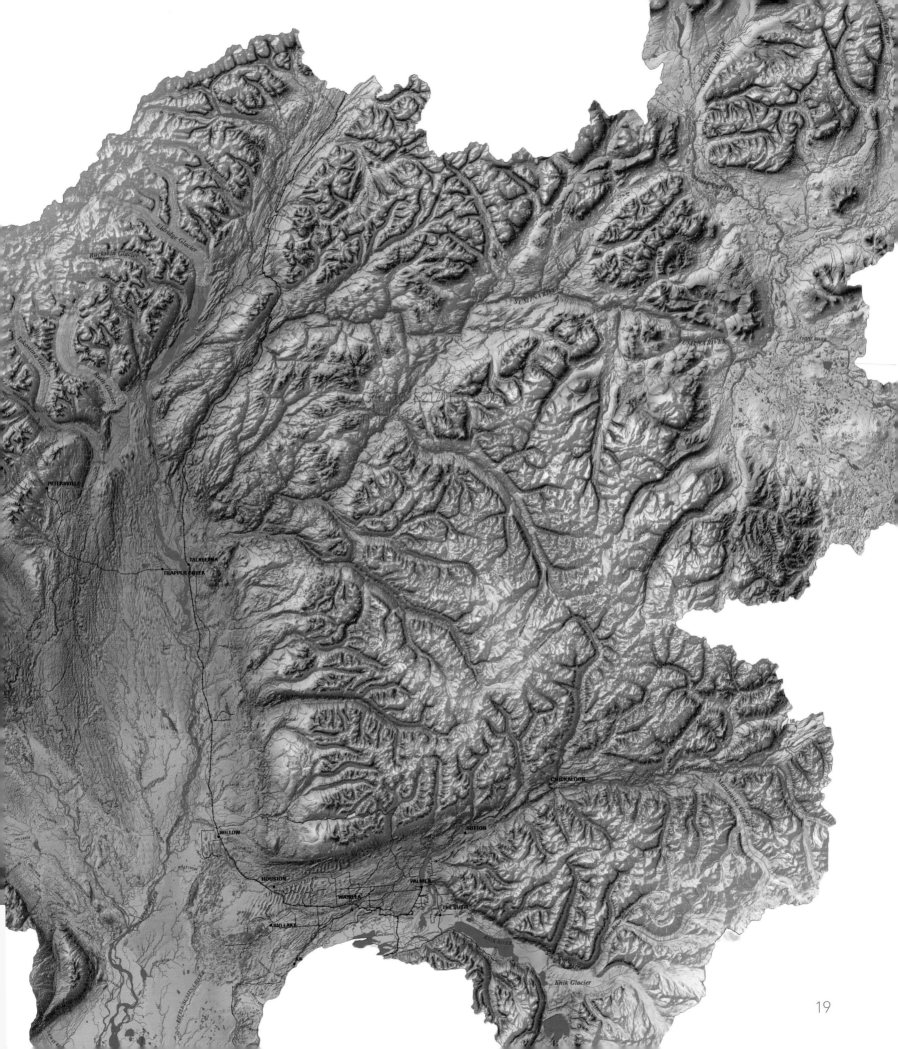

Red Relief Image Map of Mount Usu Volcano

Asia Air Survey Co., Ltd.
Kawasaki , Kanagawa, Japan
By Tatsuro Chiba

This map shows Mount Usu, one of the most active volcanoes in Japan. During the eruption of 2000, one cryptodome was created and formed a number of faults and small craters on it. A red relief image map (RRIM) was used to visualize such complicated topographic information. On the RRIM image, it was expressed as more red colored on steeper slopes, brighter on ridges, and darker in valleys. The RRIM is useful for volcano topographic interpretation and field investigation.

Asia Air Survey developed the original method to create the image map, on the basis of parameters of positive openness, negative openness, and slope angle. Using ArcGIS software, the RRIM can be easily overlapped with contour maps and overview images. This map was created from a one-meter digital elevation model acquired by lidar scanning in 2005. It was an academic research project demonstrating RRIM as a simple yet effective technique to visualize terrain.

Contact
Tatsuro Chiba
ta.chiba@ajiko.co.jp

Software
ArcGIS for Desktop 10.3.1

Data Source
Asia Air Survey

Courtesy of Asia Air Survey Co., Ltd.

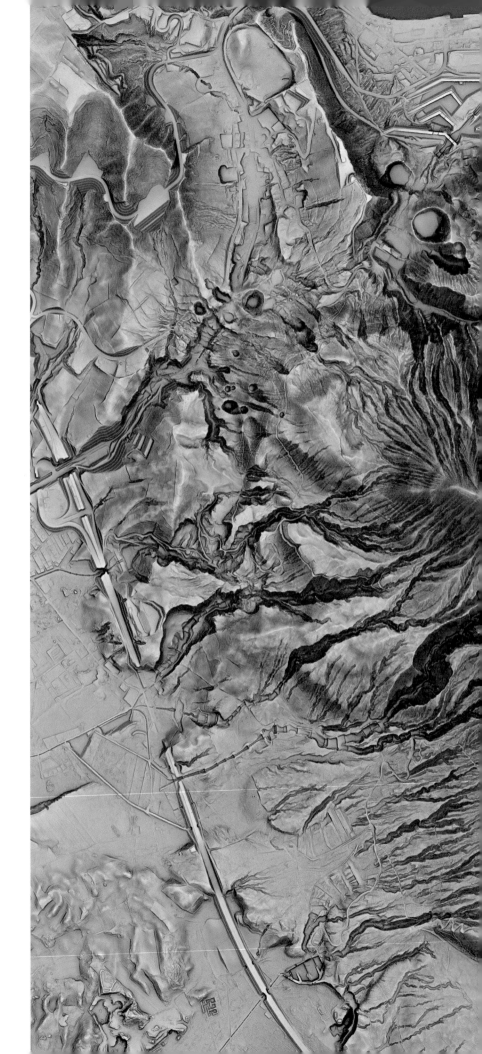

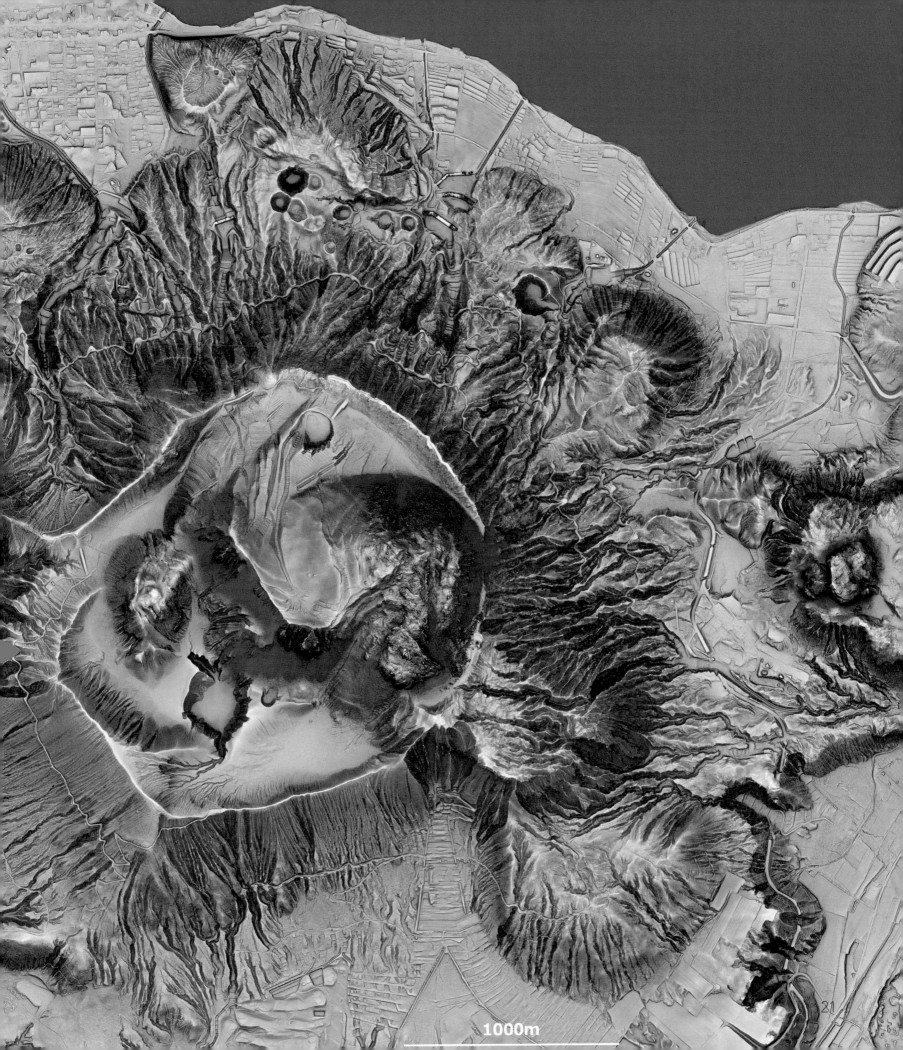

1000m

Visualization Tool: Scenario Planning Enhanced with 3D GIS

Southern California Association of Governments (SCAG)
Los Angeles, California, USA
By Ping Wang and Tuo Sun

This visualization planning model integrates the scenario planning model with 3D GIS technologies (ArcGIS® Pro and Esri® CityEngine®) to design, view, and assess land developments at a variety of planning scales (project, community, city, region). The model enhances land-use scenario planning for sustainable economic development. This is a suite of tools that intends to help users understand, measure, and evaluate impacts on various policies, such as zoning, and programs related to transportation, land use, housing, demographics, fiscal revenues, public health, and air quality.

Contact
Ping Wang
wangp@scag.ca.gov

Software
ArcGIS for Desktop 10.2, ArcGIS Pro 1.2, CityEngine 2015.1

Data Source
SCAG

Courtesy of SCAG.

WORKFLOW

1 Input LU/GP by parcel
Input SED by TAZ

[Create Scenario Planning format] python tool

2 Scenario Planning format parcel

Paint scenarios

3 User scenario

[Scenario Planning + CE] python tool

KEY FEATURES

Realistic Model with texture

Schematic Model in SCAG Land-Use

Accurate street model

SED comparison to SCAG policy

VISUALIZATION TOOL
SCENARIO PLANNING

EXISTING

SCENARIO PLAN

Single Family
Multi-family
Town house
Mixed-Use Residential
Office
Retail
Public
Industry

hanced user plan
with 3D features

5 SED comparison (user
plan to policy goals)

Updated Scenario
anning report / ROI
model

F.A.R

9.8   Office 30
5.1   Office 15
4.8   Mixed-Use Residential 15
2.6   Mixed-Use Residential 5
       Main Street Retail LifeStyle

Difference after enhanced with CityEngine

Population
24,747   7%

Job
9,152   26%

Property Tax Revenue
$2,100,000
Sales Tax Revenue
$3,450,000   50%

Displacement population
998
Displacement value
$110,600,000   10%   5%

Energy Use
58 per household   8%
19 per job   7%

Water Consumption
215 per household   5%

Carbon Emission
CO_2 5.4 per household   8%

Solid Waste
6.0 per household
3.6 per job   5%

Olympic Blvd.

SAMPLE PLACE:

Over Plan Zone

Western Ave.

MID-CITY,
LOS ANGELES
CALIFORNIA

NHANCED WITH 3D GIS

Global Tree Density

Yale University
New Haven, Connecticut, USA
By Henry B. Glick and Charlie Bettigole

These maps depict the first global model of tree density and the first statistically robust estimate of the number of trees globally: 3.041 trillion. They were produced by evaluating thousands of spatially explicit generalized linear regression models created from dozens of topographic, vegetative, climatic, and anthropogenic variables, and 429,775 forest tree density measurements from around the world.

This research was a collaborative effort over eighteen months, bringing together field work and expertise from over fifty countries and more than sixty organizations and individuals. The data contained in these maps helps further our understanding of terrestrial ecosystems by supporting ongoing research into biodiversity, species distributions, and ecosystems services, and by describing perceivable structural characteristics that influence habitat suitability. This data also supplies critical information on forest loss, contributes to projections of forest change and carbon accounting under different climate change scenarios, and provides a baseline against which a number of international tree planting initiatives can better gauge their efforts.

Contact
Henry B. Glick
henry.glick@gmail.com

Software
ArcGIS for Desktop 10.1/10.3, ArcGlobe 10.3, R 3.1.x, Photoshop CS6

Data Sources

Global Map of Tree Density (Crowther et al 2015, Glick et al 2016); GMTED2010 (US Geological Survey/National Geospatial-Intelligence Agency); VIIRS Day/Night Band Composites (Earth Observation Group, National Oceanic and Atmospheric Administration National Geophysical Data Center), Esri World Ocean Basemap

Courtesy of Henry B. Glick.

Trees per km^2

1,000,000+

0

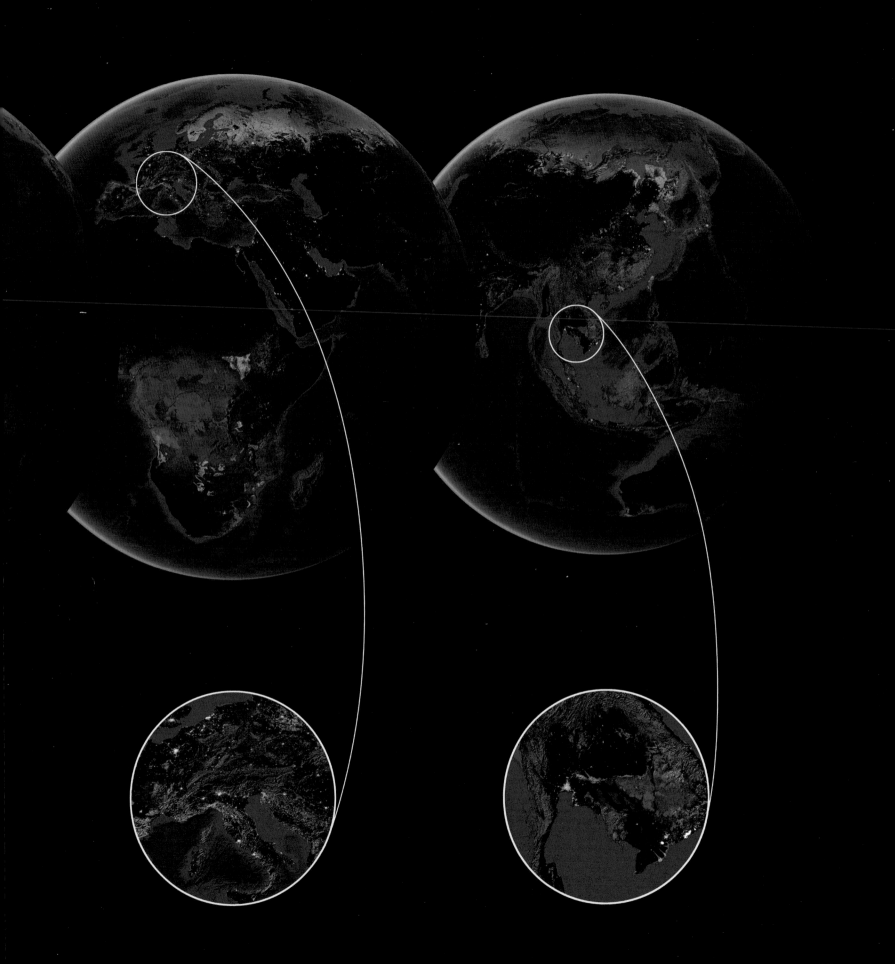

CARTOGRAPHY

Lake Whatcom Watershed

City of Bellingham
Bellingham, Washington, USA
By Chris Behee

This map depicts the topographic features of the Lake Whatcom Watershed and surrounding areas, including the South Fork Nooksack River to the east; Lake Samish to the southwest, and Squalicum Creek to the north. Vegetation is derived from 2013 color-infrared imagery using the normalized difference vegetation index. Topography is derived from 2013 high-resolution lidar terrain data. This data includes surface models for bare-earth and top-of-canopy elevations.

Using the difference between the lidar surface models allows calculation of vegetation height depicted as varying shades of green on the map. Lake depth (bathymetric) data for Lake Whatcom was derived from digital sonar soundings collected by the US Bureau of Reclamation for a 1999 reservoir study. Bathymetric data for the surrounding lakes was derived from the Washington State Department of Ecology and US Geological Survey.

Contact
Chris Behee
cbehee@cob.org

Software
ArcGIS for Desktop 10.3.1

Data Sources
City of Bellingham GIS, US Bureau of Reclamation, Washington State Department of Ecology, US Geological Survey

Courtesy of Chris Behee.

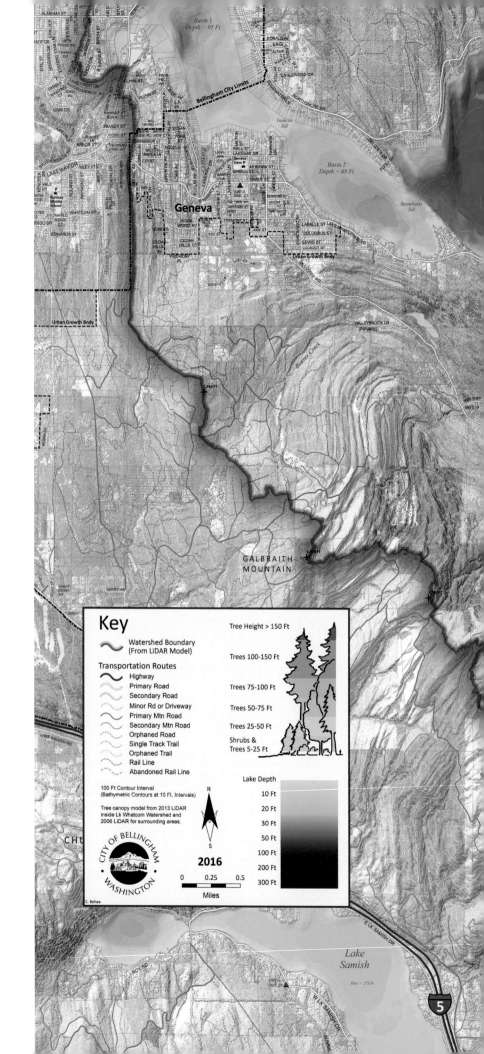

Lake Whatcom
Elev. = 314 Ft

North Basin 3
Depth = 266 Ft

NORTHSHORE RD

NORTHSHORE DR

Smith Creek

B.P.A. TRANSMISSION LINES

WATERSHED BOUNDARY

Sunnyside Sill

**Sudden
Valley**

Austin Cr.

*Reveille
Island*

*Lake
Louise*

GATE 2

GATE 2B

South Basin 3
Depth = 328 Ft

OKOUT
UNTAIN

S BAY DR

S BAY DR

South Bay

WCFD 18
Stat. 25

RENEE DR

B.P.A. TRANSMISSION LINES

PARK RD

Anderson Creek

S LAKE WHATCOM PK

WATERSHED BOUNDARY

Solar Potential in Kenton County

Planning and Development Services (PDS) of Kenton County,
LINK-GIS
Fort Mitchell, Kentucky, USA
By Louis Hill Jr., Ryan Kent, and Trisha Brush

Solar energy is becoming an increasingly economical
energy choice for American homeowners and
businesses. The US Energy Department's SunShot
Initiative works to drive down costs, making it faster and
more affordable for families and businesses to go solar.

To help homeowners determine whether solar would
be feasible for their homes, OKI launched an online
interactive solar map project funded by a grant from the
SunShot Initiative. The solar map provides information
about the solar potential of buildings. The term "solar
potential" includes usable roof space, kilowatt-hours of
electricity generated, and annual cost savings.

This Northern Kentucky mapLAB project explores the
solar potential in Kenton County. It identifies the total
solar potential of Kenton County as a whole, the solar
potential of individual cities, and the solar potential of
city- and county-owned buildings. Finally, this project
identifies the five areas of the county that have the most
solar potential, and what the key assumptions are in
determining solar potential.

Contact
Louis Hill Jr.
lhill@pdskc.org

Software
ArcGIS for Desktop 10.3.1, CorelDRAW X7

Data Sources
PDS, LINK-GIS, Ohio-Kentucky-Indiana Regional Council of
Governments (OKI)

Courtesy of PDS, LINK-GIS, and OKI.

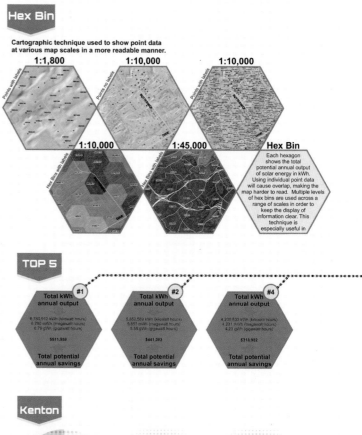

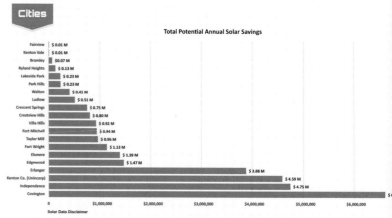

TOP 5

#3 Total kWh
annual output

4,715,680 kWh (a kilowatt hours)
4,716 mWh (megawatt hours)
4.72 gWh (gigawatt hours)

$305,562

Total potential
annual savings

#5 Total kWh
annual output

4,649,592 kWh (kilowatt hours)
4,650 mWh (megawatt hours)
4.65 gWh (gigawatt hours)

$305,339

Total potential
annual savings

In recent years, the solar industry has been a rapidly growing
market. Rooftop solar PV installations can have positive
impacts on the local economy and job market, provide a stable
source of energy immune to traditional energy price volatility,
increase property values, reduce electricity costs for homes,
businesses, and governments, and augment utility energy
needs during peak hours. More information can be found
at: linkgis.org

NKYmapLAB

August 2015   Volume 1: Map 8

Northern Kentucky mapLAB is a copyrighted, published product of Planning and Development Services of Kenton County.
The goal of the initiative is to analyze a wide variety of tabular data and present them in a more visual format that
facilitates understanding by the public and its elected leaders. Suggestions for future analyses are always welcome.

**Total Annual Potential
Output kWh**

- 0.00 - 2.00
- 2.01 - 133,523
- 133,524 - 252,465
- 252,466 - 420,670
- 420,671 - 715,949
- 715,950 - 1,210,497
- 1,210,498 - 1,929,066
- 1,929,067 - 3,045,714
- 3,045,714 - 6,789,912

Featured Data Sources

www.direction2030.org

www.linkgis.org

www.oki.org

www.nrel.gov

Solar Assumptions

- Buildings less than 230 sq ft. are
  considered too small for a PV array.

- Less than 1,146 kWh/sq meter/year of solar
  insolation is considered too shaded for solar.

- Cost of electricity: averaged across the
  residential, commercial, & industrial sectors.
  9.16 cents / kWh for Ohio
  7.54 cents / kWh for Kentucky
  8.63 cents / kWh for Indiana.

- System Efficiency: 15% percent efficiency,
  for standard crystalline Silicon PV modules.

- Shading based off of LiDAR data.

- Weather based off of data collected at
  Cincinnati's Lunken Airport.

 **PDS**

direction 2030
Your Voice. Your Choice.

Plan Goals & Objectives

C Community Identity   H Health   N Natural Systems
E Economy   HC Healthy Communities ■ Primary Goal
G Governance   M Mobility   ■ Secondary Goal

How Does This Topic
Apply to Direction 2030?

HC Encourage a variety of housing types
throughout the County to meet the needs
of all generations and income levels.

M Balance the need to maintain existing infrastructure
and build new infrastructure while being mindful of
cost, economic conditions and return on investment.

N Strive to achieve a balance between
E development and preservation.

HC Encourage innovative design on sites with
constraints based on the presence of natural
systems and incentivize the protection of quality
open space.

G Encourage cooperative governance.

G Continue to encourage the sharing of technical tools
and resources effectively reducing the cost of the
system.

Key Quote:

"Local communities can play a critical role in
reducing these soft costs (of installing solar
panels) by streamlining and standardizing the
permitting process and by providing accessible
information to the public."

– OKI "Go Solar Ready" initiative

Multicriteria Evaluation to Determine Forest Bird Habitat during Spring Migration

Environment and Climate Change Canada
Delta, British Columbia, Canada
By Amos Chow, Adam Lee, Kathleen Moore, Wendy Easton, Krista De Groot, and Ivy Whitehorne

The regional office of the Canadian Wildlife Service (CWS) in British Columbia, Canada, identifies priority conservation areas for migratory birds in the province; several of which are listed under Canada's Species at Risk Act.

This map highlights broad zones important to land birds during spring migration. Particularly important are low-elevation areas in April where trees and shrubs leaf out earlier, making insects and seeds available earlier than on adjacent mountains. These areas highlighted also coincide with urban populated areas, posing a conservation concern. The CWS works with different levels of government and nongovernmental organizations to concentrate conservation actions in these key areas.

Contact
Amos Chow
amos.chow@canada.ca

Software
ArcGIS for Desktop 10.1, IDRISI Selva

Data Sources
Bird Studies Canada and Cornell Lab of Ornithology. 2008. eBird Canada. Data accessed from NatureCounts, Canadian Wildlife Service, Natural Resources Canada, Province of British Columbia, University of British Columbia

Courtesy of Environment and Climate Change Canada.

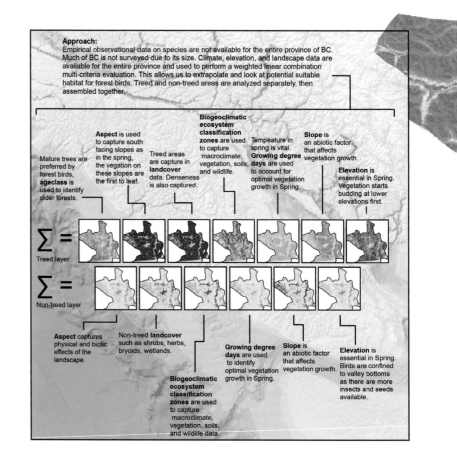

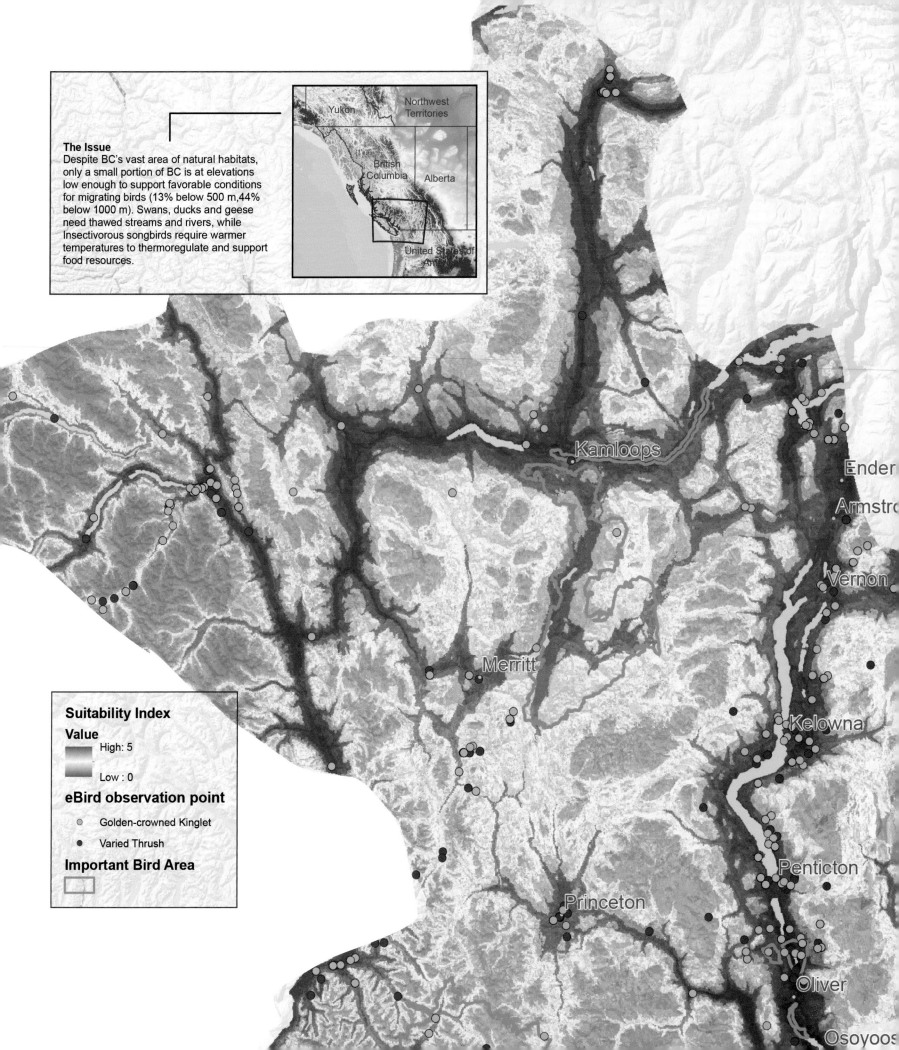

The Issue
Despite BC's vast area of natural habitats, only a small portion of BC is at elevations low enough to support favorable conditions for migrating birds (13% below 500 m, 44% below 1000 m). Swans, ducks and geese need thawed streams and rivers, while Insectivorous songbirds require warmer temperatures to thermoregulate and support food resources.

Yukon

Northwest Territories

British Columbia

Alberta

United States of America

Kamloops

Ender

Armstro

Vernon

Merritt

Kelowna

Penticton

Princeton

Oliver

Osoyoos

Suitability Index

Value

High: 5

Low : 0

eBird observation point

● Golden-crowned Kinglet

● Varied Thrush

Important Bird Area

CONSERVATION AND SUSTAINABLE DEVELOPMENT

Sandpoint Greenprint Priorities

The Trust for Public Land
Santa Fe, New Mexico, USA
By Fred Gifford, Carolyn Ives, Lindsay Withers, and Tom Dudley (AllPoints GIS)

The communities of Greater Sandpoint in Bonner County, Idaho, want to encourage sustainable economic development and retain the livability and spectacular scenery that make it such a special place. This all depends on protecting the small-town character and natural and recreational resources that are essential to the local quality of life.

The Trust for Public Land worked with Idaho Conservation League, the planning departments of the City of Ponderay and the City of Sandpoint, and the Kaniksu Land Trust to coordinate the Greater Sandpoint greenprint process. Hundreds of residents participated in a community survey in the fall of 2014, and many others were reached through speak-outs at local committee meetings held throughout 2015.

The goals of the greenprint are to maintain water quality, provide recreation, protect wildlife habitat, and preserve working lands. Greenprinting tools identify local priorities and help guide future investments in trails, parks, and open spaces to help the region plan for growth, while retaining its livability and scenic character.

Contact
Fred Gifford
fred.gifford@tpl.org

Software
ArcGIS for Desktop 10.3

Data Sources
The Trust for Public Land, Idaho Conservation League, Bonner County, City of Sandpoint, Esri, National Conservation Easement Database,
National Hydrography Dataset

Copyright © The Trust for Public Land. Information on these maps is provided for purposes of discussion and visualization only.

Provide Recreation

Maintain Water Quality

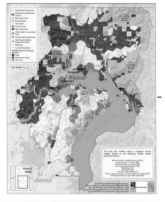

Protect Wildlife Habitat

Preserve Working Lands

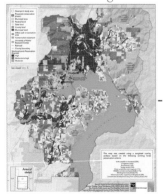

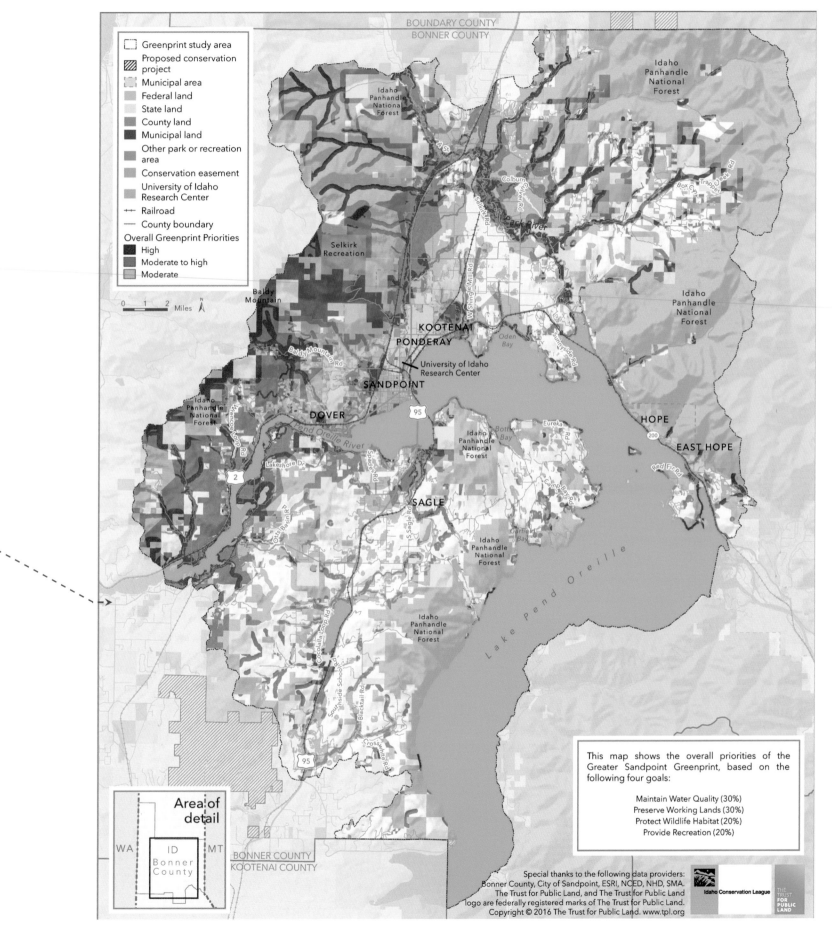

Greenprint study area
Proposed conservation project
Municipal area
Federal land
State land
County land
Municipal land
Other park or recreation area
Conservation easement
University of Idaho Research Center
Railroad
County boundary

Overall Greenprint Priorities
High
Moderate to high
Moderate

0 1 2 Miles
N

BOUNDARY COUNTY
BONNER COUNTY

Idaho Panhandle National Forest

Idaho Panhandle National Forest

Idaho Panhandle National Forest

Colburn

Pack River

Box Cyn

Trappers Creek Rd

Selkirk Recreation

Baldy Mountain

Baldy Mountain Rd

KOOTENAI
PONDERAY

University of Idaho Research Center

SANDPOINT

Oden Bay

Sunnyside Rd

95

DOVER

Pend Oreille River

Idaho Panhandle National Forest

Bottle Bay

Eureka

HOPE

200

EAST HOPE

Lakeshore Dr

2

Wrencoe Loop Rd

Otts Basin Rd

Spades Rd

SAGLE

S Sagle Rd

Idaho Panhandle National Forest

Garfield Bay

Camp Bay Rd

Red Fir Rd

Lake Pend Oreille

Cocolalla Loop Rd

Sourhinside School Rd

Blacktail Rd

Idaho Panhandle National Forest

Crosswhite Rd

95

Area of detail

WA   ID   MT
Bonner County

BONNER COUNTY
KOOTENAI COUNTY

This map shows the overall priorities of the Greater Sandpoint Greenprint, based on the following four goals:

Maintain Water Quality (30%)
Preserve Working Lands (30%)
Protect Wildlife Habitat (20%)
Provide Recreation (20%)

Special thanks to the following data providers:
Bonner County, City of Sandpoint, ESRI, NCED, NHD, SMA.
The Trust for Public Land, and The Trust for Public Land logo are federally registered marks of The Trust for Public Land.
Copyright © 2016 The Trust for Public Land. www.tpl.org

Idaho Conservation League

THE TRUST FOR PUBLIC LAND

CONSERVATION AND SUSTAINABLE DEVELOPMENT

Creating a Conservation Blueprint for Cuba

Brigham Young University (BYU)
Provo, Utah, USA
By Teresa Gomez, Steve Schill, John Knowles, and Steve Petersen

Cuba is the largest country in the insular Caribbean. Though the archipelago boasts some of the best preserved island biodiversity in the world, it is under increasing threat with the prospect of sudden and massive growth in tourism with the lifting of the US embargo. Consequently, it is critical to develop a detailed conservation blueprint for Cuba identifying and prioritizing the most important places to preserve across terrestrial, freshwater, and marine realms.

BYU is working with experts to identify and map biodiversity elements to identify a suite of high-value areas that meet representation goals for species and ecosystems across Cuba. As a decision-support system, the blueprint will prioritize guide efforts to focus conservation on important areas and help Cuba make informed decisions about future development in ways that will promote sustainable use without sacrificing ecological integrity.

Contact
Teresa Gomez
trs.gomez@gmail.com

Software
ArcGIS for Desktop 10.3

Data Sources
Nature Serve, The Nature Conservancy (TNC),
World Database of Protected Areas

Courtesy of BYU and TNC.

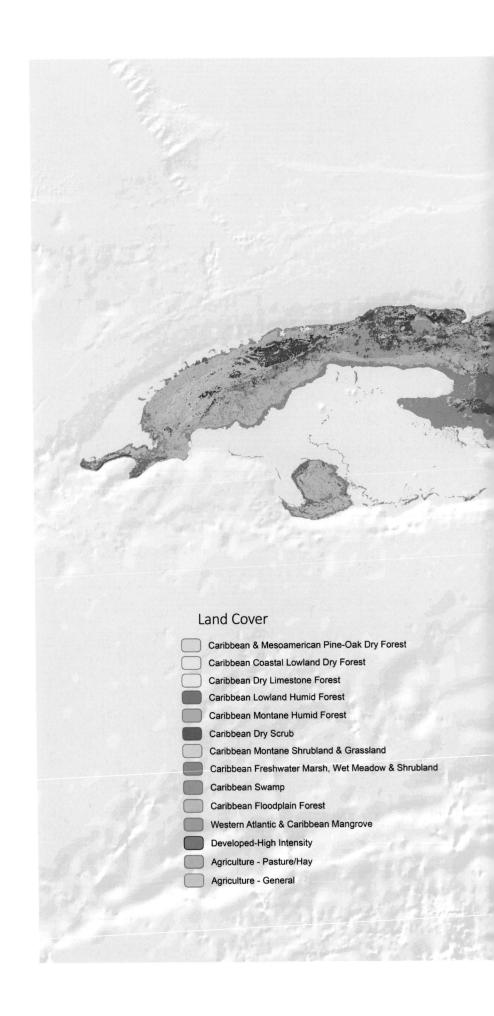

Land Cover

- Caribbean & Mesoamerican Pine-Oak Dry Forest
- Caribbean Coastal Lowland Dry Forest
- Caribbean Dry Limestone Forest
- Caribbean Lowland Humid Forest
- Caribbean Montane Humid Forest
- Caribbean Dry Scrub
- Caribbean Montane Shrubland & Grassland
- Caribbean Freshwater Marsh, Wet Meadow & Shrubland
- Caribbean Swamp
- Caribbean Floodplain Forest
- Western Atlantic & Caribbean Mangrove
- Developed-High Intensity
- Agriculture - Pasture/Hay
- Agriculture - General

Natura 2000 at Iroise Marine Natural Park

Agence Française de la Biodiversit
(The French Agency for Biodiversity),
Parc Naturel Marin d'Iroise (Iroise Marine Natural Park)
Vincennes, France
By Elodie Giacomini

The Natura 2000 network is a collection of natural European sites, terrestrial and marine, identified for the rarity or fragility of wild animal or plant species and their habitats. Natura 2000 reconciles nature conservation and socioeconomic concerns. In France, the Natura 2000 network includes 1758 sites.

This map of the Iroise Marine Natural Park, established in 2007 as France's first marine park, focuses on protecting marine birds' nesting sites. Sailboats and kite surfers cannot be closer than 100 meters from nesting sites and motorboats 300 meters, according to Natura 2000 directives.

Contact
Elodie Giacomini
elodie.giacomini@afbiodiversite.fr

Software
ArcGIS Desktop

Data Sources
Agence des Aires Marines Protégées (Agency for Marine Protected Areas), Iroise Marine Natural Park, Service Hydrographique et Océanographique de la Marine (The Naval Hydrographic and Oceanographic Service), Institut national de l'information Géographique et Forestière (National Institute of Geographic and Forest Information)

Courtesy of Agence Française de la Biodiversite and Parc Naturel Marin d'Iroise.

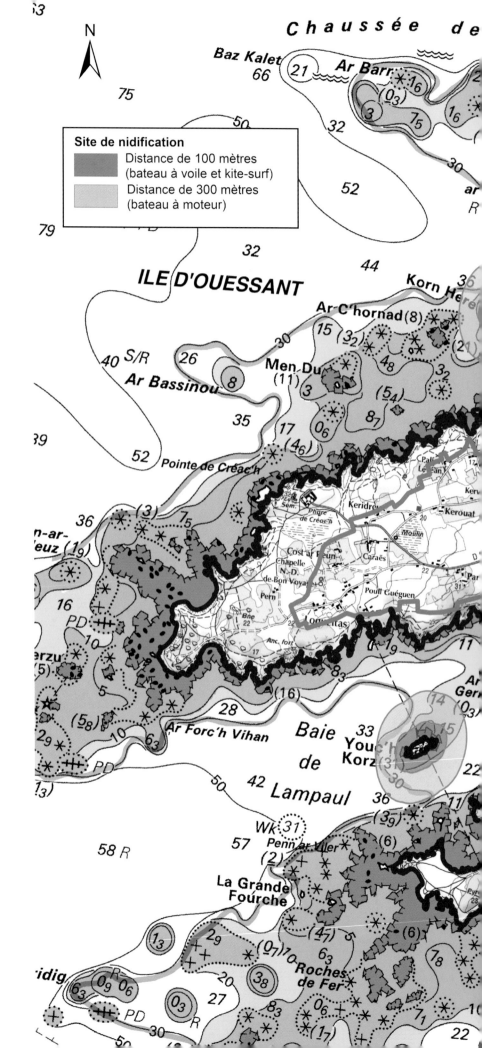

Site de nidification
Distance de 100 mètres (bateau à voile et kite-surf)
Distance de 300 mètres (bateau à moteur)

University of Minnesota Twin Cities Interactive Campus Map

University of Minnesota Twin Cities
Minneapolis, Minnesota, USA
By Sharvari Sangle

This interactive campus map was a student project enabling users to explore the University of Minnesota campus at their fingertips. It's a mobile responsive environment, made available to the students, staff, and others affiliated with the university.

The application was built with Esri's Web AppBuilder Developer's Edition 1.1 and has a pleasing campus basemap, zoom in/out, search tool, measure tool, and GPS location on the front end along with an interactive side panel giving it a simple and neat look. The interactive side panel allows users to explore more features including legends, print, and bookmarks. They can click/hover on the basemap for more information including directions, details page, image, and address of the building.

Contact
Sharvari Sangle
sangl003@umn.edu

Software
ArcGIS® Web AppBuilder 1.1

Data Sources
University of Minnesota, University Services; Hennepin County; Esri

Courtesy of Sharvari Sangle.

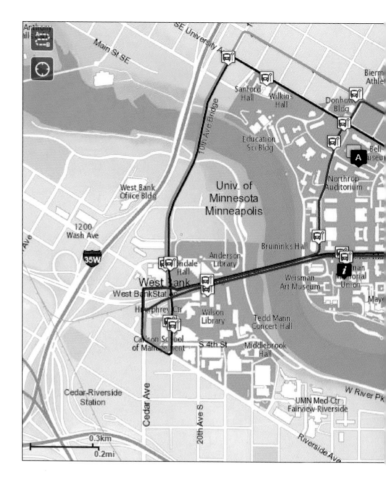

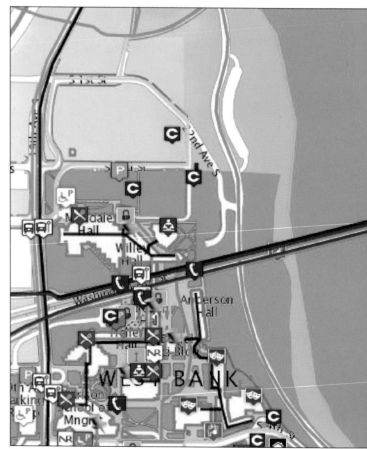

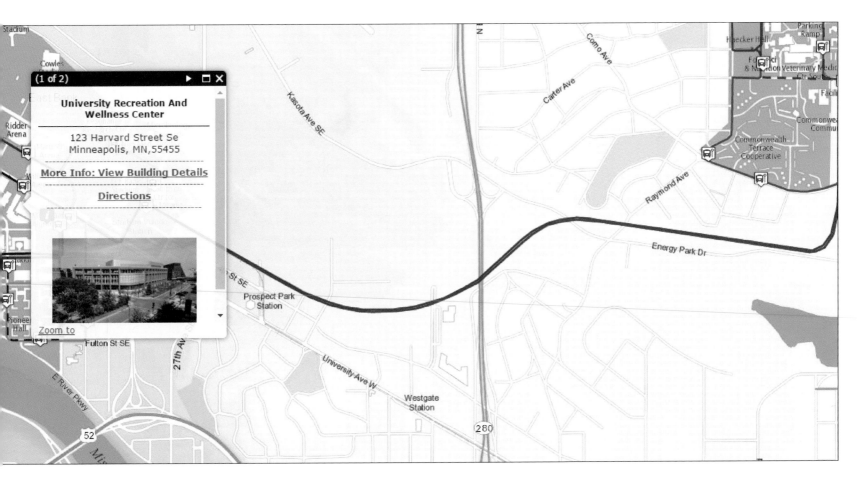

University Recreation And Wellness Center

123 Harvard Street Se
Minneapolis, MN,55455

More Info: View Building Details

Directions

Zoom to

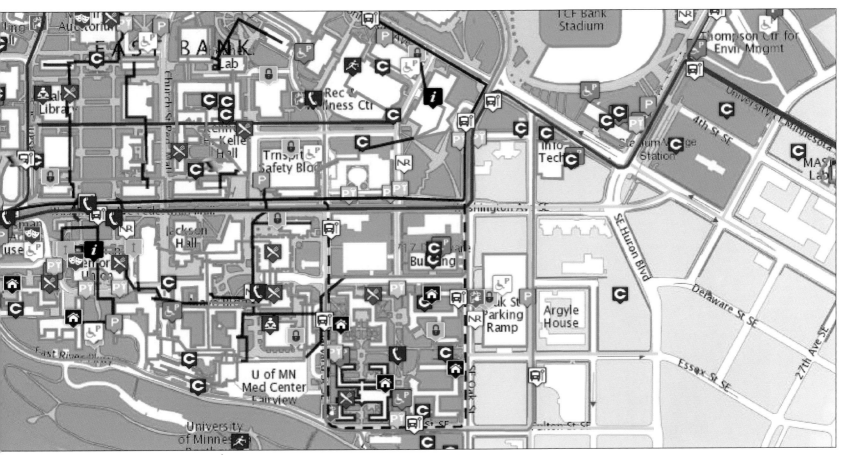

Creating Safe Routes to School with Survey123

Jacksonville Transportation Authority (JTA)
Jacksonville, Florida, USA
By Alexander Traversa

This project assisted local Jacksonville schools by creating an interactive way for students to identify possible hazards while walking to school. JTA explored Survey123 as a possible solution for field data collection. JTA's GIS team created a survey to capture infrastructure deficiencies in a half-mile radius around Andrew A. Robinson Elementary School. The school was selected on the basis of safety criteria including such factors as pedestrian fatalities and surrounding speed limits. The survey was tested by JTA's GIS team members, who walked the roads and sidewalks surrounding the elementary school to document deficiencies such as damaged or missing sidewalks, crosswalk locations, pedestrian signals and signage, ramps for the handicapped, and other safety concerns.

The collected data was processed and used to determine areas with a high density of deficiencies, as well as the total deficiencies on each block. A cost analysis using the collected data determined where funding would create the most benefit. This pilot project was submitted in a Safe Routes to School grant application and could be used for future projects.

Contact
Patty Richters
prichters@jtafla.com

Software
ArcGIS for Desktop 10.3

Data Sources
JTA, Florida Department of Transportation, University of Florida Geoplan Center, Duval County School Board

Courtesy of JTA.

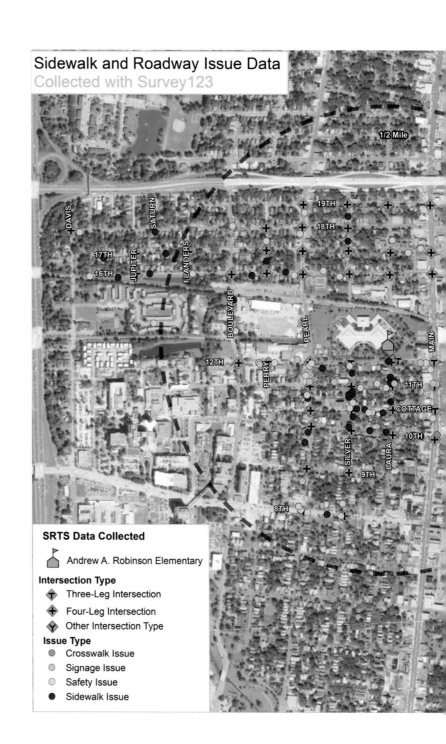

Sidewalk and Roadway Issue Data
Collected with Survey123

SRTS Data Collected

⚑ Andrew A. Robinson Elementary

Intersection Type
⬧ Three-Leg Intersection
✛ Four-Leg Intersection
◆ Other Intersection Type

Issue Type
⬤ Crosswalk Issue
◐ Signage Issue
◯ Safety Issue
● Sidewalk Issue

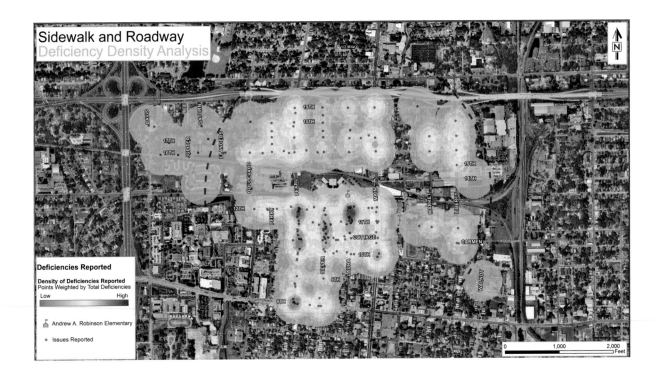

Sidewalk and Roadway
Deficiency Density Analysis

Deficiencies Reported

Density of Deficiencies Reported
Points Weighted by Total Deficiencies

Low ▭ High

🚩 Andrew A. Robinson Elementary

• Issues Reported

0   1,000   2,000
Feet

Issue Type	Count
✝ Three-Leg Intersection	9
✛ Four-Leg Intersection	46
◈ Other Intersection Type	1
● Crosswalk Issue	1
○ Signage Issue	11
○ Safety Issue	48
● Sidewalk Issue	67

0   760   1,520
Feet

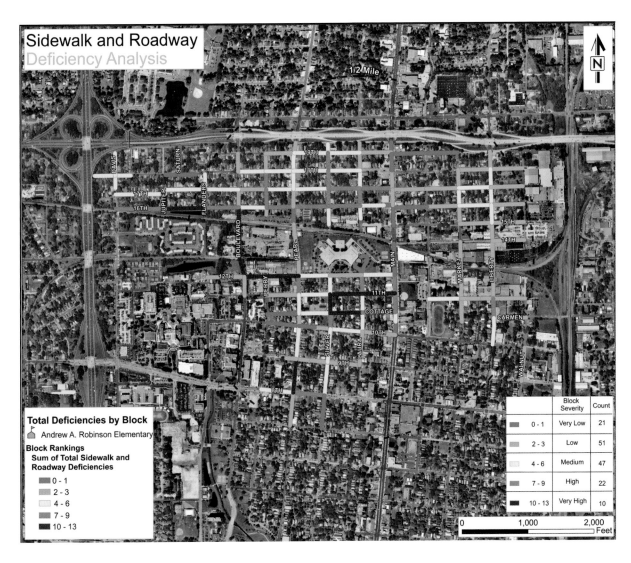

Sidewalk and Roadway
Deficiency Analysis

Total Deficiencies by Block

🚩 Andrew A. Robinson Elementary

Block Rankings
Sum of Total Sidewalk and
Roadway Deficiencies

▬ 0 - 1
▬ 2 - 3
▬ 4 - 6
▬ 7 - 9
▬ 10 - 13

	Block Severity	Count
0 - 1	Very Low	21
2 - 3	Low	51
4 - 6	Medium	47
7 - 9	High	22
10 - 13	Very High	10

0   1,000   2,000
Feet

University of Maryland Facilities Management

University of Maryland
College Park, Maryland, USA
By Geoff Caruso and Mary Kate Bland

University of Maryland Facilities Management plans, designs, constructs, equips, maintains, and operates buildings, infrastructure, and grounds, and provides related services to support the university's mission of education, research, and public service. This map was created for the Facilities Management Customer Response Center, which generates work orders for facilities on campus. The map is used as a visual reference for the locations of buildings, parking lots, and recreational facilities. In order to get the best scale for the main campus, outlying properties are shown as inset maps.

Repurposing map templates gives University of Maryland maps a consistent design appearance. The same palette and design elements used in the Facilities Management map appear in other maps including a large billboard map located at main entrances to campus and a smaller Campus Visitor Center map. The same basemap data for the campus web map is also used to fill the demand for hard copy mapping.

Contact
Mary Kate Bland
mcannist@umd.edu

Software
ArcGIS for Desktop 10.3.1

Data Source
University of Maryland, Facilities Planning

Courtesy of University of Maryland.

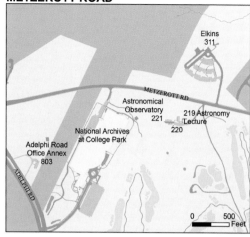

METZEROTT ROAD

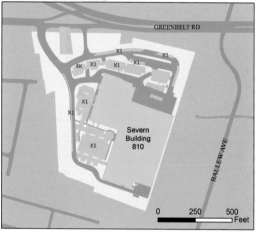

SEVERN BUILDING

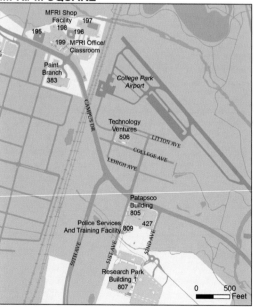

MFRI/ M SQUARE

Map courtesy of Department
of Facilities Planning
www.facilities.umd.edu
www.maps.umd.edu/map

Date: 11/4/2016

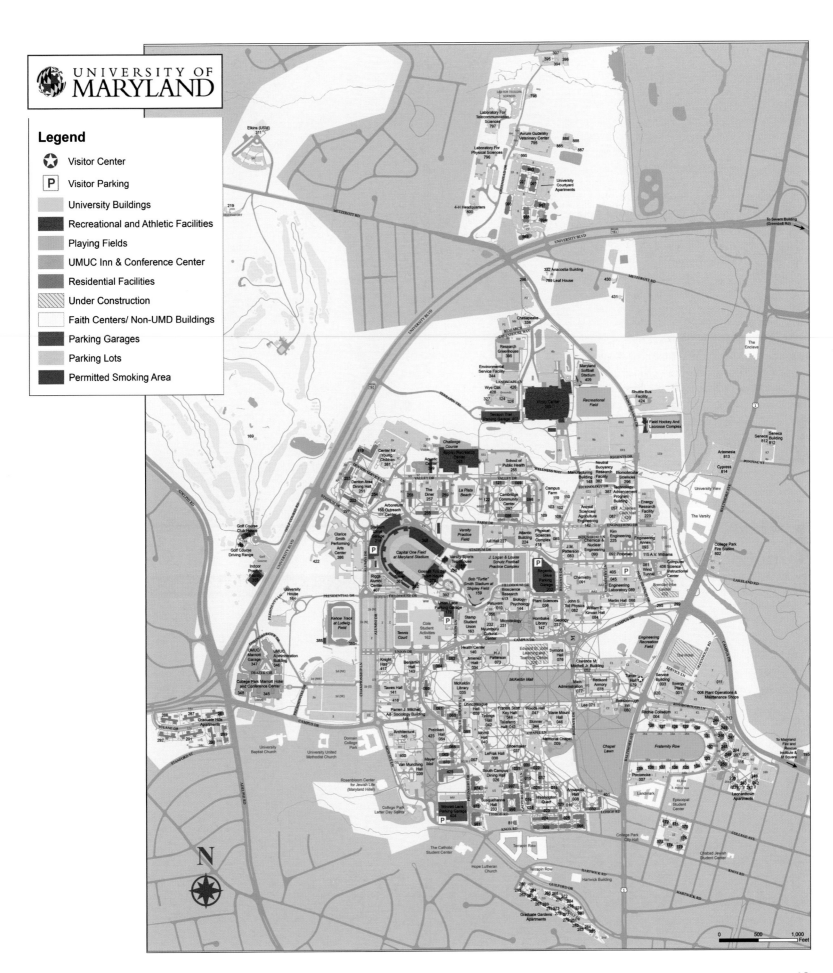

These three student projects were completed as part of the geospatial science course taught at Loudoun County high schools in Virginia in association with the Geospatial Semester program at James Madison University (JMU).

The Geospatial Semester is a unique partnership between high schools in Virginia and the Integrated Science and Technology Department at JMU. High school seniors participating in the Geospatial Semester learn about GIS software, geospatial analysis, remote sensing, and satellite imaging, and apply their knowledge to a final project of their own choosing. A key aspect of the program is a focus on local projects connecting students, technology, and their community. Nearly 3,000 students on thirty-four high school campuses have earned college credit while learning geospatial technologies through this program.

Rerouting the Iterarod

Science Office, Loudoun County Public Schools
Ashburn, Virginia, USA
By Henry Hall and Lauren Granata

This project looks to reroute the Iditarod, the annual long-distance sled dog race in Alaska, due to complications resulting from climate change.

Contact
Michael Wagner
Michael.Wagner@lcps.org

Software
ArcGIS Desktop

Data Sources
US Geological Survey, Alaska Department of Natural Resources

Courtesy of Science Office, Loudoun County Public Schools.

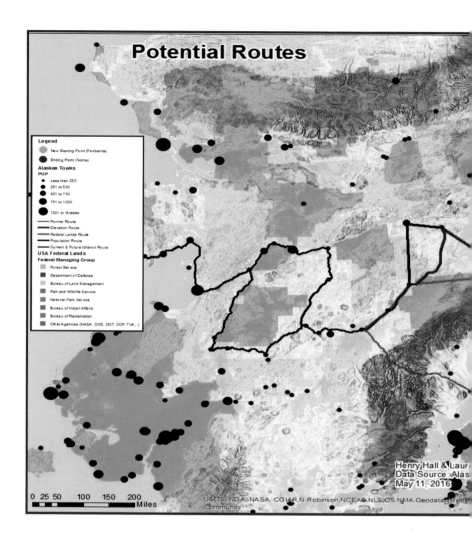

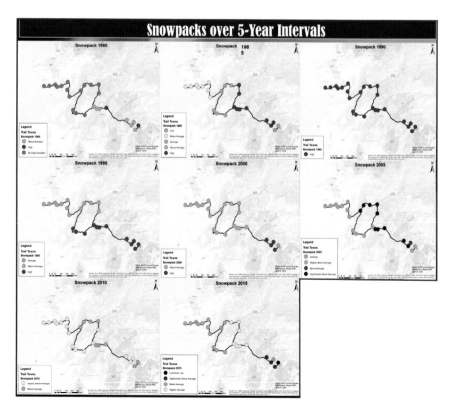

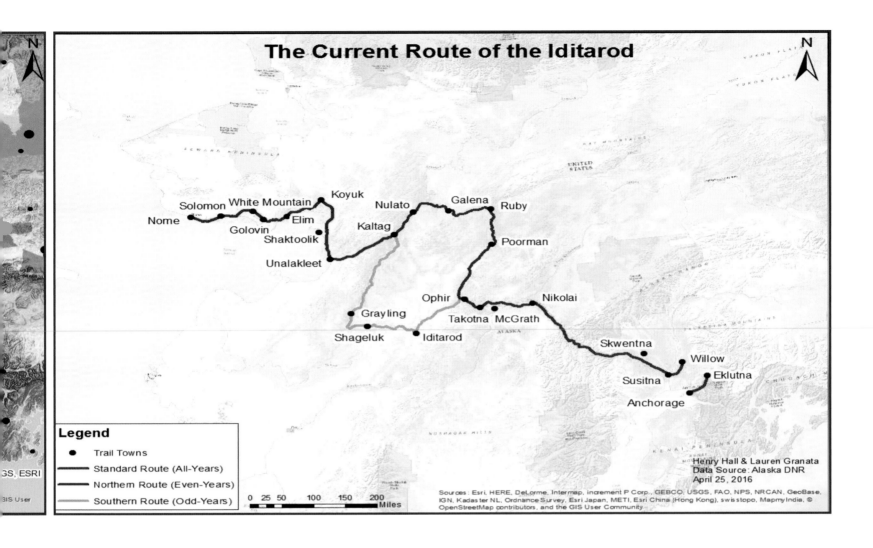

The Current Route of the Iditarod

Legend
- ● Trail Towns
- ▬ Standard Route (All-Years)
- ▬ Northern Route (Even-Years)
- ▬ Southern Route (Odd-Years)

0 25 50 100 150 200 Miles

Henry Hall & Lauren Granata
Data Source: Alaska DNR
April 25, 2016

Sources: Esri, HERE, DeLorme, Intermap, increment P Corp., GEBCO, USGS, FAO, NPS, NRCAN, GeoBase, IGN, Kadaster NL, Ordnance Survey, Esri Japan, METI, Esri China (Hong Kong), swisstopo, MapmyIndia, © OpenStreetMap contributors, and the GIS User Community

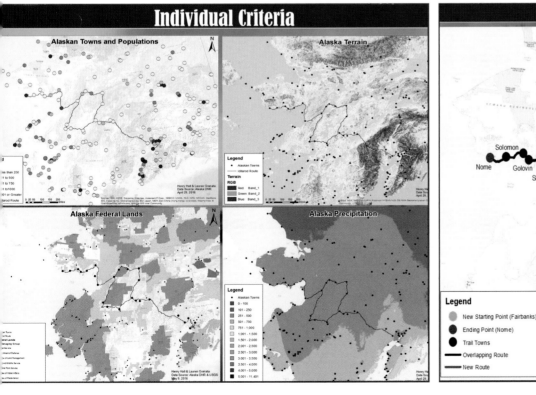

Individual Criteria

Alaskan Towns and Populations

Alaska Terrain

Alaska Federal Lands

Alaska Precipitation

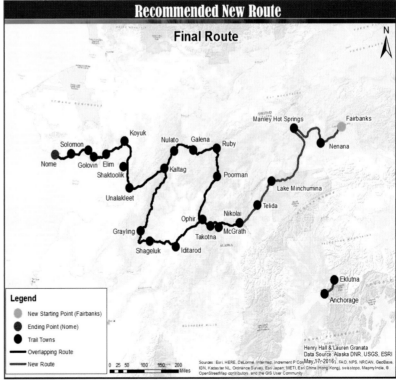

Recommended New Route

Final Route

Legend
- ● New Starting Point (Fairbanks)
- ● Ending Point (Nome)
- ● Trail Towns
- ▬ Overlapping Route
- ▬ New Route

0 25 50 100 150 200 Miles

Henry Hall & Lauren Granata
Data Source: Alaska DNR, USGS, ESRI
May 17, 2016

Sources: Esri, HERE, DeLorme, Intermap, increment P Corp., FAO, NPS, NRCAN, GeoBase, IGN, Kadaster NL, Ordnance Survey, Esri Japan, METI, Esri China (Hong Kong), swisstopo, MapmyIndia, © OpenStreetMap contributors, and the GIS User Community

Risk Assessment of Climate-Induced Sea Level Rise in Virginia Beach by 2100

Science Office, Loudoun County Public Schools
Ashburn, Virginia, USA
By Aaron Agena and Vivek Ramakrishnan

Using sea level rise predictions for the year 2100, this project attempts to show areas of Virginia Beach, Virginia, that would be most at risk if predictions are correct.

Contact
Michael Wagner
Michael.Wagner@lcps.org

Software
ArcGIS Desktop

Data Sources
Virginia LiDAR, Virginia Institute of Marine Science, City of Virginia Beach GIS

Courtesy of Science Office, Loudoun County Public Schools.

Virginia Beach Elevation

Elevation

High : 1643
Low : -42

0   0.175   0.35   0.7 Miles

This map shows the elevation of the study area in Virginia Beach. The darker colors on the map represent buildings or geography that have high elevation, while the lighter colors represent low elevation. Based on the color scheme of this map, this area of Virginia Beach has typically low elevation, with some tall infrastructure. In addition, there are no natural buffers that could help prevent this area from flooding and storms.

Virginia Beach Flooring and Building Damage

Effects of High Estimate Sea Level Rise

☐ Buildings Affected
▨ Flooded Areas (<12m)

0   0.075   0.15   0.3 Miles

This map shows a zoomed in area of the study area so that it is easier to see what buildings would be affected with the high estimate sea level rise. It is easy to see that the roads are flooded along with the areas around each building. This only contains half of the buildings within the study area, and already a great number of infrastructure would be damaged, and possibly destroyed.

Virginia Beach High Estimate–Sea Level Rise (2100)

Sea Level Rise Extent (High)

■ Flooded Areas (<12 m)

This map shows the area of flooding based on a high estimate of sea level rise. This required a two part analysis. Bruun's law was used to determine what the mean water level would be after a complete erosion of the coastline. Then the remaining amount of sea level rise after the 85 cm to erode the sea level was added to the mean water level at the top of the coastline–equaling approximately 12m of sea level rise. The horizontal extent of flooding was determined by historical flooding trends during storm surges (800m from the coastline)

Virginia Beach Risk Assessment of–High Estimate Sea Level Rise (2100)

Effects of High Estimate Sea Level Rise

■ Buildings Affected

0   0.25   0.5   1 Miles

1387 buildings/infrastructure will be affected in the study area.

Including:

191 commercial buildings	935 single family homes/duplex's	Average property value of Boardwalk area/study area is 360,000–resulting in almost $500 million dollars of damage in the study area alone (Zillow.com).
196 multi-family homes	3 town house developments	
7 office buildings	1 elementary school	
37 public/semi public spaces	The entire boardwalk area	

The Effects of Deforestation on the Amazon Rain Forest

Science Office, Loudoun County Public Schools
Ashburn, Virginia, USA
By C.J. Monroe

This project analyzed deforestation in the Amazon Rain Forest between 2000 and 2010 using data found in ArcGIS Online.

Contact
Michael Wagner
Michael.Wagner@lcps.org

Software
ArcGIS Desktop

Data Sources
NASA, ArcGIS Online Deforestation maps

Courtesy of Science Office, Loudoun County Public Schools.

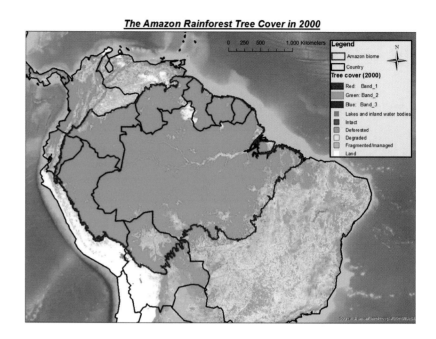

The Amazon Rainforest Tree Cover in 2000

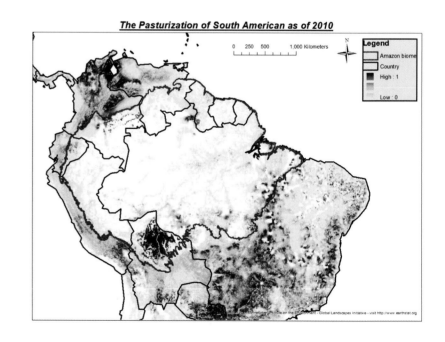

The Pasturization of South American as of 2010

The Amazon Rainforest Tree Cover as of 2010

The Amazon Rainforest Deforestation from 2000 to 2010 in Sq.Km.

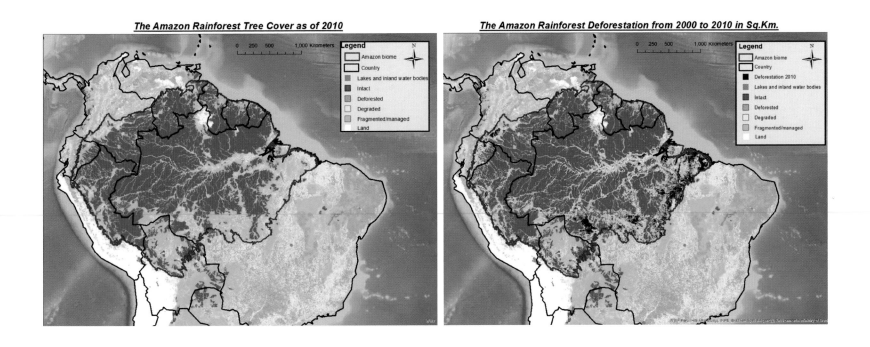

Population Density of South America as of 2010

South American's Annual Average Percepitation from 2000 to 2010 in mm.

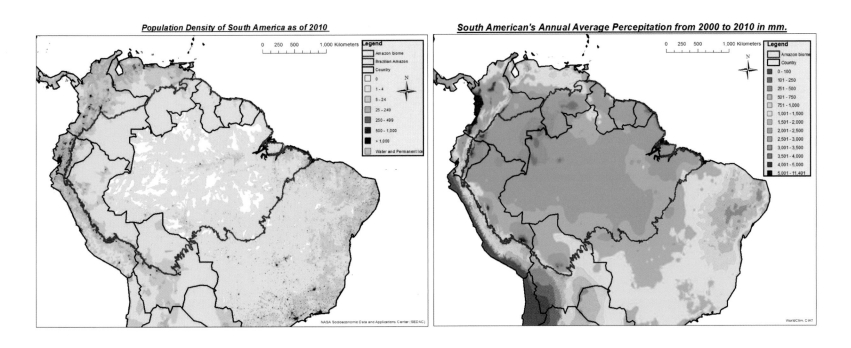

Russian River Salmon and Steelhead Monitoring Map

University of California, San Diego, California
Sea Grant Extension
Santa Rosa, California, USA
By Andrew Bartshire

In 2004, native coho salmon were on the brink of elimination from the Russian River watershed, located 50 miles north of San Francisco. The Russian River Coho Salmon Captive Broodstock Program began releasing juvenile coho salmon into tributaries of the Russian River with the goal of reestablishing self-sustaining populations.

University of California Cooperative Extension and California Sea Grant worked with local, state, and federal biologists to design and implement a coho salmon monitoring program to track the survival and abundance of hatchery-released fish. In 2013, the Cooperative Extension and Sea Grant partnered with the Sonoma County Water Agency and California Department of Fish and Wildlife to begin implementation of the California Coastal Monitoring Program, a statewide effort to document status and trends of migrating salmon populations using standardized methods and a centralized statewide database.

Sea Grant biologists now monitor over 145 miles of stream in forty Russian River tributaries. This map provides an overview of the coho salmon monitoring program and is used by Sea Grant biologists to plan and coordinate monitoring efforts.

Contact
Andrew Bartshire
abartshire@ucsd.edu

Software
ArcGIS for Desktop 10.3

Data Sources
County of Sonoma, California Department of
Fish and Wildlife

*Courtesy of University of California, San Diego, California
Sea Grant Extension.*

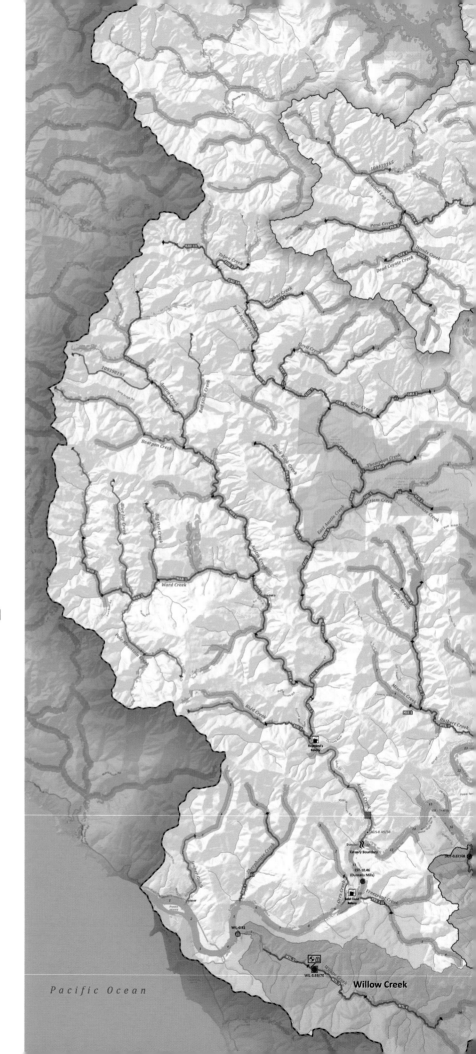

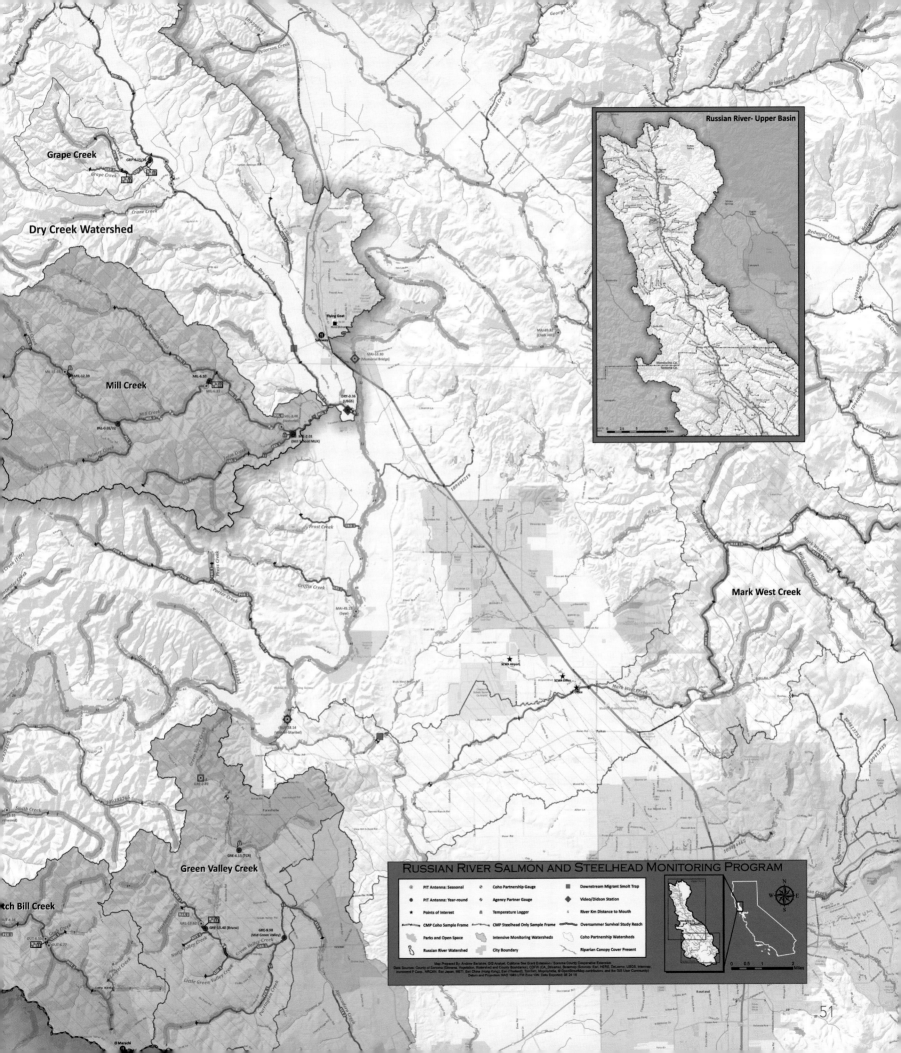

RUSSIAN RIVER SALMON AND STEELHEAD MONITORING PROGRAM

Russian River- Upper Basin

Grape Creek

Dry Creek Watershed

Mill Creek

Green Valley Creek

Mark West Creek

tch Bill Creek

Legend		
PIT Antenna: Seasonal	Coho Partnership Gauge	Downstream Migrant Smolt Trap
PIT Antenna: Year-round	Agency Partner Gauge	Video/Didson Station
Points of Interest	Temperature Logger	River Km Distance to Mouth
CMP Coho Sample Frame	CMP Steelhead Only Sample Frame	Oversummer Survival Study Reach
Parks and Open Space	Intensive Monitoring Watersheds	Coho Partnership Watersheds
Russian River Watershed	City Boundary	Riparian Canopy Cover Present

Map Prepared By: Andrew Bartshire, GIS Analyst, California Sea Grant Extension / Sonoma County Cooperative Extension
Data Sources: County of Sonoma (Streams, Vegetation, Watershed and County Boundaries), CDFW (CA_Streams), Basemap (Sources: Esri, HERE, DeLorme, USGS, Intermap, increment P Corp., NRCAN, Esri Japan, METI, Esri China (Hong Kong), Esri (Thailand), TomTom, Mapmyindia, © OpenStreetMap contributors, and the GIS User Community)
Datum and Projection: NAD 1983 UTM Zone 10N Date Exported: 08 24 16

The Environmental Burden Index

Centers for Disease Control and Prevention (CDC)
Atlanta, Georgia, USA
By Jessica Kolling, Olivia Leach, Ian Dunn, and Brian Lewis

The Environmental Burden Index (EBI) is the first nationwide estimate of environmental quality available at the census tract level to support public health research and practice. The methods used to create the EBI are an innovative development in the way environmental datasets are analyzed, visualized, and used. The EBI makes environmental data more approachable and easier to use for data-driven decision-making, policy initiatives, and hypothesis generation to support environmental public health. This visualization displays EBI data in Georgia and describes the data and methods used to create the index and associated peer groups.

Contact
Jessica Kolling
jkolli10@gmail.com

Software
ArcGIS for Desktop 10.3

Data Sources
CDC's Environmental Health Tracking Program, US Environmental Protection Agency, TomTom, National Drought Mitigation Center, US Department of Agriculture, National Oceanic and Atmospheric Administration, Multi-Resolution Land Characteristics Consortium, US Census Bureau.

Courtesy of CDC.

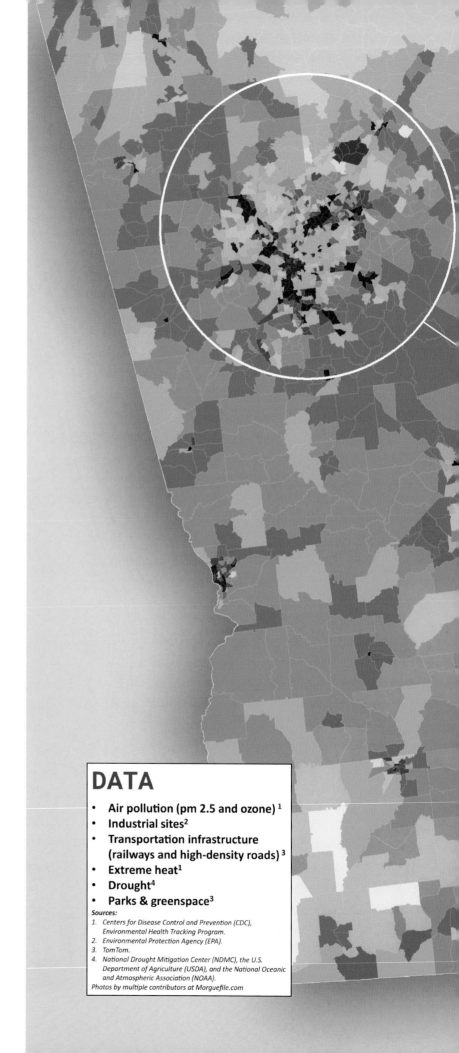

DATA

- **Air pollution (pm 2.5 and ozone)** [1]
- **Industrial sites** [2]
- **Transportation infrastructure (railways and high-density roads)** [3]
- **Extreme heat** [1]
- **Drought** [4]
- **Parks & greenspace** [3]

Sources:
1. *Centers for Disease Control and Prevention (CDC), Environmental Health Tracking Program.*
2. *Environmental Protection Agency (EPA).*
3. *TomTom.*
4. *National Drought Mitigation Center (NDMC), the U.S. Department of Agriculture (USDA), and the National Oceanic and Atmospheric Association (NOAA).*
Photos by multiple contributors at Morguefile.com

ENVIRONMENTAL PEER GROUPS

Environmental data are often proxies for urbanicity. If Index scores were ranked at a state or national level census tracts with the "worst" environmental quality would be located in urban areas. Environmental Peer Groups were derived from National Land Cover Database Data (NLCD). The NLCD is a land cover classification scheme that uses 16 classes to define the US geography at a spatial resolution of 30 meters. We used the "Tabulate Features to Percent" tool (developed by USGS) to calculate each census tract's predominate land cover class. We then condensed classification schemes to the following peer groups:

1. Developed Open
2. Developed Low
3. Developed Medium
4. Developed High

5. Forest
6. Shrubland*
7. Herbaceous*
8. Planted/Cultivated

9. Wetlands
10. Water/Barren

*not found in Georgia

Atlanta

Marine Munitions Survey

HDR, Inc.
San Diego, California, USA
By Bryan Hosford and Kira Lofgren

In response to evidence of World War II-era munitions on the Florida site, marine-based remote sensing surveys were conducted to locate, identify, and characterize ferrous items on and near the seafloor. This multidisciplinary approach to finding unexploded ordinance involved geophysics, former Navy explosive ordinance disposal technicians, and GIS. An array of technologies was used, including side scanning sonar, remotely operated vehicles, and a specially designed magnetometer array that profile-mapped the bay floor. Side scan sonar was used to assist in site characterization to locate underwater hazards prior to deploying magnetometer array.

Ferrous metal objects were detected and mapped as anomalies shown on the map. GIS was used to integrate side scan sonar results with the magnetometer anomalies. Dive teams and remotely operated vehicles were deployed to investigate a percentage of the anomalies for the characterization of the site. GIS was used in all stages of the multiyear project from site suitability to data collection and verification to analysis of results.

Contact
Anders Burvall
anders.burvall@hdrinc.com

Software
ArcGIS for Desktop 10.3, Adobe Photoshop

Data Source
HDR, Inc.

Courtesy of HDR, Inc.

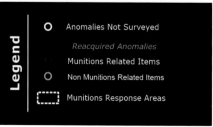

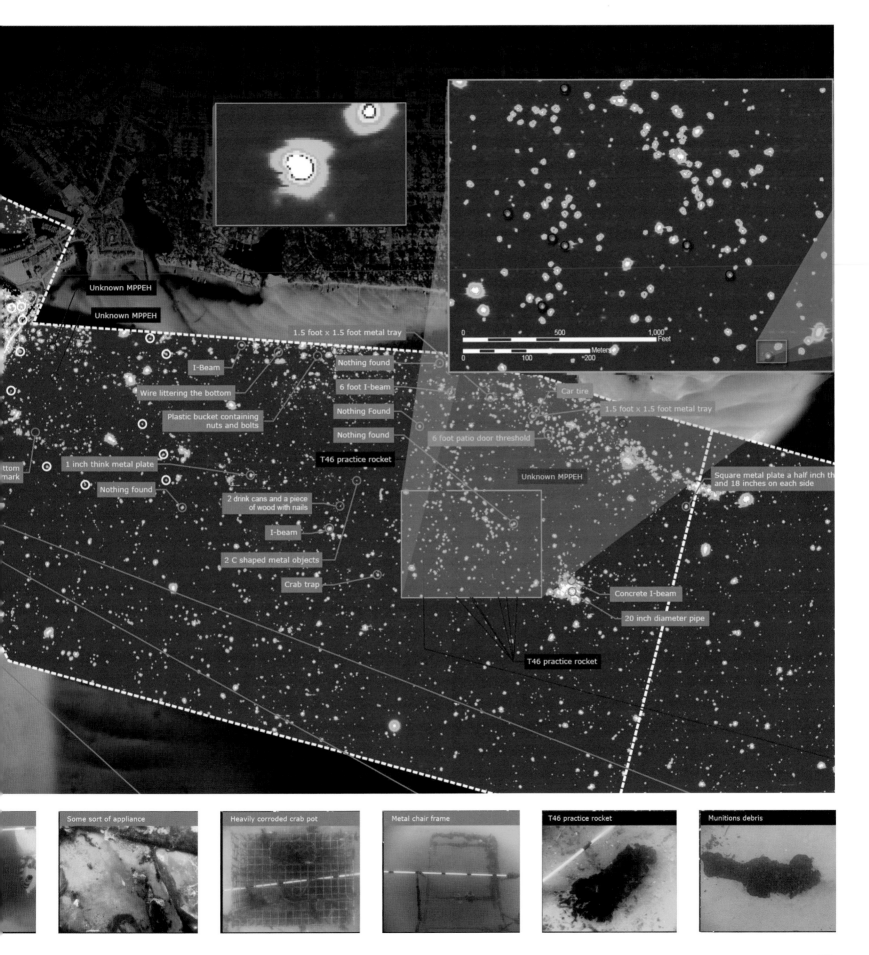

Unknown MPPEH

Unknown MPPEH

1.5 foot x 1.5 foot metal tray

I-Beam

Wire littering the bottom

Plastic bucket containing nuts and bolts

Nothing found

6 foot I-beam

Nothing Found

Nothing found

T46 practice rocket

Car tire

1.5 foot x 1.5 foot metal tray

6 foot patio door threshold

Unknown MPPEH

Square metal plate a half inch th and 18 inches on each side

1 inch think metal plate

Nothing found

2 drink cans and a piece of wood with nails

I-beam

2 C shaped metal objects

Crab trap

Concrete I-beam

20 inch diameter pipe

T46 practice rocket

ttom mark

0   500   1,000
Feet
0   100   200
Meters

Some sort of appliance

Heavily corroded crab pot

Metal chair frame

T46 practice rocket

Munitions debris

Las Vegas Metropolitan Police Disorder Calls

Las Vegas Metropollitan Police Department
Las Vegas, Nevada, USA
By Amy McCarthy

Disorder calls for service such as reckless drivers, vandalism, and public intoxication are important to track for a number of reasons. Disorder calls make up a significant amount of overall call volume to the 9-1-1 emergency line. By tracking the density of disorder calls, the Las Vegas Metropolitan Police Department can ensure the most effective deployment of resources, thereby lowering response times. Also, addressing smaller crimes in a neighborhood theoretically prevents the area from escalating to more serious crimes. By mapping both the density of disorder calls as well as spatial trends, analysts are able to identify hot spots of disorder activity and provide more in-depth analysis of those problem areas.

Contact
Amy McCarthy
A15360M@lvmpd.com

Software
ArcGIS for Desktop 10.0

Data Source
Las Vegas Metropolitan Police Department Computer-Aided Dispatch

Courtesy of Las Vegas Metropolitan Police Department and Southern Nevada Counter Terrorism Center, Analytical Section

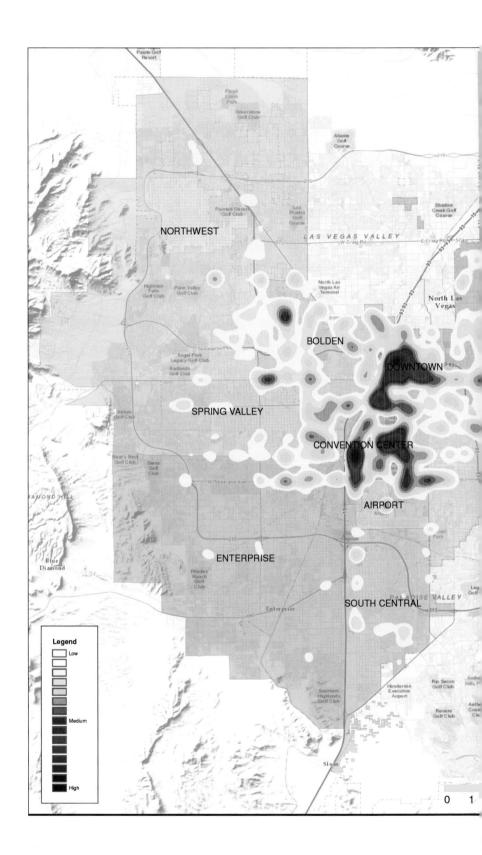

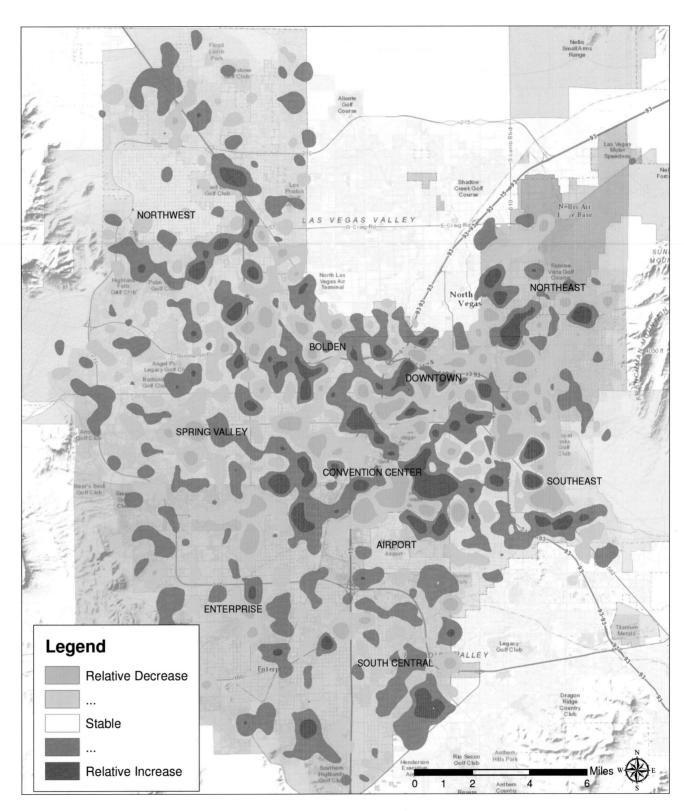

Legend

Relative Decrease

...

Stable

...

Relative Increase

City of Phoenix Enhanced Flood Risk Analysis

Michael Baker International
Lakewood, Colorado, USA
By Jason Isherwood and Daniel Aragon

Determining relative flood risk to structures is an essential community planning tool. GIS makes performing this type of analysis for large metropolitan areas such as Phoenix more approachable and effective than ever. Michael Baker International analyzed 100-year flood return interval spatial data and developed estimated flood depth grids based on floodplain boundaries and cross-sectional data. The resulting depth data was then spatially compared with assessor parcel information (including replacement costs and building/foundation types) to determine potentially impacted structures.

Hazus software provided by the Federal Emergency Management Agency (FEMA) was used to estimate losses as a result of this hazard event. Additionally, these parcel-based (representing individual structure) loss results were then compared with the Hazus default aggregated inventory to be used by the city and FEMA for planning purposes. This map layout summarizes the technical approach to this project by outlining the basic steps undertaken from start to finish as well as visualizes the qualitative results extruded on a 3D landscape.

Contact
Jason Isherwood
jisherwood@mbakerintl.com

Software
ArcGIS for Desktop 10.2.2, ArcGIS Pro 1.1,
Hazus 3.0, Adobe Photoshop CS6,
Adobe Illustrator CS6

Data Sources
Federal Emergency Management Agency, City of Phoenix, Maricopa County, Flood Control District of Maricopa County

Courtesy of Michael Baker International.

City of Phoenix Boundary

State of Arizona Building,
1901 West Madison Street

High Losses

Low Losses

Downtown Phoenix

Salt River

Parcel Based Structural Losses

Agriculture
Residential   Commercial
               Education
               Government
               Industrial
               Religious

General Building Stock - Census Block Based Structural Losses

Agriculture
Residential   Commercial
                   Education
                   Government
                   Industrial
                   Religious

59

Tsunami Vulnerability: Crescent City, California

Michael Baker International
Lakewood, Colorado, USA
By Aron Langely, Daniel Aragon, Jason Isherwood, and Nicole Metz

Michael Baker International developed a series of 3D and 2D map visualizations and analysis results for Crescent City, California, showing the city's potential vulnerability to a tsunami. Based on the raw results of a pilot study conducted by the Federal Emergency Management Agency, the University of Washington, and BakerAECOM as part of the Risk MAP program, the GIS team developed potential tsunami inundation extents and depth grids. Following that effort, the team analyzed the potential vulnerabilities and impacts to notable infrastructure and existing land use for the areas in and around Crescent City. The results were presented as an informational poster and made available to local and regional decision-makers to aid with future hazard mitigation and planning efforts.

Contact

Jason Isherwood
jisherwood@mbakerintl.com

Software

ArcGIS for Desktop 10.2.2, ArcGIS Pro 1.1, GeoClaw, Adobe Photoshop CS6, Adobe Illustrator CS6

Data Sources

Federal Emergency Management Agency, University of Washington Probabilistic Tsunami Hazard Assessment, City of Crescent City, Michael Baker International, National Oceanic and Atmospheric Administration

Courtesy of Michael Baker International.

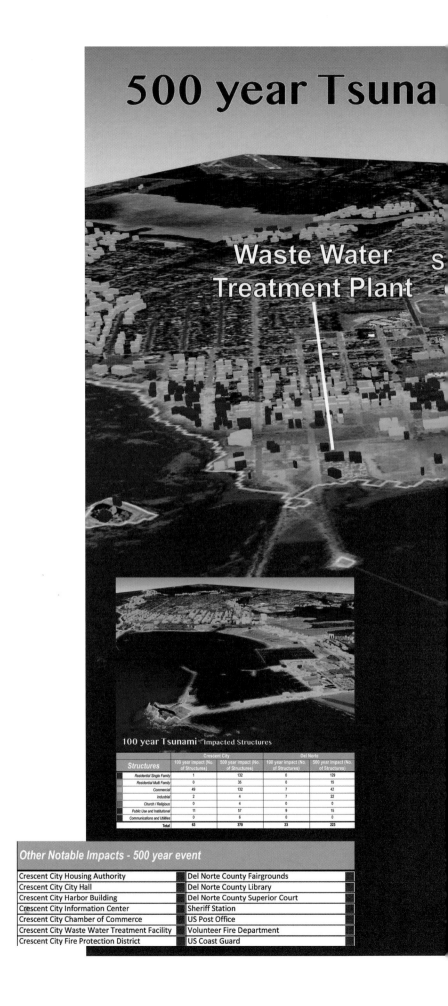

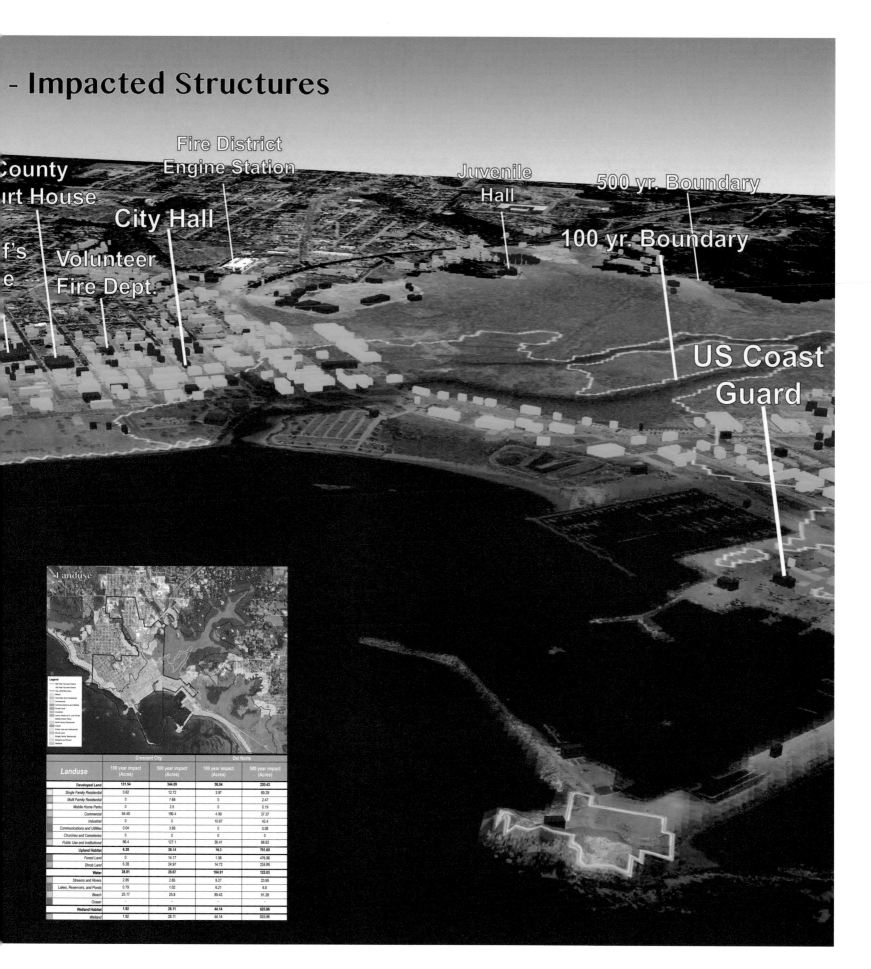

- Impacted Structures

County
rt House

f's
e

Volunteer
Fire Dept.

City Hall

Fire District
Engine Station

Juvenile
Hall

500 yr. Boundary

100 yr. Boundary

US Coast
Guard

Landuse

Landuse	Crescent City		Del Norte	
	100 year impact (Acres)	500 year impact (Acres)	100 year impact (Acres)	500 year impact (Acres)
Developed Land	**131.54**	**344.09**	**56.04**	**220.43**
Single Family Residential	0.62	12.72	3.97	69.29
Multi Family Residential	0	7.68	0	2.47
Mobile Home Parks	0	2.5	0	0.19
Commercial	64.48	190.4	4.99	37.37
Industrial	0	0	10.67	42.4
Communications and Utilities	0.04	3.69	0	0.08
Churches and Cemeteries	0	0	0	0
Public Use and Institutional	66.4	127.1	36.41	68.63
Upland Habitat	**6.28**	**39.14**	**16.3**	**701.85**
Forest Land	0	14.17	1.58	476.96
Shrub Land	6.28	24.97	14.72	224.89
Water	**28.81**	**29.67**	**104.91**	**122.03**
Streams and Rivers	2.85	2.85	9.27	23.95
Lakes, Reservoirs, and Ponds	0.79	1.02	6.21	6.8
Beach	25.17	25.8	89.43	91.28
Ocean	-	-	-	-
Wetland Habitat	**1.92**	**28.11**	**44.14**	**625.96**
Wetland	1.92	28.11	44.14	625.96

Bike Aware

Sacramento County
Sacramento, California, USA
By Kirstyn Alex

This map displays bike accidents that have occurred in Sacramento, the capital of California, from 2010 to 2015. This case study analyzes temporal and spatial results as well as the outcomes and trends of bike accidents throughout the city. Although Sacramento is ranked highly for being bicycle friendly, there is still much to be done as far as infrastructure, awareness, and education to prevent accidents from occurring.

By tracking spatial data of accidents, the dispersion and trends can more easily be seen and understood to inform policy decisions and infrastructure improvements. It is especially helpful to see the density of accidents as well as hot spots in order to target specific locations in need of safety improvements. The City of Sacramento is currently updating the Bicycle Master Plan, working with public agencies and private entities to influence policy decisions and ensure the continued improvement of its infrastructure.

Contact

Kirstyn Alex

kirstynalex@gmail.com

Software

ArcGIS for Desktop 10.4.1

Data Source

Sacramento Police Department, Crime Analysis Unit

Courtesy of Sacramento County and Kirstyn Alex.

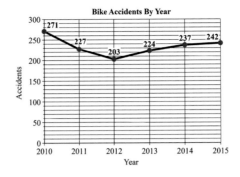

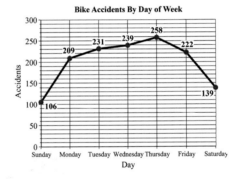

It is clear by observing the weekly chart that workday commuting is the most popular time for biking and therefore, bike accidents. The number of accidents on weekdays is about double the number of accidents on weekends.

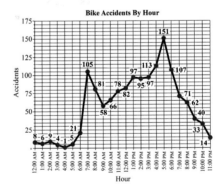

The number of accidents by hour again shows that the most dangerous time for bikers is in rush hour traffic.

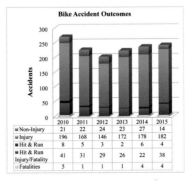

The distribution of bike accident outcomes is mostly expected. The most shocking numbers are the counts of hits-and-runs.

Arena Boulevard

Bell Avenue

Boulevard

TruxelRoad

Northgate Boulevard

Norwood Avenue

Marysville Boulevard

Auburn Boulevard

West El Camino Avenue

El Camino Avenue

Garden Highway

Arden Way

Elvas Avenue

Howe Avenue

7th Street

E Street

North 5th Street

H Street

T Street

T Street

N Street

P Street

T Street

H Street

J Street

M Street

28th Street

Folsom Boulevard (36)

Folsom Boulevard (36)

5th Street

Riverside Boulevard

Land Park Drive

21st Street

Broadway (30)

Alhambra Boulevard (33)

Stockton Boulevard (56)

Jackson Road

Powerinn Road

Florin Perkins Road

Fruitridge Road (30)

Martin Luther King Jr. Boulevard

Freeport Boulevard

24th Street (32)

Elder Creek Road

Florin Road (35)

Franklin Boulevard

Pocket Road

63

Landslide Susceptibility and Element at Risk Assessment

GeoBC
Victoria, British Columbia, Canada
By Azadeh Ramesh

Landslide susceptibility mapping and identifying the risk zonation are required for urban and rural development, land-use planning, natural-disaster management, and emergency responses. Modeling and mapping the landslide disaster and risk zonation, in combination with advanced new technologies such as web maps and mobile apps, is extremely helpful for stakeholders, land planning, and decision-support managers.

This project explores the opportunities for using GIS to assess landslide susceptibility and elements at risk. The resulting maps showing landslide susceptibility zonation and elements at risk classified the area into five relative susceptibility classes: very high, high, moderate, low, and very low. The final map helps planners select suitable areas for development and implement appropriate mitigation measures in the landslide-prone areas. A mobile app was developed for landslide field investigation and data monitoring in real time, enabling users to make timely decisions in emergency situations, respond to landslide events, and take immediate action.

Contact

Azadeh Ramesh
azadeh.ramesh@gov.bc.ca

Software

ArcGIS for Desktop 10.2.2, ArcGIS Pro 1.2.0

Data Source

BC Geographic Warehouse

Courtesy of GeoBC, Decision Support Section.

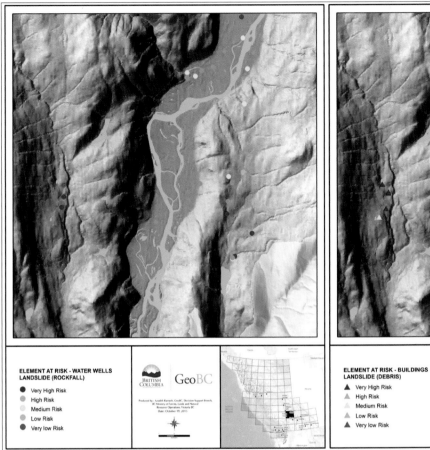

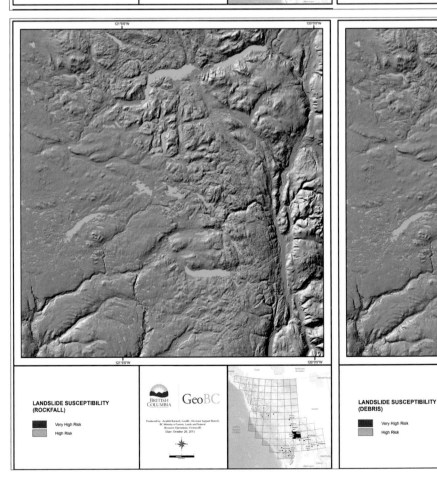

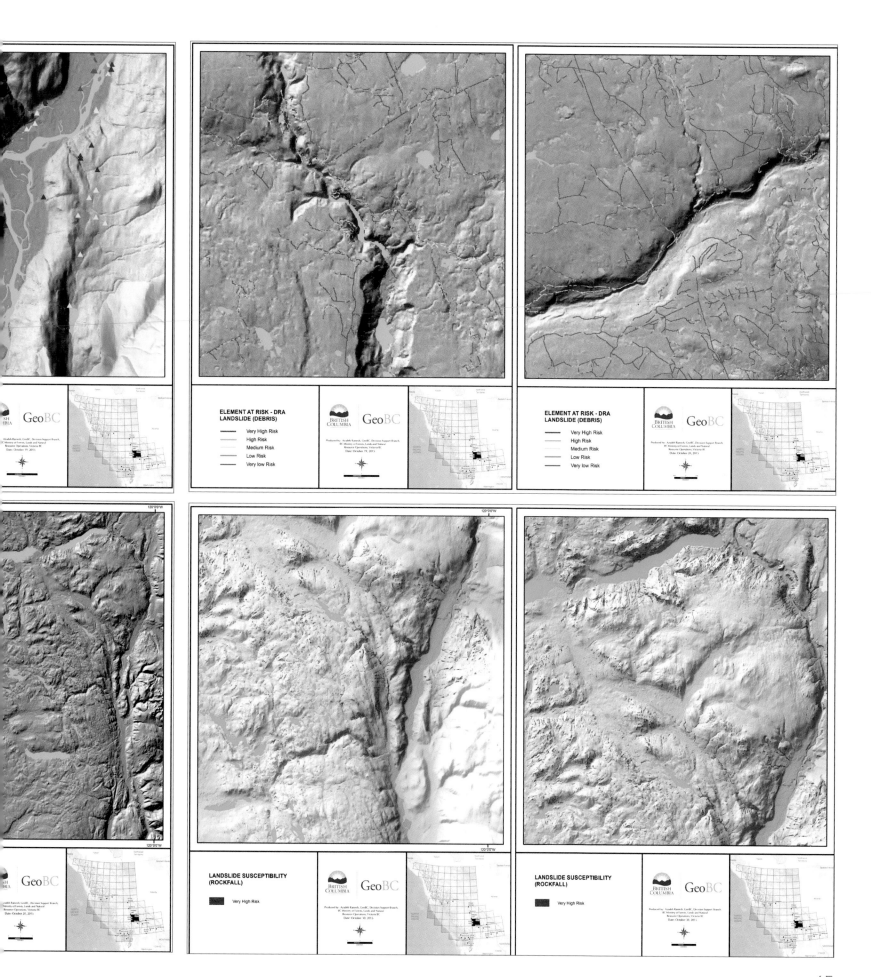

ELEMENT AT RISK - DRA
LANDSLIDE (DEBRIS)

— Very High Risk
— High Risk
— Medium Risk
— Low Risk
— Very low Risk

GeoBC

ELEMENT AT RISK - DRA
LANDSLIDE (DEBRIS)

— Very High Risk
— High Risk
— Medium Risk
— Low Risk
— Very low Risk

GeoBC

LANDSLIDE SUSCEPTIBILITY
(ROCKFALL)

▪ Very High Risk

GeoBC

LANDSLIDE SUSCEPTIBILITY
(ROCKFALL)

▪ Very High Risk

GeoBC

First Creek, Wolverine, and Chelan Complex Wildfire Map

US Department of Agriculture (USDA) Forest Service
Albuquerque, New Mexico, USA
By Jarl Moreland

This map of the Chelan Complex, Wolverine, First Creek, and Blankenship wildfires depicts the geographic extent and operational details of fire operations as of September 8, 2015 in North Central Washington. That was an extremely, active year for wildland fire in the Pacific Northwest. Maps like this were used to convey information about the incidents to fire personnel, the public, and private entities to influence policy decisions and ensure the continued improvement of the infrastructure.

Contact

Jarl Moreland
jmoreland@fs.fed.us

Software

ArcGIS for Desktop 10.1.1

Data Source

USDA Forest Service

Courtesy of USDA Forest Service.

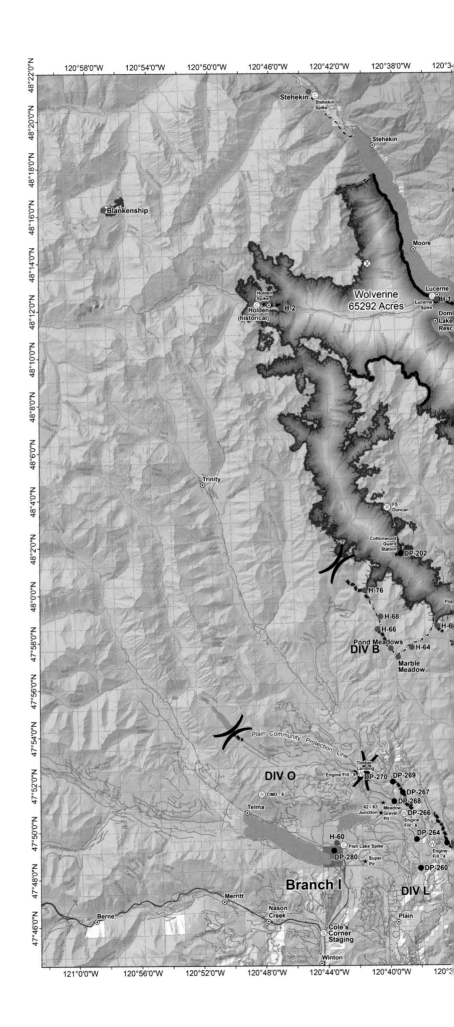

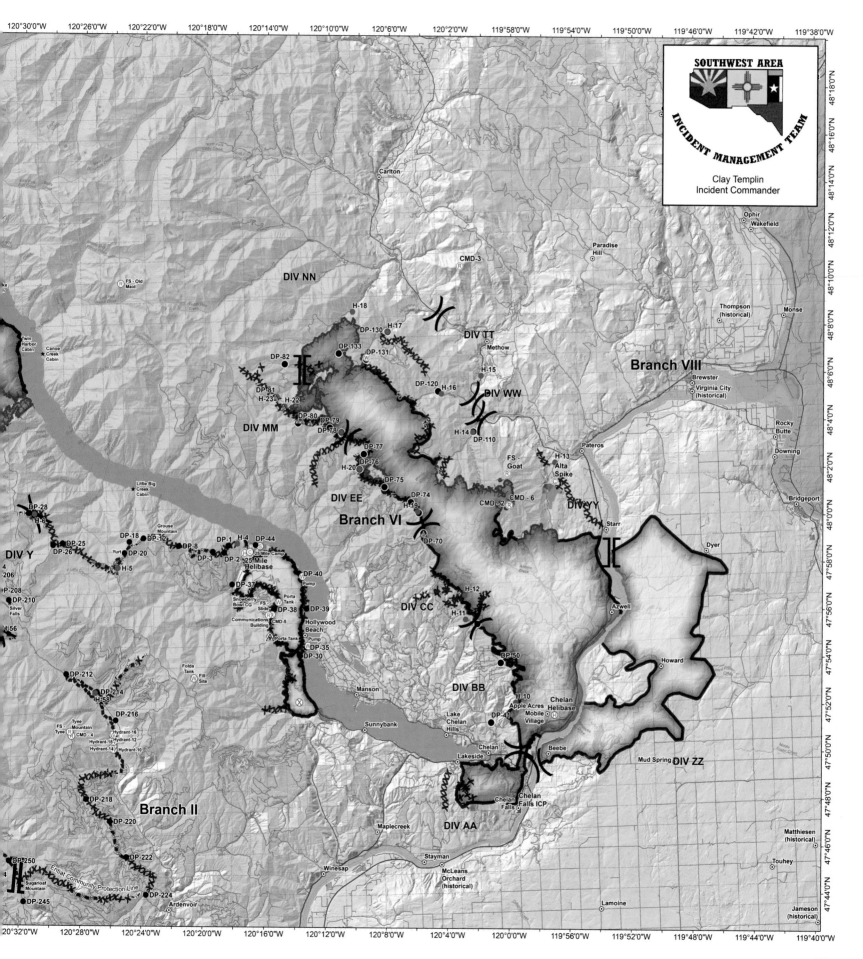

Current Weather and Forecasts Web App

Property & Liability Resource Bureau (PLRB)
Downers Grove, Illinois, USA
By Andrew Louchios

PLRB is a not-for-profit association of property and casualty insurance companies. PLRB's "Current Weather and Forecasts" web app provides current radar, severe weather outlooks, tropical storm disturbances and probability formation areas, active tropical storms, watches/warnings, snow/precipitation forecasts, and more.

Using the GeoLookup widget, users can upload their policyholder data points to the map and overlay any of the layers. Also, as the default, the data points will be enriched using the severe weather outlook data (the image displays data points that fall within and outside the polygon severe weather outlook areas). Users can then download the csv and do further analysis to determine how many policyholders may be affected by severe weather for the current day.

Contact

Andrew Louchios
alouchios@plrb.org

Software

Web AppBuilder for ArcGIS (Developer Edition), Version 2.0

Data Sources

Esri, National Oceanic and Atmospheric Administration, Nationall Weather Service, nowCOAST

Courtesy of PLRB.

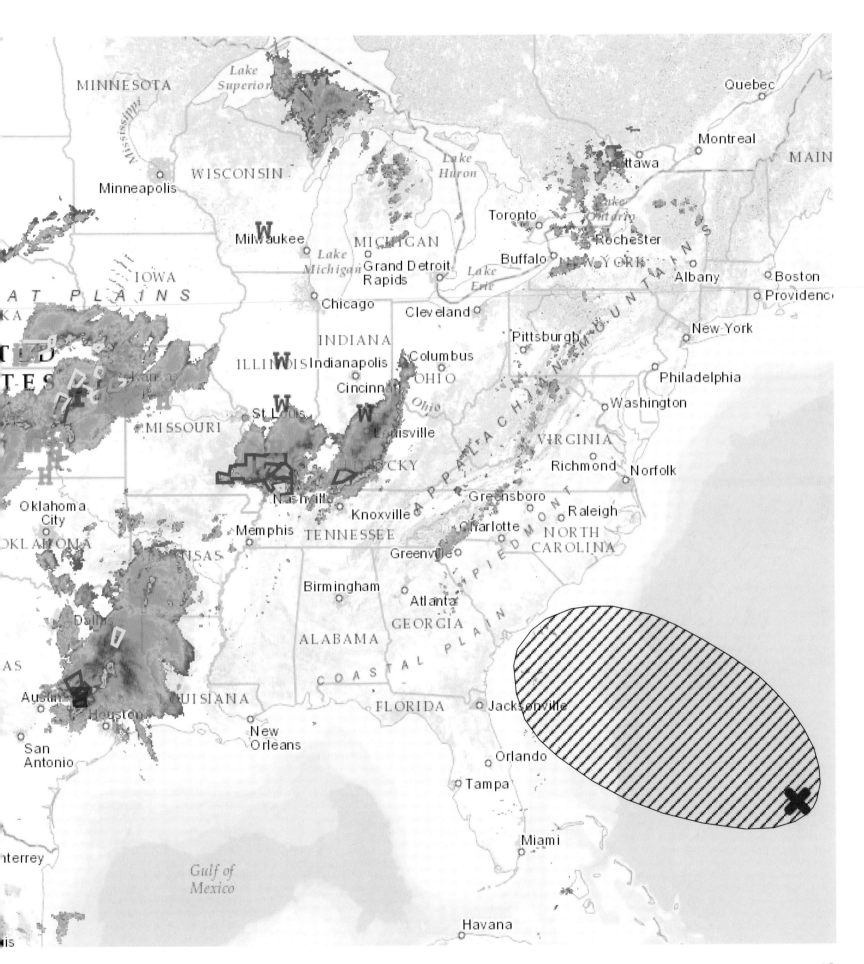

Arlington Expressway Mobility Corridor

Jacksonville Transportation Authority (JTA)
Jacksonville, Florida, USA
By Tom Blush

The purpose of this project was to identify and propose solutions to pedestrian safety and accessibility deficiencies along thirteen key mobility corridors throughout Jacksonville, Florida. The Arlington Expressway Mobility Corridor was using criteria relating to density, land-use diversity, pedestrian environment design, key destinations, and distance to bus stops. Ultimately, project areas within the corridor were identified, and prioritized using additional criteria including mobility and safety, funding leveragability, public health/livability, and economic development potential. Pedestrian safety and accessibility improvements that came out of this project included way finding, sidewalk replacement, lighting upgrades, and crosswalk striping.

Contact

Tom Blush
tblush@jtafla.com

Software

ArcGIS for Desktop 10.3

Data Sources

JTA, University of Florida Geoplan Center, Google, Esri

Courtesy of JTA.

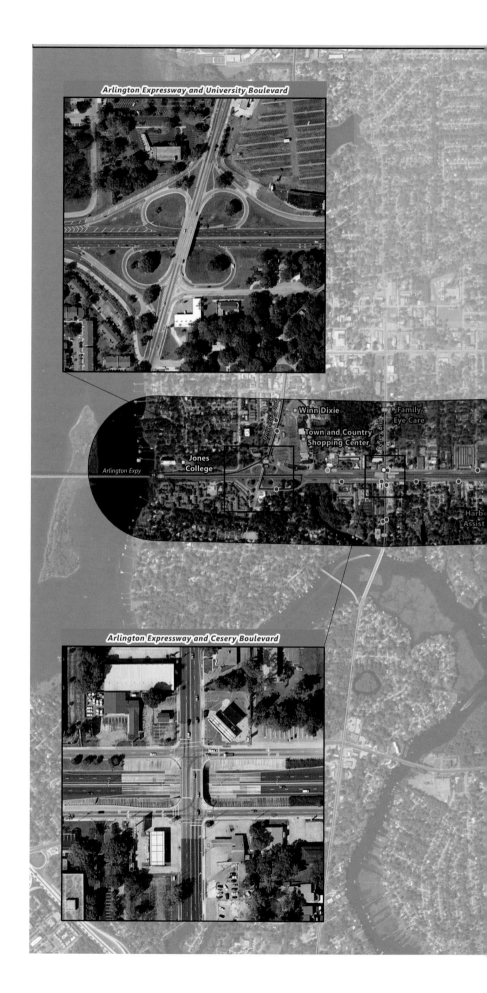

Arlington Expressway and Arlington Road

Arlington Expressway and Southside Connector

Purpose

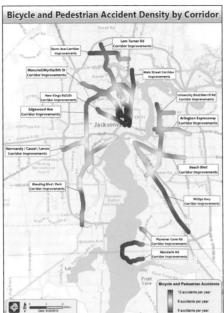

Bicycle and Pedestrian Accident Density by Corridor

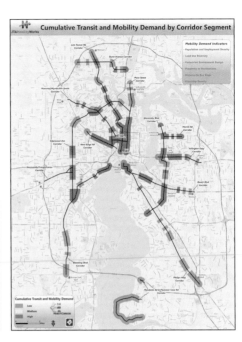

Cumulative Transit and Mobility Demand by Corridor Segment

Analysis

Arlington Expressway Mobility Corridor

Arlington Expressway Mobility Corridor

Results

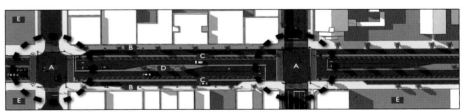

Arlington Expressway at University Boulevard

Existing

Proposed

71

Sidewalk Hazard Data Collection in City of West Jordan

City of West Jordan
West Jordan, Utah, USA
By Sheldon Baumgartner

This project analyzed sidewalks in West Jordan to identify potential tripping hazards for pedestrian safety, prioritizing repairs and reducing the city's liability. The city leveraged ArcGIS Online and the ArcGIS Collector App to complete the project. Inspectors used a wireless MiFi device with an IPad or cell phone and the Collector App to collect hazards in each district of the city. They collected different types of hazards, recorded the attributes, and attached photographs of each hazard to the point or line feature. The city's GIS staff created a hotspot map to show areas with a higher concentration of hazards collected, helping the Capital Improvements Project group to prioritize areas to fix and improve sidewalk conditions.

Contact

Cllint Hutchings
clinthu@wjordan.com

Software

ArcGIS for Desktop 10.3.1, Collector for ArcGIS®,
Adobe Acrobat Pro

Data Sources

City of West Jordan, Google Image Service

Courtesy of City of West Jordan.

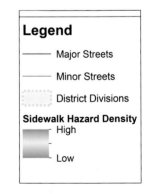

Legend

——— Major Streets

——— Minor Streets

⋯⋯ District Divisions

Sidewalk Hazard Density
High

Low

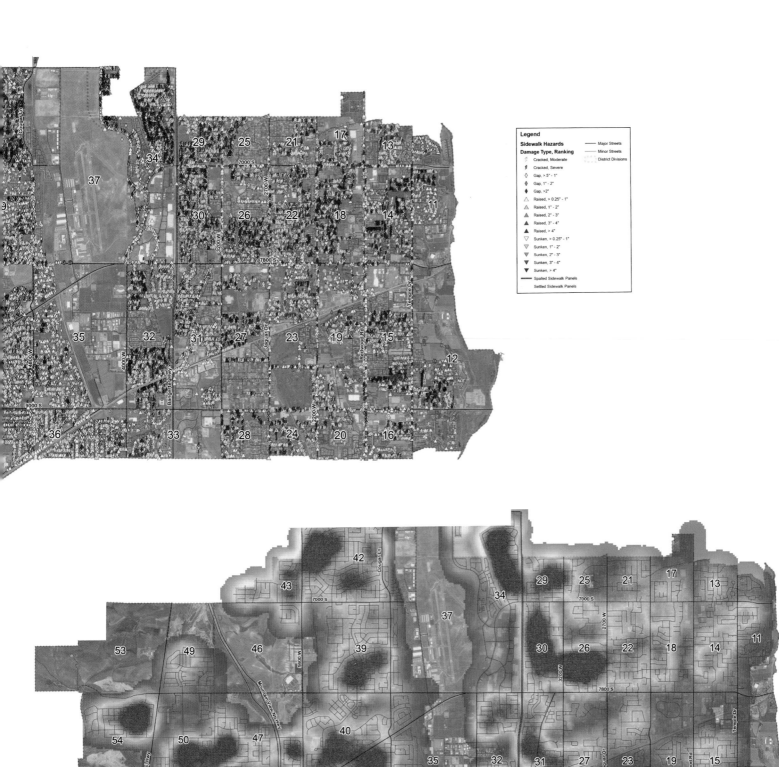

Building Data for Climate Change Adaptation

Center for International Earth Science Information Network (CIESIN), Columbia University
Palisades, New York, USA
By Alyssa Fico, Kytt MacManus, Jane Mills, and Greg Yetman

Coastal storms are among the world's costliest disasters. The destructive impacts of Hurricane Irene and Superstorm Sandy on the Hudson River Valley and Long Island demonstrate that New York is unprepared for future intensified coastal storms and sea level rise caused by climate change. Through a project funded by New York State Energy Research & Development, CIESIN partnered with the Stevens Institute of Technology and the Columbia Water Center to produce the Hudson River Flood Impact Decision Support System, version 1, a free online mapping tool that allows users to better understand the impacts of flood inundation posed by sea level rise, storm surge, and rain events.

Users can explore the interactive map to estimate potential environmental, social, and financial impacts of future flooding for decision-making purposes. They can download maps and statistical estimates of flooding impacts on populations, facilities, and buildings. The project website and mapping tool will help inform community planners, public officials, resource managers, and others who assess risk.

Contact

Alyssa Fico
afico@ciesin.columbia.edu

Software

ArcGIS for Desktop 10.3.1

Data Sources

Cornell University and the New York State Department of Environmental Conservation, Hudson River Estuary Program; Dutchess County Office of Central and Information Services; New York State GIS Program Office, Ulster County Planning Department

Courtesy of CIESIN, Columbia University.

Flood zones for 5-year to 1000-year storm events were created using statistical analysis of data for a set of 881 historical and synthetic storms.

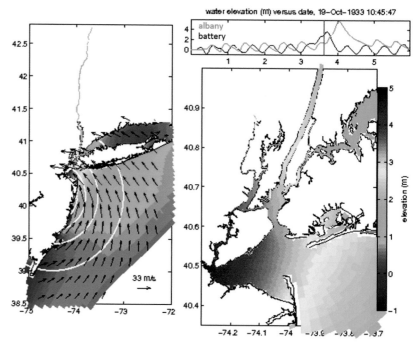

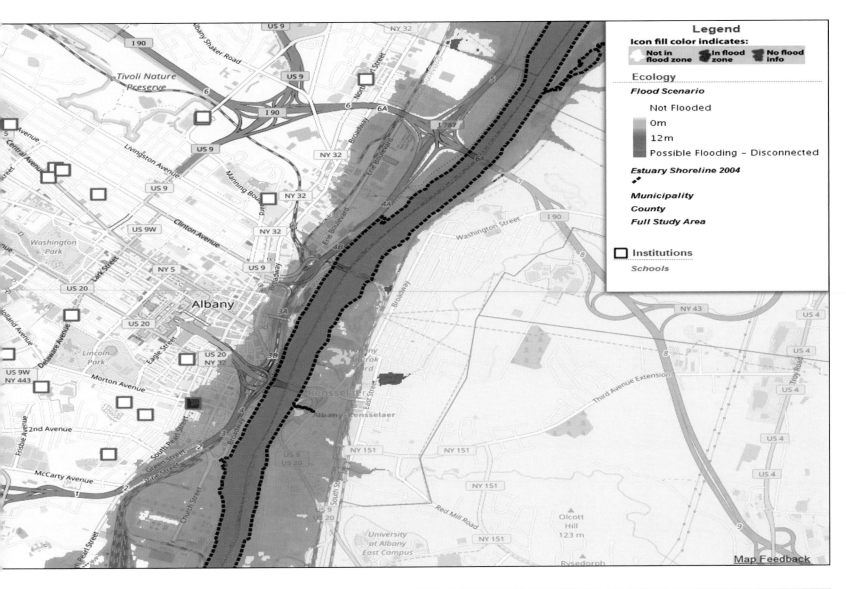

Legend

Icon fill color indicates:

Not in flood zone	In flood zone	No flood info

Ecology

Flood Scenario

Not Flooded

0m

12m

Possible Flooding – Disconnected

Estuary Shoreline 2004

Municipality

County

Full Study Area

Institutions

Schools

Map Feedback

Flood modeling combines sea level rise estimates and 5-year to 1000-year storm return periods resulting in a variety of flood scenarios.

GIS at the Office of the Assessor

Los Angeles County Office of the Assessor
Los Angeles, California, USA
By Mapping and GIS Services

The Los Angeles County Office of the Assessor uses GIS to analyze property values and tax rates as shown in these examples. The map showing the property tax rates for parts of Los Angeles County enables current and potential property owners to see their tax rates compared to nearby areas. The Arcadia map shows the location and severity of the impact of the housing market crash on property values while the Pasadena map shows a pattern of higher single-family property values in areas farther from commercial property. The map showing the location of the assessor's branch offices and their respective service areas helps the public find the one closest to them as well as alternate locations.

Contact

Emilio Solano
ejsolano@assessor.lacounty.gov

Software

ArcGIS for Desktop 10.3

Data Source

Los Angeles County Office of the Assessor

Courtesy of Los Angeles County Office of the Assessor.

2006 and 2015 Property Value Comparison in Arcadia, Californ

Single Family Property Assessed Value in City of Pasadena

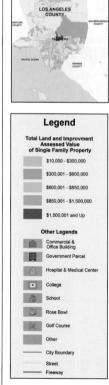

Assessor District Offices and Service Areas

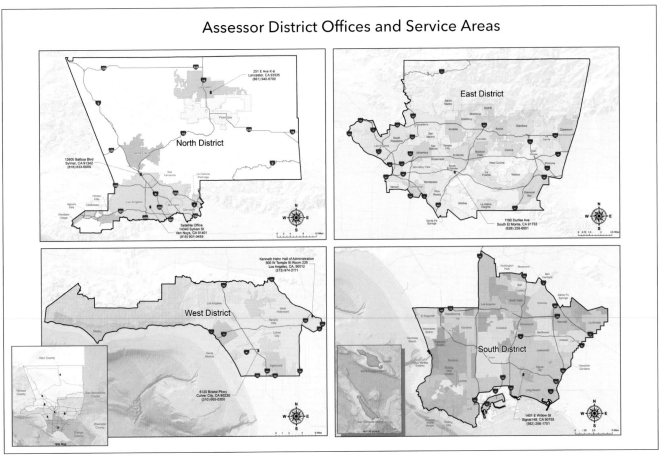

Comparison of Los Angeles County Property Tax Rates

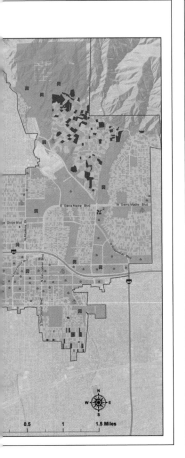

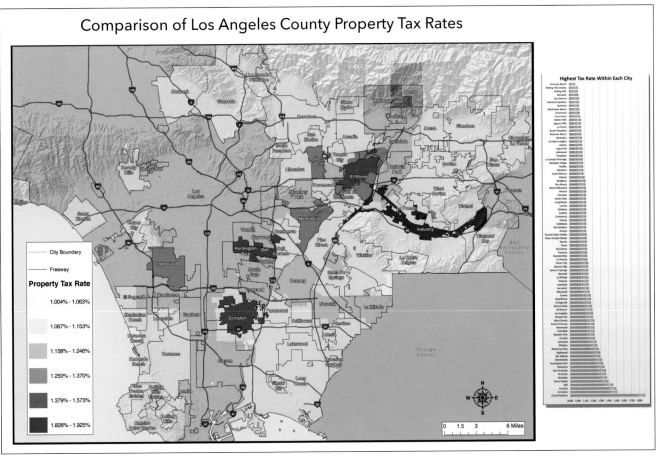

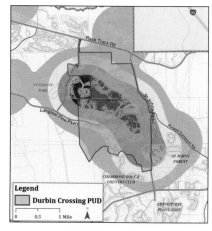

St. Johns County Residential Building Permits

St. Johns County
St. Augustine, Florida, USA
By Michael Campbell and Paul Clement

St. Johns County, located in northeast Florida, has been listed as the sixteenth fastest-growing county in the United States with a population increase of 19.3 percent for the years 2010 to 2015, according to the US Census Bureau. Several reasons for the population increase include top-rated schools, low crime rate, low unemployment rate, and proximity to jobs and recreation sites.

This map depicts the 2015 residential building permits for St. Johns County. The map was created using ArcGIS® Pro 1.2 application to show the concentration of the approximately 2,500 residential building permits that received certificates of occupancy in 2015 and the areas of the county that are currently experiencing population growth.

Contact

Michael Campbell
mcampbell@sjcfl.us

Software

ArcGIS Pro 1.2

Data Sources

St. Johns County GIS Division, US Census Bureau

Courtesy of St. Johns County GIS Division.

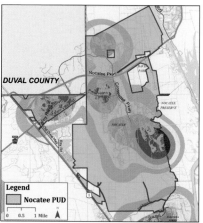

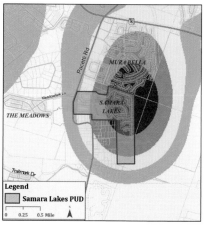

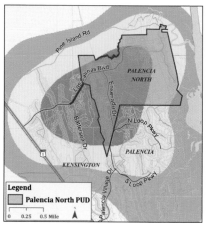

78

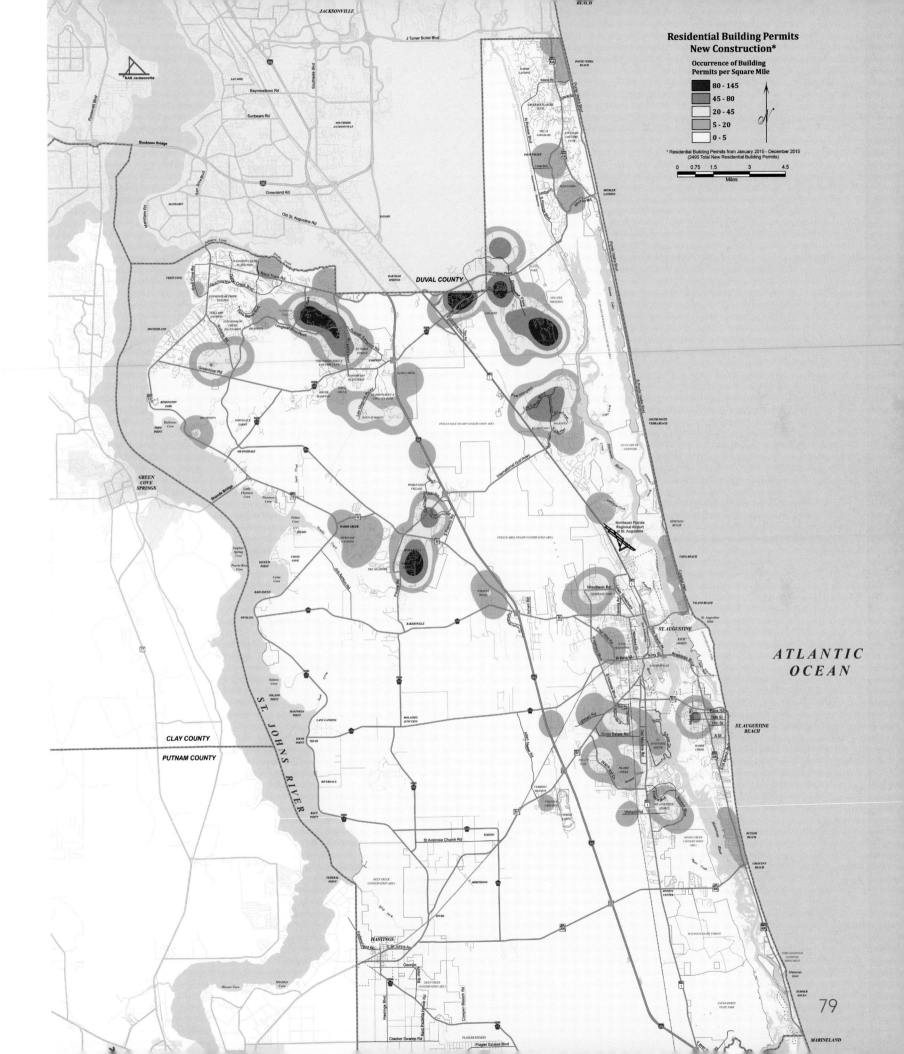

Tree Canopy Coverage and Change Detection for the City of Avondale Estates

InterDev
Atlanta, Georgia, USA
By Michael Edelson, GISP

In recent years, many cities in the Atlanta metro area have been creating standards to protect their trees, often using ordinances that require a detailed tree inventory as well as a quantitative method for monitoring tree canopies.

In 2016, the City of Avondale Estates, Georgia, commissioned a study of the urban tree canopy. The purpose of the study was to establish a baseline and monitor trends in the tree canopy. The study, which used aerial imagery from the US Department of Agriculture, measured tree canopy throughout the city and arrived at an overall percent coverage. This information will provide critical data to assist key decision-makers and citizens. Performing this study over the course of several years is a powerful tool for understanding and monitoring important trends in tree canopy change.

Contact

Michael Edelson
medelson@interdev.com

Software

ArcGIS for Desktop 10.3, ArcGIS Spatial Analyst 10.3

Data Sources

US Department of Agriculture, National Agriculture Imagery Program; DeKalb County GIS; Atlanta Regional Commission GIS

Courtesy of the City of Avondale Estates and InterDev.

2009 Tree Canopy Coverage
City-wide - 53.5%
Residential Area - 58.5%
Central Business District - 25.5%

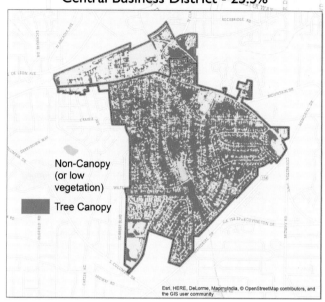

2015 Tree Canopy Coverage
City-wide - 54.0%
Residential Area - 59.0%
Central Business District - 27.6%

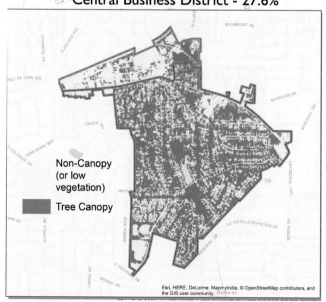

Oxnard Zoning Map

City of Oxnard
Oxnard, California, USA
By Salvador Mancha

The City of Oxnard Zoning Map is a visual
representation of zoning designations as described
in the Oxnard City Code. The map also illustrates
designations of adopted specific plans. Zoning is
the division of a jurisdiction into districts (zones)
within which permissible uses are prescribed and
development standards are defined. Zoning is
the principal tool for implementing the goals and
policies of the general plan by translating land-use
categories and standards into regulations.

Contact

Salvador Mancha
salvador.mancha@oxnard.org

Software

ArcGIS for Desktop 10.0, Adobe Illustrator CS4

Data Sources

City of Oxnard, County of Ventura

Courtesy of City of Oxnard GIS.

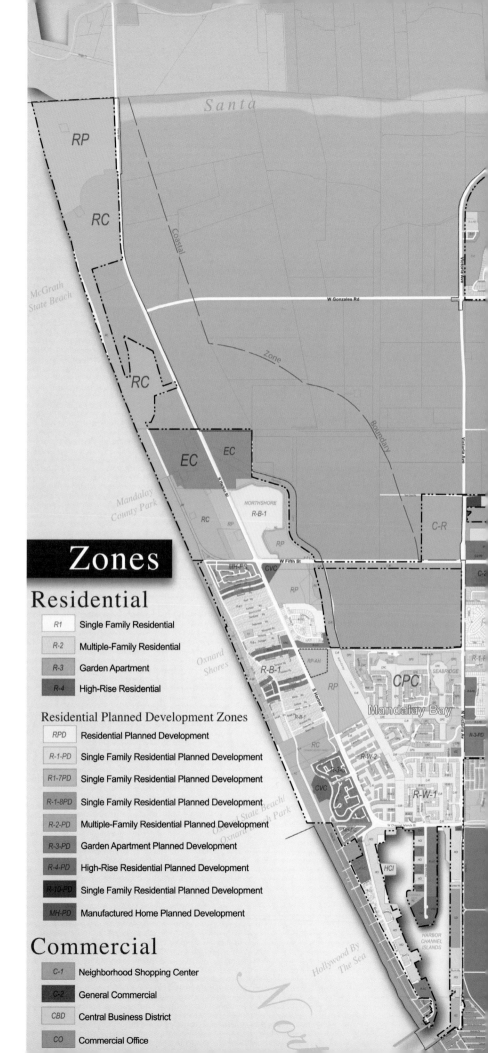

Zones

Residential

R1	Single Family Residential
R-2	Multiple-Family Residential
R-3	Garden Apartment
R-4	High-Rise Residential

Residential Planned Development Zones

RPD	Residential Planned Development
R-1-PD	Single Family Residential Planned Development
R1-7PD	Single Family Residential Planned Development
R-1-8PD	Single Family Residential Planned Development
R-2-PD	Multiple-Family Residential Planned Development
R-3-PD	Garden Apartment Planned Development
R-4-PD	High-Rise Residential Planned Development
R-10-PD	Single Family Residential Planned Development
MH-PD	Manufactured Home Planned Development

Commercial

C-1	Neighborhood Shopping Center
C-2	General Commercial
CBD	Central Business District
CO	Commercial Office

Island of Maui, Hawai'i, Parcel Value

County of Maui
Kahului, Hawaii, USA
By Daniel Keali'i Sereno

Using colors in the yellow, orange, and red range, this map depicts the average parcel value of the years 2001 through 2016 for the County of Maui. This yearly range was chosen because it was the most complete range of data available in the computer-assisted mass appraisal (CAMA) system. The Z dimension shows the amount of absolute value change for each parcel over the specified time period. This is used to detect parcels with values over time that are not consistent and could indicate an issue with the parcel's method of assessment or an issue with a parcel's data entry into the CAMA system.

Contact

Daniel Keali'i Sereno
daniel.sereno@co.maui.hi.us

Software

ArcGIS Pro 1.2.0

Data Source

County of Maui

Courtesy of County of Maui.

**AVERAGE PARCEL VALUE
FOR THE PERIOD 2001 - 2016**
 ≤ $4,000,000
 ≤ $15,000,000
 ≤ $56,000,000
 ≤ $200,000,000
 ≤ $350,000,000

ISLAND OF MAUI, HAWAI'I

APPRAISED PARCEL VALUE AVERAGE AND VALUE CHANGE WITH
RELATIVE TOTAL VALUE CHANGE FOR YEARS 2001 - 2016 SHOWN IN THE Z DIMENSION

Map by Dan Sereno
County of Maui, Department of Finance
daniel.sereno@co.maui.hi.us

Automation of Lithuanian Geodata

National Land Service under the Ministry
of Agriculture Vilnius, Lithuania
By SE GIS-Centras, JSC Institute of Aerial Geodesy

The Republic of Lithuania initiated research to
automate and update geodata and map production
generalization in 2012. The state enterprise GIS-
Centras took the leading role in this research and
further implementation of automated processes. That
work was finalized with the automated production
of the Lithuanian Topographic Map (TOP50LKS) in
2016. Flexible automated technology (models for
cartographic generalization and visualization) vector
dataset and map sheets in print-suitable format were
created during this project. TOP50LKS covers the whole
territory of Lithuania and consists of 131 map sheets.
Automation is expected to allow faster updating of
geodata, production of topographic maps, and cost
savings in the near future.

Contact

Eugenija Sleiteryte-Viluniene
eugenija.viluniene@nzt.lt

Software

ArcGIS for Desktop 10.3.1, Adobe Illustrator CS6

Data Source

For Lithuanian territory: National Land Service,
Environmental Protection Agency, State Forest Survey
Service under the Ministry of Environment, Lithuanian
Geological Service under the Ministry of Environment,
Lithuanian Hydrometeorological Survey under the Ministry
of Environment, Lithuanian Road Administration under the
Ministry of Transport and Communications, State Enterprise
GIS-Centras, AB LESTO, LitGRID, other public sources
(WWW).
For abroad territories: Latvian Geospatial information
Agency, Ministry of National Defence Republic of Poland,
OpenStreetMap

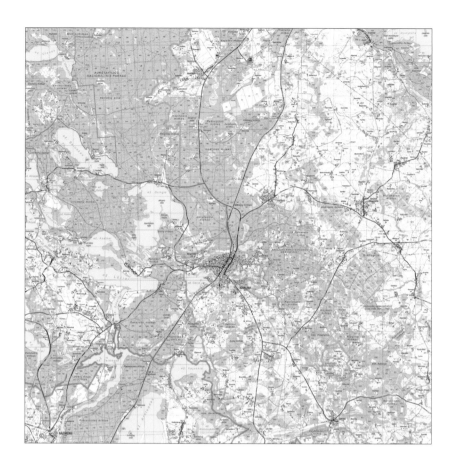

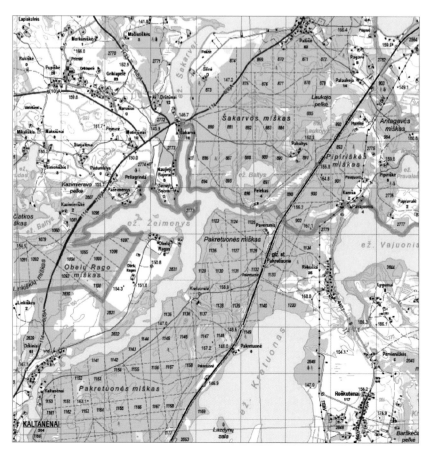

LIETUVOS RESPUBLIKOS TOPOGRAFINIS ŽEMĖLAPIS (TOP50LKS-SR)

1994 METŲ LIETUVOS KOORDINAČIŲ SISTEMA (LKS-94)

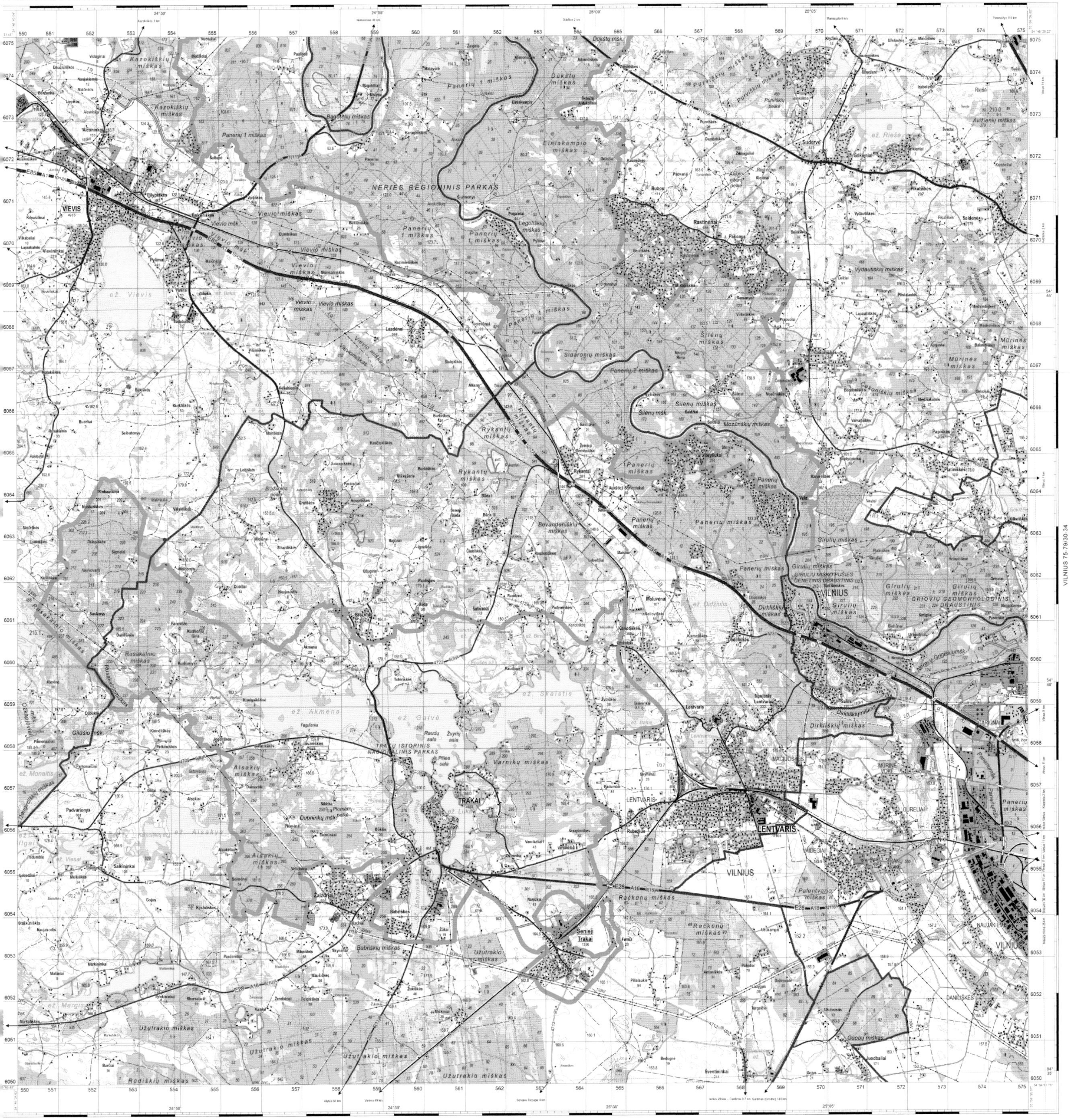

VIEVIS

NERIES REGIONINIS PARKAS

VILNIUS

LENTVARIS

TRAKAI

TRAKŲ ISTORINIS NACIONALINIS PARKAS

Senieji Trakai

European Union Referendum Results (Brexit)

The Times of London
By Sam Joiner, Callum Christie, and Ben Flanagan

The United Kingdom European Union (EU) membership referendum, also known as the EU referendum or Brexit, took place on June 23, 2016. This was held to decide whether the country should leave or remain in the EU. The leave vote won by 52 percent to 48 percent with more than 30 million people voting.

The Times of London used the ArcGIS platform to map real time data feeds of the referendum results throughout the night. For clarity and aesthetics, their news editors and web developers opted to use a cartogram, where each local authority is represented by a single hexagon, rather than its actual geographic boundary. This method accommodates for the difference in size of local authorities. The map also displays the strength of the vote in each local authority, taking advantage of the smart mapping capabilities in ArcGIS Online. The Times' map was featured at the heart of its referendum coverage. This helped readers to get the most accurate, up-to-date information and analysis as easily and quickly as possible.

Contact

Ben Flanagan
bflanagan@esriuk.com

Software

ArcGIS for Desktop 10.4, ArcGIS℠ Online, ArcGIS® API for JavaScript™, Adobe Illustrator

Data Source

The Press Association

Courtesy of The Times of London.

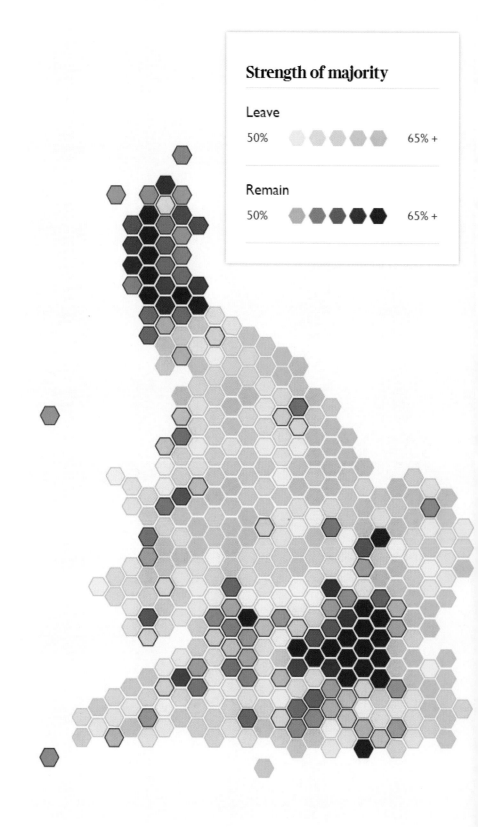

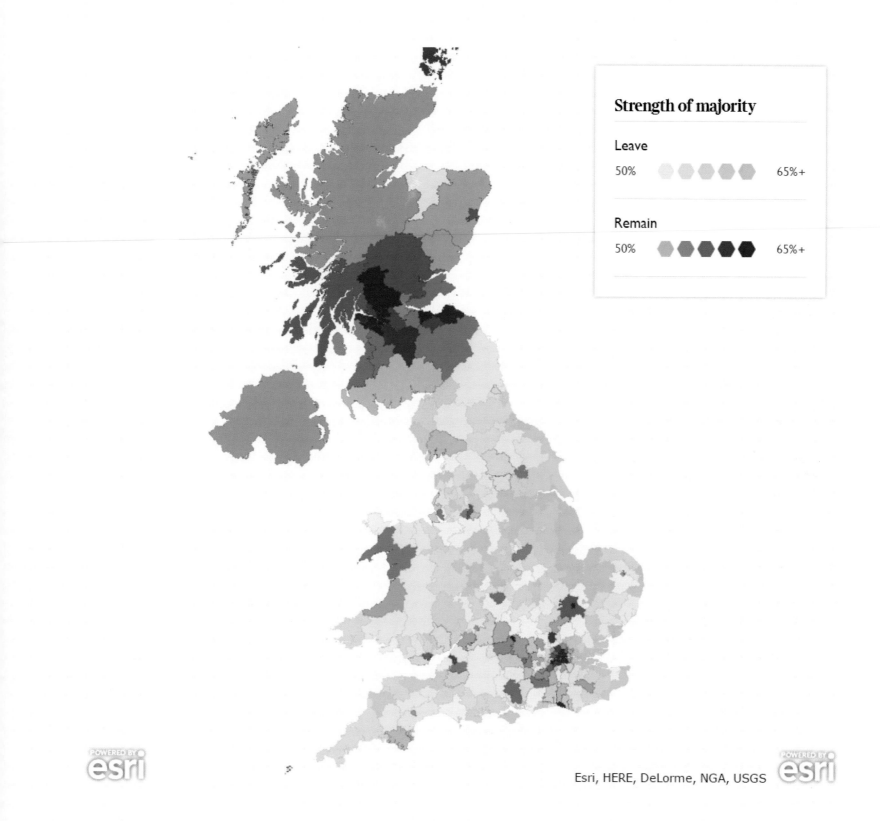

Strength of majority

Leave
50% 65%+

Remain
50% 65%+

Esri, HERE, DeLorme, NGA, USGS

North Carolina Low Birth Weight Analysis

North Carolina State Center for Health Statistics
Raleigh, North Carolina, USA
By Dianne Enright

Low birth weight can be a predictor for health consequences not only for an infant but also as that infant grows into adulthood. These maps show where low birth weight and very low birth weight are occurring in North Carolina. The North Carolina State Center for Health Statistics is responsible for data collection, health-related research, production of reports, and maintenance of a comprehensive collection of health statistics. The center provides high-quality health information for better informed decisions and effective health policies.

Contact

Dianne Enrighte
dianne.enright@dhhs.nc.gov

Software

ArcGIS for Desktop 10.3

Data Sources

North Carolina State Center for Health Statistics Birthfile 2000-2010; Census American Community Survey, 2014

Courtesy of North Carolina State Center for Health Statistics.

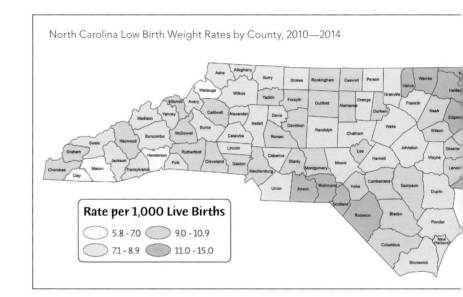

North Carolina Low Birth Weight Rates by County, 2010—2014

Rate per 1,000 Live Births
5.8 - 7.0   9.0 - 10.9
7.1 - 8.9   11.0 - 15.0

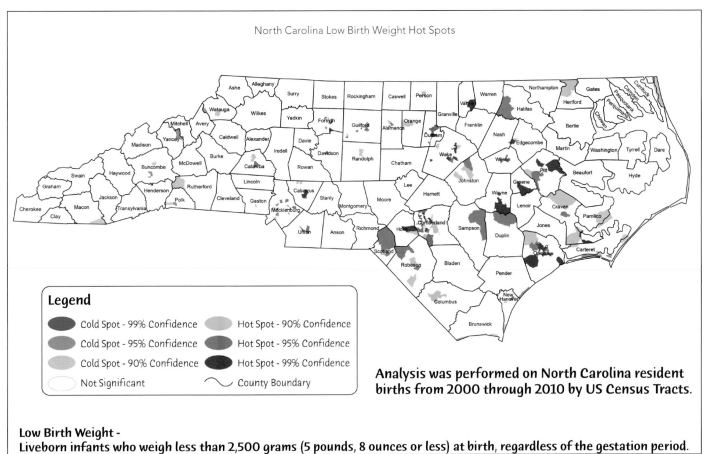

North Carolina Low Birth Weight Hot Spots

Legend

Cold Spot - 99% Confidence
Cold Spot - 95% Confidence
Cold Spot - 90% Confidence
Not Significant
Hot Spot - 90% Confidence
Hot Spot - 95% Confidence
Hot Spot - 99% Confidence
County Boundary

Analysis was performed on North Carolina resident births from 2000 through 2010 by US Census Tracts.

Low Birth Weight -
Liveborn infants who weigh less than 2,500 grams (5 pounds, 8 ounces or less) at birth, regardless of the gestation period.

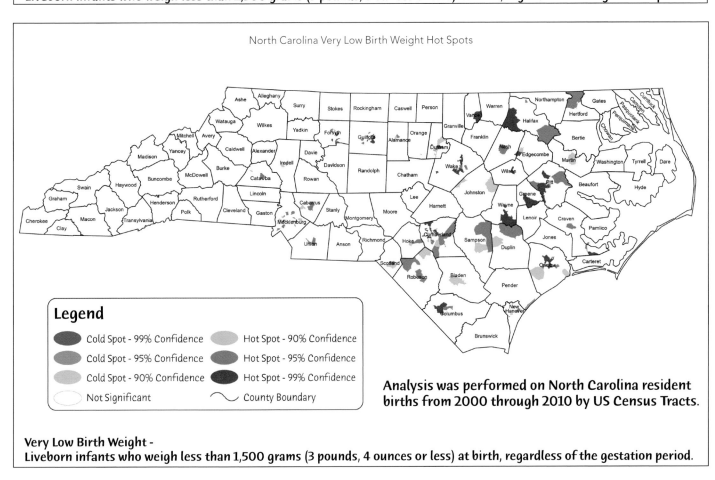

North Carolina Very Low Birth Weight Hot Spots

Legend

Cold Spot - 99% Confidence
Cold Spot - 95% Confidence
Cold Spot - 90% Confidence
Not Significant
Hot Spot - 90% Confidence
Hot Spot - 95% Confidence
Hot Spot - 99% Confidence
County Boundary

Analysis was performed on North Carolina resident births from 2000 through 2010 by US Census Tracts.

Very Low Birth Weight -
Liveborn infants who weigh less than 1,500 grams (3 pounds, 4 ounces or less) at birth, regardless of the gestation period.

County Performance Outcomes by Mental Health Provider Agencies

Los Angeles County Department of Mental Health
Los Angeles, California, USA
By Vandana Joshi and Yoko Myers

This map shows the percentage of consumers who reported satisfaction with their mental health services in specific satisfaction domains. The data was tracked at the provider level to see which agencies' rate of satisfaction were above or below the Los Angeles County average. Data revealed specific geographic patterns related to consumer satisfaction. Provider agencies in the North County/Antelope Valley scored below the county average on general satisfaction, participation in treatment planning, outcomes, and improved functioning.

Contact

Vandana Joshi
vjoshi@dmh.lacounty.gov

Software

ArcGIS for Desktop 10.3.1

Data Source

Los Angeles County Department of Mental Health

Courtesy of Los Angeles County.

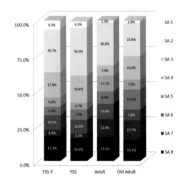

Percent of Surveys
Received by Service
Area (SA) and Age Group

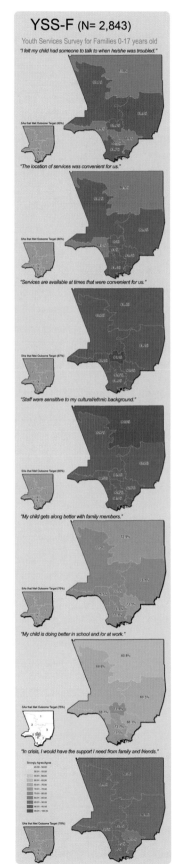

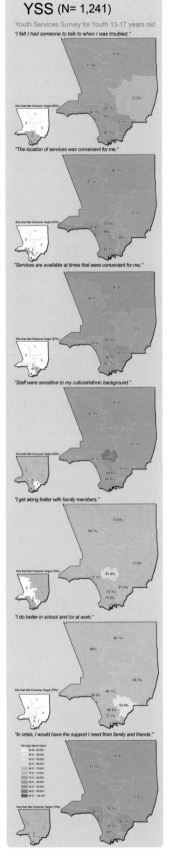

Surveys Received (Number of Responses)
by Service Area (SA**) and Age Group

SA 1:
Antelope Valley

5

53

178

42

SA 2:
San Fernando

426

873

64

992

509

45

SA 3:
San Gabriel
Valley

241

238

187

SA 4:
Metro

289

39

58

359

19

SA 5:
West

170

298

SA 6:
South

91

21

349

37

414

SA 7:
East

125

131

40

201

41

SA 8:
South Bay

555

503

Number of Surveys Received

10   50   100   500   1,000

* Percent of Clients who responded "Agree or Strongly Agree" to Survey Questions.

** The Department of Mental Health Service Area (SA) boundaries are identical to the SPA boundaries.

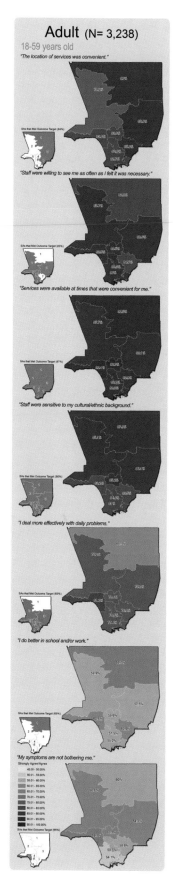

Adult (N= 3,238)
18-59 years old

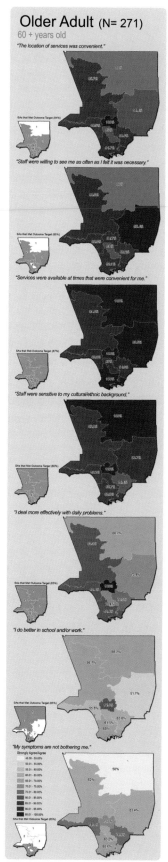

Older Adult (N= 271)
60 + years old

93

Built Environment and Asthma in Southern California

Southern California Association of Governments (SCAG)
Los Angeles, California, USA
By Sean O. Calvin, Michael Mroczek, Tom Vo, and Jung Seo

The objective of this research was to analyze the relationship between the built environment and potential risk of asthma. This research tests a hypothesis that living in transit-oriented communities of urban centers may be associated with the higher car and truck emissions and the disproportionately high risk of asthma. Data for the research came from the California Environmental Protection Agency's CalEnviroScreen, a screening methodology to identify communities disproportionately burdened by multiple sources of pollution, the California Environmental Health Tracking Program for children's asthma status, and SCAG's transportation and emission models for the development of 2016 regional transportation plan/ sustainable communities strategy. The research estimates traffic volumes and emissions and examines the spatial correlation between the transit-oriented development pattern and children's potential risk of asthma in the region.

Contact

Jung Seo
seo@scag.ca.gov

Software

ArcGIS for Desktop 10.3

Data Sources

SCAG, Office of Environmental Health Hazard Assessment CalEnviroScreen Version 2.0, US Environmental Protection Agency Toxics Release Inventory Program

Courtesy of SCAG.

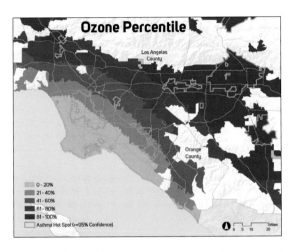

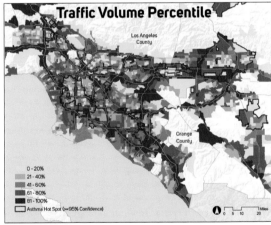

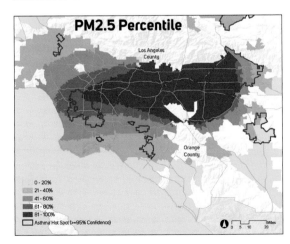

Poverty Rate Percentile

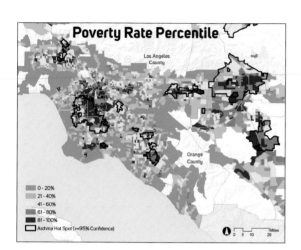

Legend:
- 0 - 20%
- 21 - 40%
- 41 - 60%
- 61 - 80%
- 81 - 100%
- Asthma Hot Spot (>=95% Confidence)

Diesel PM Percentile

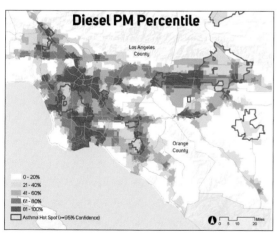

Legend:
- 0 - 20%
- 21 - 40%
- 41 - 60%
- 61 - 80%
- 81 - 100%
- Asthma Hot Spot (>=95% Confidence)

Minority Percentile

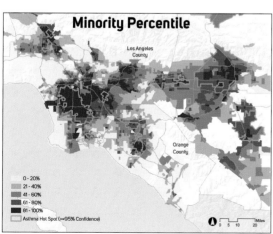

Legend:
- 0 - 20%
- 21 - 40%
- 41 - 60%
- 61 - 80%
- 81 - 100%
- Asthma Hot Spot (>=95% Confidence)

Children's Asthma ED Visit Rate Hot Spot

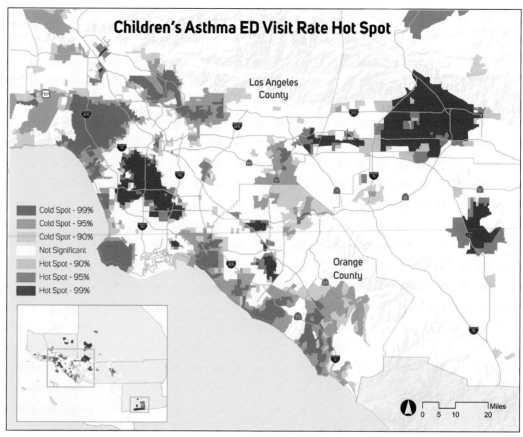

Legend:
- Cold Spot - 99%
- Cold Spot - 95%
- Cold Spot - 90%
- Not Significant
- Hot Spot - 90%
- Hot Spot - 95%
- Hot Spot - 99%

ED Visit for Asthma Percentile

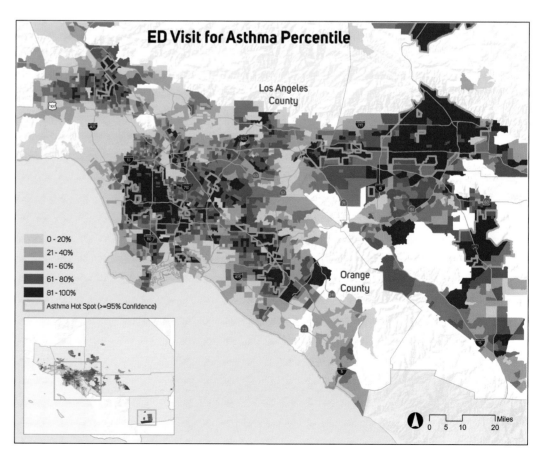

Legend:
- 0 - 20%
- 21 - 40%
- 41 - 60%
- 61 - 80%
- 81 - 100%
- Asthma Hot Spot (>=95% Confidence)

Twin Cities Urban Heat Islands and Social Vulnerability

The Trust for Public Land
Santa Fe, New Mexico, USA
By Chris David, Carolyn Ives, and Lindsay Withers

The Climate-Smart Cities™ program of the Trust for Public Land helps cities nationwide create parks and protect land to meet the climate challenge. The program helps cities use parks and natural lands as "green infrastructure" serving four objectives: connect, cool, absorb, and protect. The "cool" objective consists of creating shady green spaces that reduce the urban "heat island" effect, protecting people from heat waves, and reducing summer energy use.

These maps of the Twin Cities (Minneapolis and St. Paul) highlight daytime and nighttime Urban Heat Island Hotspots as well as block groups with a high percentage of people of color, households in poverty, and seniors, all socially vulnerable populations identified as a key demographic indicator in the Environmental Protection Agency's Environmental Justice Screening and Mapping Tool. These maps are currently used to help communicate and shape the Climate-Smart Cities strategy in the Twin Cities.

Contact

Chris David
Chris.David@tpl.org

Software

ArcGIS for Desktop 10.3

Data Sources

Esri, MetroGIS DataFinder, City of Minneapolis, City of St. Paul, US Geological Survey Land Processes Distributed Active Archive Center

Copyright © The Trust for Public Land. Information on these maps is provided for purposes of discussion and visualization only.

PEOPLE OF COLOR

POVERTY

SENIORS

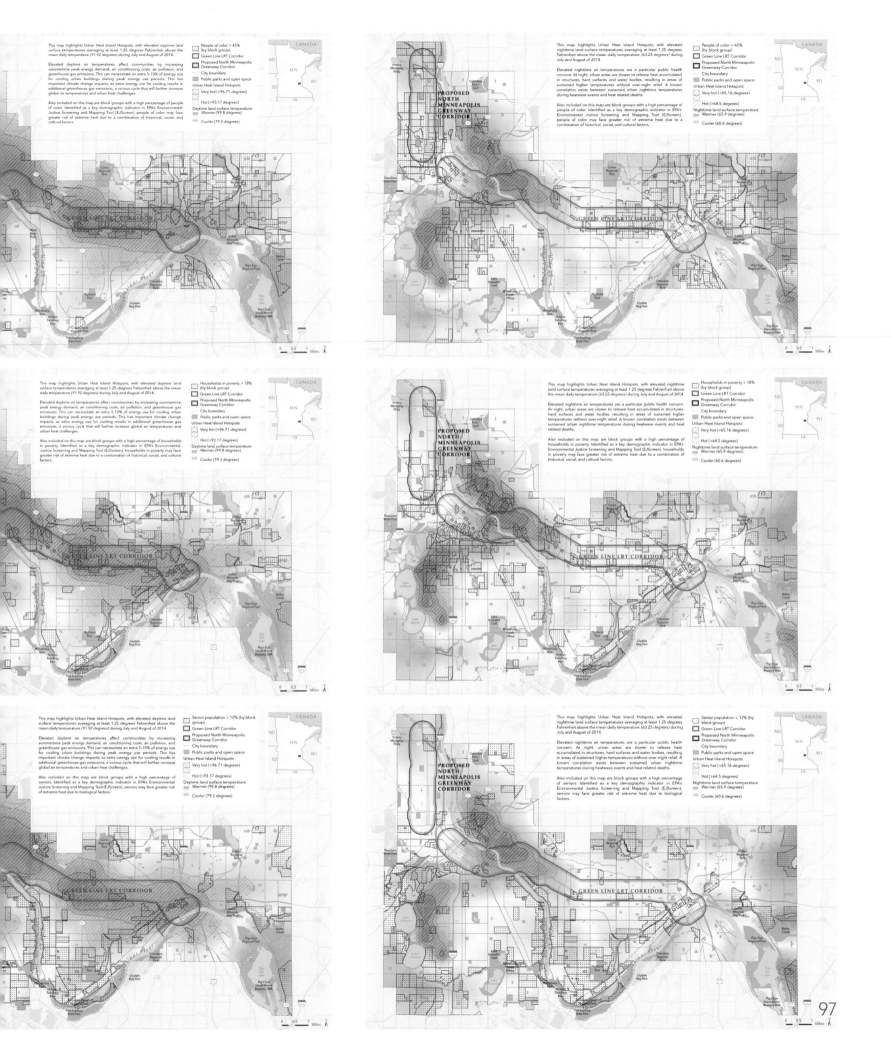

This map highlights Urban Heat Island Hotspots, with elevated daytime land surface temperatures averaging at least 1.25 degrees Fahrenheit above the mean daily temperature (91.92 degrees) during July and August of 2014.

Elevated daytime air temperatures affect communities by increasing summertime peak energy demand, air conditioning costs, air pollution, and greenhouse gas emissions. This can necessitate an extra 5-10% of energy use for cooling urban buildings during peak energy use periods. This has important climate change impacts, as extra energy use for cooling results in additional greenhouse gas emissions, a vicious cycle that will further increase global air temperatures and urban heat challenges.

Also included on this map are block groups with a high percentage of people of color. Identified as a key demographic indicator in EPA's Environmental Justice Screening and Mapping Tool (EJScreen), people of color may face greater risk of extreme heat due to a combination of historical, social, and cultural factors.

People of color > 45% (by block group)
Green Line LRT Corridor
Proposed North Minneapolis Greenway Corridor
City boundary
Public parks and open space
Urban Heat Island Hotspots
Very hot (>96.71 degrees)
Hot (>93.17 degrees)
Daytime land surface temperature
Warmer (99.8 degrees)
Cooler (79.3 degrees)

This map highlights Urban Heat Island Hotspots, with elevated nighttime land surface temperatures averaging at least 1.25 degrees Fahrenheit above the mean daily temperature (63.25 degrees) during July and August of 2014.

Elevated nighttime air temperatures are a particular public health concern. At night, urban areas are slower to release heat accumulated in structures, hard surfaces and water bodies, resulting in areas of sustained higher temperatures without over-night relief. A known correlation exists between sustained urban nighttime temperatures during heatwave events and heat related deaths.

Also included on this map are block groups with a high percentage of people of color. Identified as a key demographic indicator in EPA's Environmental Justice Screening and Mapping Tool (EJScreen), people of color may face greater risk of extreme heat due to a combination of historical, social, and cultural factors.

People of color > 45% (by block group)
Green Line LRT Corridor
Proposed North Minneapolis Greenway Corridor
City boundary
Public parks and open space
Urban Heat Island Hotspots
Very hot (>65.16 degrees)
Hot (>64.5 degrees)
Nighttime land surface temperature
Warmer (65.9 degrees)
Cooler (60.6 degrees)

This map highlights Urban Heat Island Hotspots, with elevated daytime land surface temperatures averaging at least 1.25 degrees Fahrenheit above the mean daily temperature (91.92 degrees) during July and August of 2014.

Elevated daytime air temperatures affect communities by increasing summertime peak energy demand, air conditioning costs, air pollution, and greenhouse gas emissions. This can necessitate an extra 5-10% of energy use for cooling urban buildings during peak energy use periods. This has important climate change impacts, as extra energy use for cooling results in additional greenhouse gas emissions, a vicious cycle that will further increase global air temperatures and urban heat challenges.

Also included on this map are block groups with a high percentage of households in poverty. Identified as a key demographic indicator in EPA's Environmental Justice Screening and Mapping Tool (EJScreen), households in poverty may face greater risk of extreme heat due to a combination of historical, social, and cultural factors.

Households in poverty > 18% (by block group)
Green Line LRT Corridor
Proposed North Minneapolis Greenway Corridor
City boundary
Public parks and open space
Urban Heat Island Hotspots
Very hot (>96.71 degrees)
Hot (>93.17 degrees)
Daytime land surface temperature
Warmer (99.8 degrees)
Cooler (79.3 degrees)

This map highlights Urban Heat Island Hotspots, with elevated nighttime land surface temperatures averaging at least 1.25 degrees Fahrenheit above the mean daily temperature (63.25 degrees) during July and August of 2014.

Elevated nighttime air temperatures are a particular public health concern. At night, urban areas are slower to release heat accumulated in structures, hard surfaces and water bodies, resulting in areas of sustained higher temperatures without over-night relief. A known correlation exists between sustained urban nighttime temperatures during heatwave events and heat related deaths.

Also included on this map are block groups with a high percentage of households in poverty. Identified as a key demographic indicator in EPA's Environmental Justice Screening and Mapping Tool (EJScreen), households in poverty may face greater risk of extreme heat due to a combination of historical, social, and cultural factors.

Households in poverty > 18% (by block group)
Green Line LRT Corridor
Proposed North Minneapolis Greenway Corridor
City boundary
Public parks and open space
Urban Heat Island Hotspots
Very hot (>65.16 degrees)
Hot (>64.5 degrees)
Nighttime land surface temperature
Warmer (65.9 degrees)
Cooler (60.6 degrees)

This map highlights Urban Heat Island Hotspots, with elevated daytime land surface temperatures averaging at least 1.25 degrees Fahrenheit above the mean daily temperature (91.92 degrees) during July and August of 2014.

Elevated daytime air temperatures affect communities by increasing summertime peak energy demand, air conditioning costs, air pollution, and greenhouse gas emissions. This can necessitate an extra 5-10% of energy use for cooling urban buildings during peak energy use periods. This has important climate change impacts, as extra energy use for cooling results in additional greenhouse gas emissions, a vicious cycle that will further increase global air temperatures and urban heat challenges.

Also included on this map are block groups with a high percentage of seniors. Identified as a key demographic indicator in EPA's Environmental Justice Screening and Mapping Tool (EJScreen), seniors may face greater risk of extreme heat due to biological factors.

Senior population > 12% (by block group)
Green Line LRT Corridor
Proposed North Minneapolis Greenway Corridor
City boundary
Public parks and open space
Urban Heat Island Hotspots
Very hot (>96.71 degrees)
Hot (>93.17 degrees)
Daytime land surface temperature
Warmer (99.8 degrees)
Cooler (79.3 degrees)

This map highlights Urban Heat Island Hotspots, with elevated nighttime land surface temperatures averaging at least 1.25 degrees Fahrenheit above the mean daily temperature (63.25 degrees) during July and August of 2014.

Elevated nighttime air temperatures are a particular public health concern. At night, urban areas are slower to release heat accumulated in structures, hard surfaces and water bodies, resulting in areas of sustained higher temperatures without over-night relief. A known correlation exists between sustained urban nighttime temperatures during heatwave events and heat related deaths.

Also included on this map are block groups with a high percentage of seniors. Identified as a key demographic indicator in EPA's Environmental Justice Screening and Mapping Tool (EJScreen), seniors may face greater risk of extreme heat due to biological factors.

Senior population > 12% (by block group)
Green Line LRT Corridor
Proposed North Minneapolis Greenway Corridor
City boundary
Public parks and open space
Urban Heat Island Hotspots
Very hot (>65.16 degrees)
Hot (>64.5 degrees)
Nighttime land surface temperature
Warmer (65.9 degrees)
Cooler (60.6 degrees)

Where Did Our Consumers Go for Vocational Rehabilitation Services?

Texas Workforce Commission
Austin, Texas, USA
By Zhaoxing "Zack" Li

Vocational rehabilitation (VR) helps individuals with disabilities gain or maintain employment. The Texas Department of Assistive and Rehabilitative Services (DARS) operated 115 field offices in seventy-two Texas counties to provide VR services in the 2015 fiscal year. This network of offices provided services to individuals living across all 254 Texas counties and together served about 107,000 consumers in that year.

This map quantitatively displays the agency's 2015 VR consumer flows by county, showing where consumers sought services relative to their home county. The map conveys eight dimensions of consumer and service data including geographic distribution of the flows (clusters), service locations (the counties where the field offices were located), and total consumers served (total flows) by county. The map discovers the pattern of real service areas—county clusters—and indicates the spatial relationship between the county clusters and current Texas Local Workforce Development Areas.

Contact

Zhaoxing "Zack" Li
zack.li@twc.state.tx.us

Software

ArcGIS for Desktop 10.3.1

Data Source

Texas Department of Assistive and Rehabilitative Services (DARS)

Many thanks to James Farris, Texas DARS GIS director, for his support and valuable comments on preparing this map.

Courtesy of Texas DARS and Texas Workforce Commission.

Consumer Flows

Total Served by County

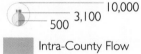

10,000
3,100
500

Intra-County Flow

Inter-County Flow

Inter-County Flows
Percent of Total* > 3

3 - 5

6 - 25

26 - 100

101 - 200

201 - 900

Percent of Total <= 3
(For Less Populated Counties Only)

1 - 15

Consumers by County

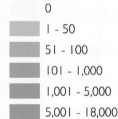

0

1 - 50

51 - 100

101 - 1,000

1,001 - 5,000

5,001 - 18,000

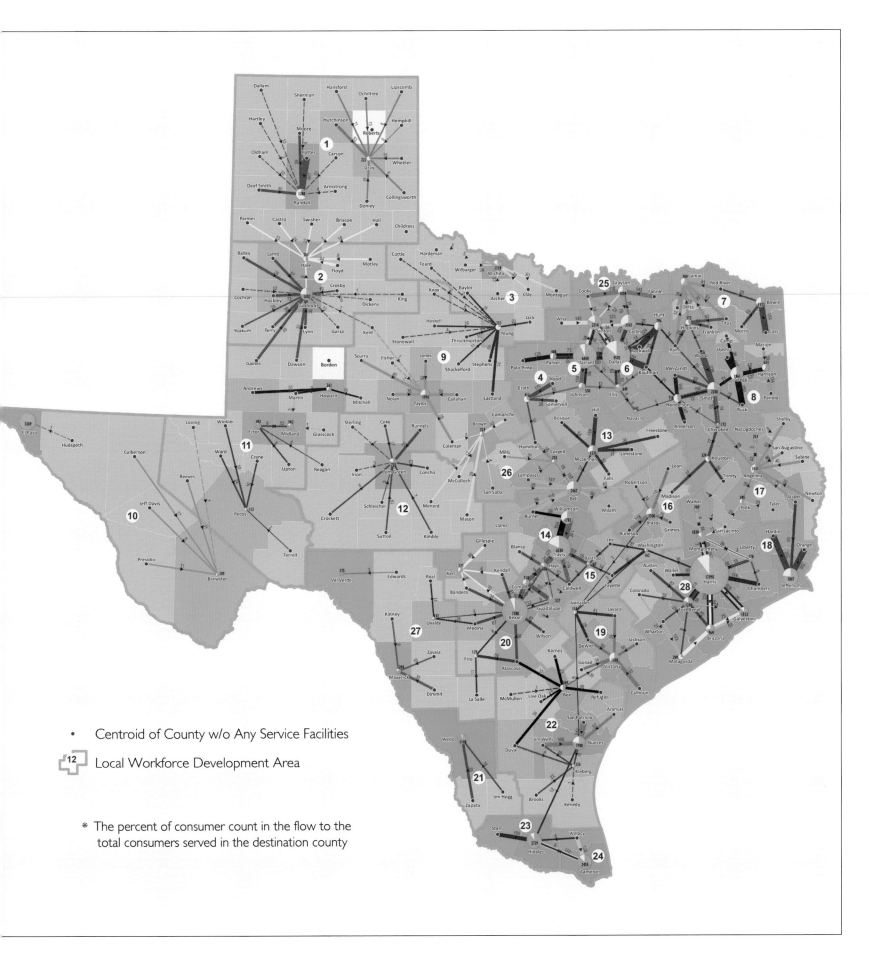

Centroid of County w/o Any Service Facilities

Local Workforce Development Area

* The percent of consumer count in the flow to the
  total consumers served in the destination county

Health Insurance Coverage

Coleman Group Inc.
Greenbelt, Maryland, USA
By Mehrshad Nourani

These maps illustrate state and county health insurance coverage on the basis of the US Census Bureau's Small Area Health Insurance Estimates (SAHIE) program, which produces timely estimates for all counties and states by detailed demographic and income groups. The SAHIE program produces single-year estimates of health insurance coverage for every county in the United States. The estimates are model-based and consistent with the American Community Survey. They are based on an "area-level" model that uses survey estimates for domains of interest, rather than individual responses. The estimates are enhanced with administrative data.

Contact

Mehrshad Nourani
mnourani8@gmail.com

Software

ArcGIS for Desktop 10.3.1

Data Source

US Census Bureau

Courtesy of Coleman Group, Inc.

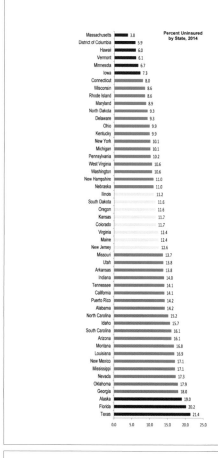

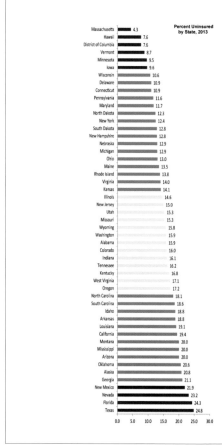

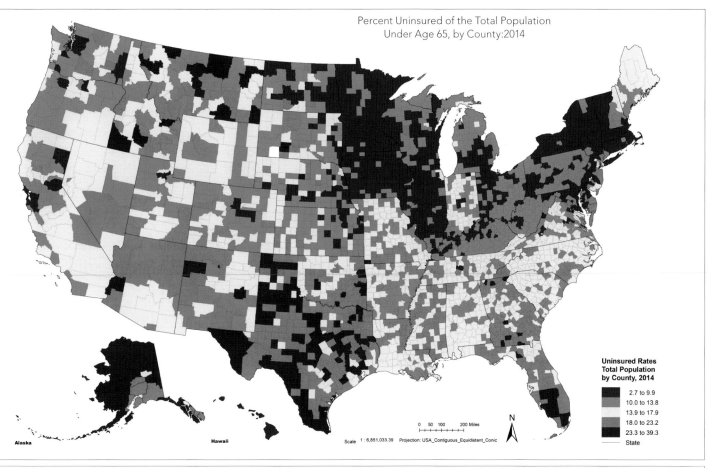

Percent Uninsured of the Total Population
Under Age 65, by County:2014

**Uninsured Rates
Total Population
by County, 2014**

2.7 to 9.9
10.0 to 13.8
13.9 to 17.9
18.0 to 23.2
23.3 to 39.3
State

Alaska   Hawaii   Scale 1 : 6,851,033.39   Projection: USA_Contiguous_Equidistant_Conic

0 50 100   200 Miles   N

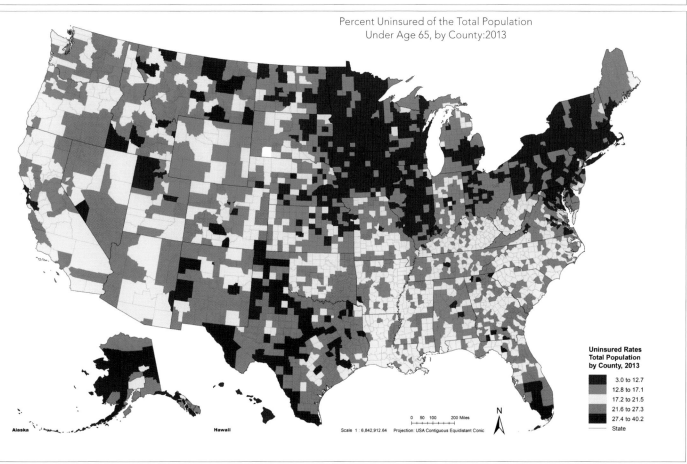

Percent Uninsured of the Total Population
Under Age 65, by County:2013

**Uninsured Rates
Total Population
by County, 2013**

3.0 to 12.7
12.8 to 17.1
17.2 to 21.5
21.6 to 27.3
27.4 to 40.2
State

Alaska   Hawaii   Scale 1 : 6,842,912.64   Projection: USA Contiguous Equidistant Conic

0 50 100   200 Miles   N

Measuring Area-Based Vulnerability to Gambling-Related Harm

Geofutures Ltd.
Bath, United Kingdom
By Gaynor Astbury, Heather Wardle, and Mark Thurstain-Goodwin

The British Gambling Act of 2005 states that youth and vulnerable people should be protected from being harmed or exploited from gambling. To date, there has been very little consideration of who may be vulnerable to gambling-related harm and where these people might be. In 2015, Geofutures was commissioned by the Westminster and Manchester City Councils in association with the Local Government Association to explore which groups of people were more likely to be vulnerable to gambling harm and where these different groups of people may be located.

The final quantitative model was based upon a qualitative scoping exercise and stakeholder engagement to define theoretical markers of harm. The risk index then drew together multiple sources of quantitative spatial information to represent different vulnerable population groups, combined into a tree-based raster-overlay model. These statistically normalized values indicate the places where people may be more vulnerable to gambling-related harm, and have been used to inform licensing decisions and targeted treatment.

Contact

Gaynor Astbury
ga@geofutures.com

Software

ArcGIS for Desktop 10, Python 2.7

Data Sources

Manchester City Council, Ordnance Survey data © Crown copyright and database right 2016

Courtesy of Geofutures Ltd., Westminster and Manchester City Councils, and the Local Government Association.

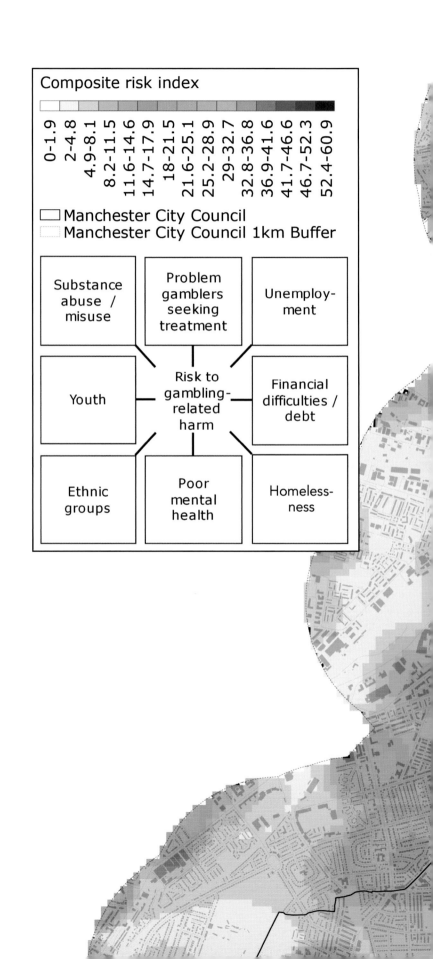

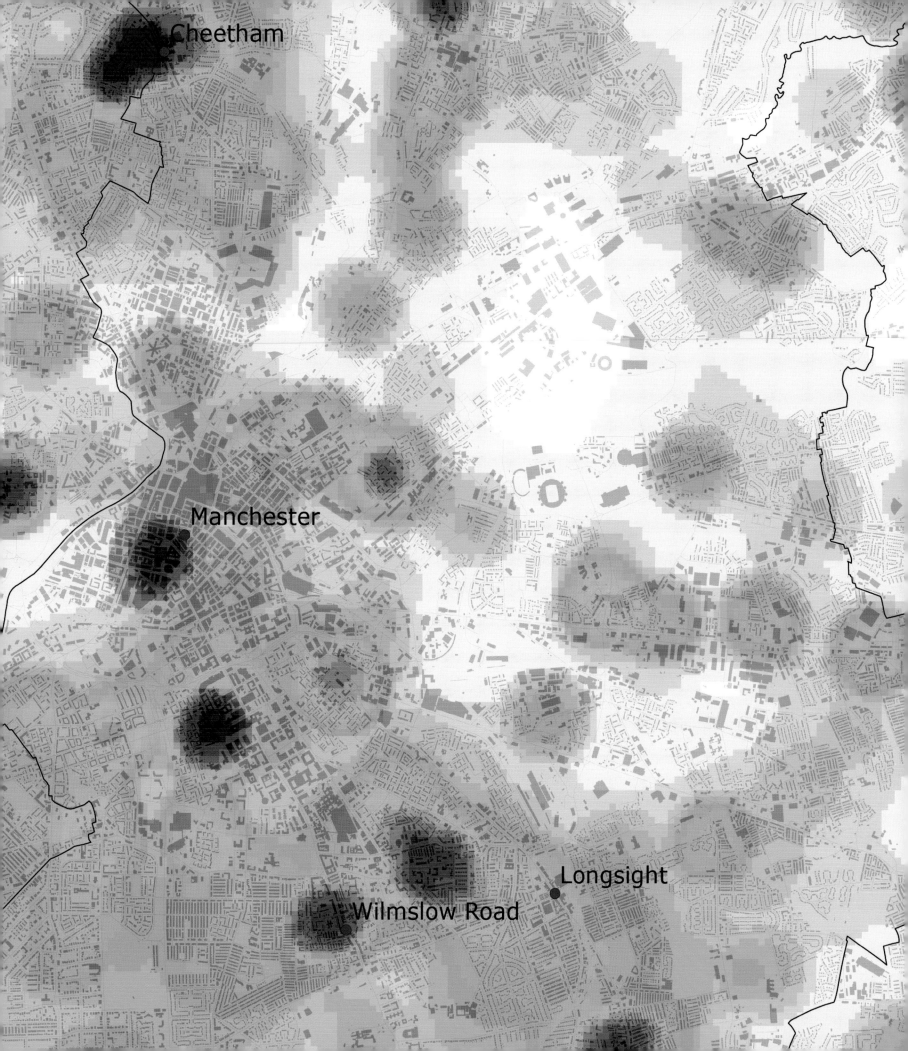

Geostatistical Analysis, Kriging, and Weighted Statistical Modeling for Archaeological Sensitivity

KAYA Associates
Huntsville, Alabama, USA
By Josh Chris, Adam Dunlap, and Wesley Norris

Ordinary Kriging, assuming a constant unknown mean over a search neighborhood of 1 kilometer, was used in a predictive model for locating prehistoric artifacts and sites. Existing data points and archaeological sites were used to define "known" or positive areas for analysis. Negative data points included specific cultural surveys, paved and named roads, buildings and concrete slabs, and areas of slope greater than 40 degrees. Positive points were buffered by 15 meters and used to clip the negative points. The resulting heat map shows ordinal rankings using seven standard deviation-based intervals to rank the potential for cultural resources.

In addition to kriging, weighted multivariate statistical modeling was used. Existing sites were overlaid with slope grids to extract a slope value, and least-cost path distances to washes and water were calculated for each point. By comparing numeric limits, a predictive equation was developed and tested for correlation. Spatial joins were used to count the instances of sites by landform and slope value. The variables were generated into grids to allow multivariate analysis to compare observed sites versus all sites with similar characteristics. Lower values (lower slope, distance to water and wash) represent a higher probability of finding prehistoric artifacts and sites.

Contact

Wesley Norris
norrisw@kayacorp.com

Software

ArcGIS Desktop, ArcGIS Spatial Analyst, System for Authomated Geoscientific Analyses

Data Sources

Cultural data from Yuma Proving Ground, National Hydrography Datasets, US Geological Survey National Elevation Dataset

Courtesy of Yuma Proving Ground, KAYA Associates, Inc.

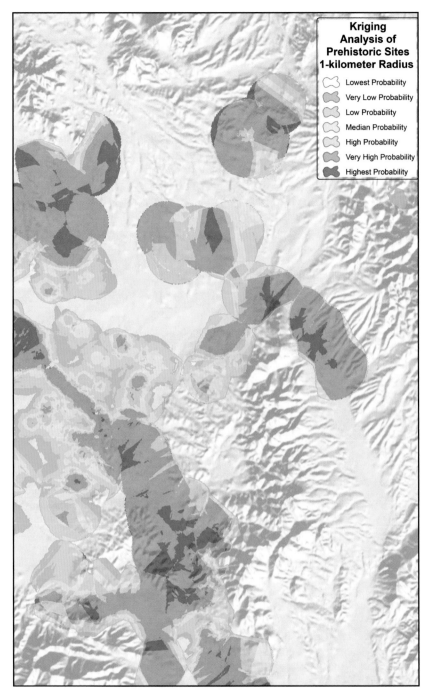

	Distance to Water*	Landform	Age	Material	Slope*	Elevation	Distance to Wash*
Distance to Water*	X	LOW	LOW	LOW	HIGH	MODERATE	HIGH
Landform	LOW	X	LOW	LOW	SLIGHT	SLIGHT	LOW
Age	LOW	LOW	X	LOW	LOW	LOW	LOW
Material	LOW	LOW	LOW	X	LOW	LOW	LOW
Slope*	HIGH	SLIGHT	LOW	LOW	X	HIGH	HIGH
Elevation	MODERATE	SLIGHT	LOW	LOW	HIGH	X	MODERATE
Distance to Wash*	HIGH	LOW	LOW	LOW	HIGH	MODERATE	X

Covariance matrix of variables via statistical analysis

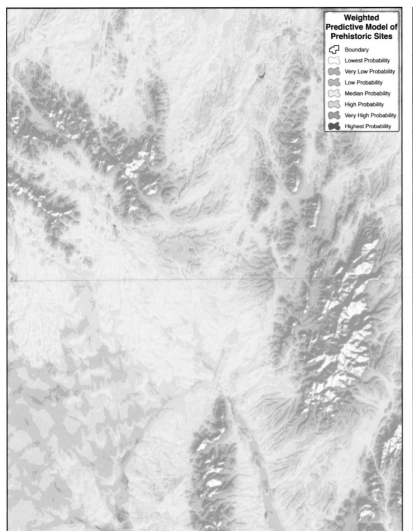

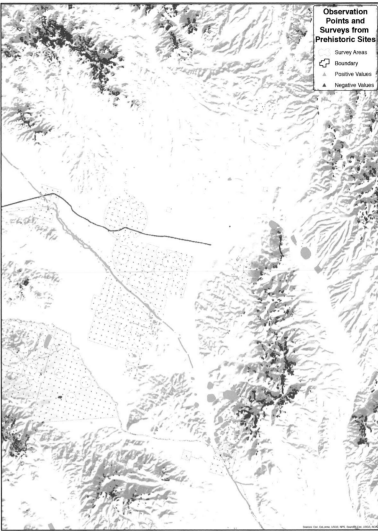

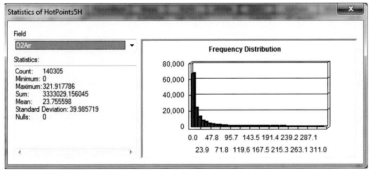

Distribution values Least Cost Path Distance to Washes

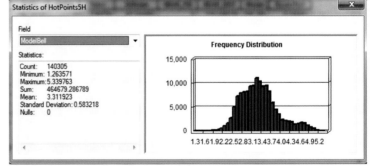

Distribution values of predictive model

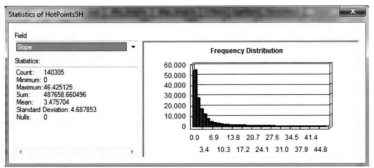

Distribution values of slope in degrees

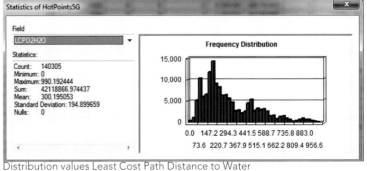

Distribution values Least Cost Path Distance to Water

UNICEF: Unless We Act Now

Blue Raster LLC
Arlington, Virginia, USA
By Blue Raster LLC

The United Nations Children's Fund (UNICEF) recently released the report, "Unless We Act Now: The Impact of Climate Change on Children," at the annual Conference of Parties. UNICEF has made putting children first its mission, and although climate change is an imminent threat to populations across the world, it is children who are hit the hardest as their bodies are most vulnerable to change.

The first step was being able to understand where these 2.3 billion children are, but taking this further to understand how environmental conditions such as droughts, floods, and extreme heat affect food and water supply, sanitation, and the spread of disease is made possible through GIS analysis. The Unless We Act Now report leveraged geospatial analysis of current demographic, environmental, and projected climate data to direct aid to child populations across the world as they face unforgiving changing weather patterns.

Contact

Kevin McMaster
kmcmaster@blueraster.com

Software

ArcGIS for Desktop 10.4, ArcGIS Online

Data Sources

Center for International Earth Science Information Network, United Nations World Population Prospects, Demographic and Health Surveys Program, World Resources Institute

Courtesy of UNICEF.

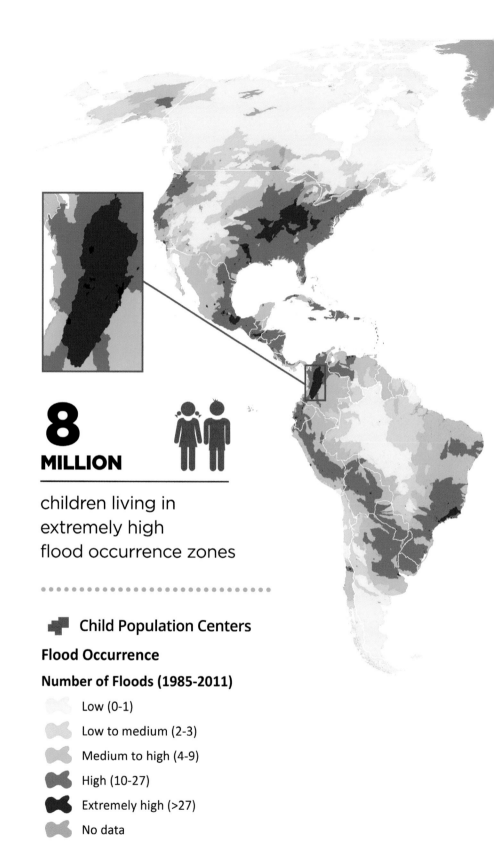

8 MILLION

children living in extremely high flood occurrence zones

Child Population Centers

Flood Occurrence

Number of Floods (1985-2011)

Low (0-1)

Low to medium (2-3)

Medium to high (4-9)

High (10-27)

Extremely high (>27)

No data

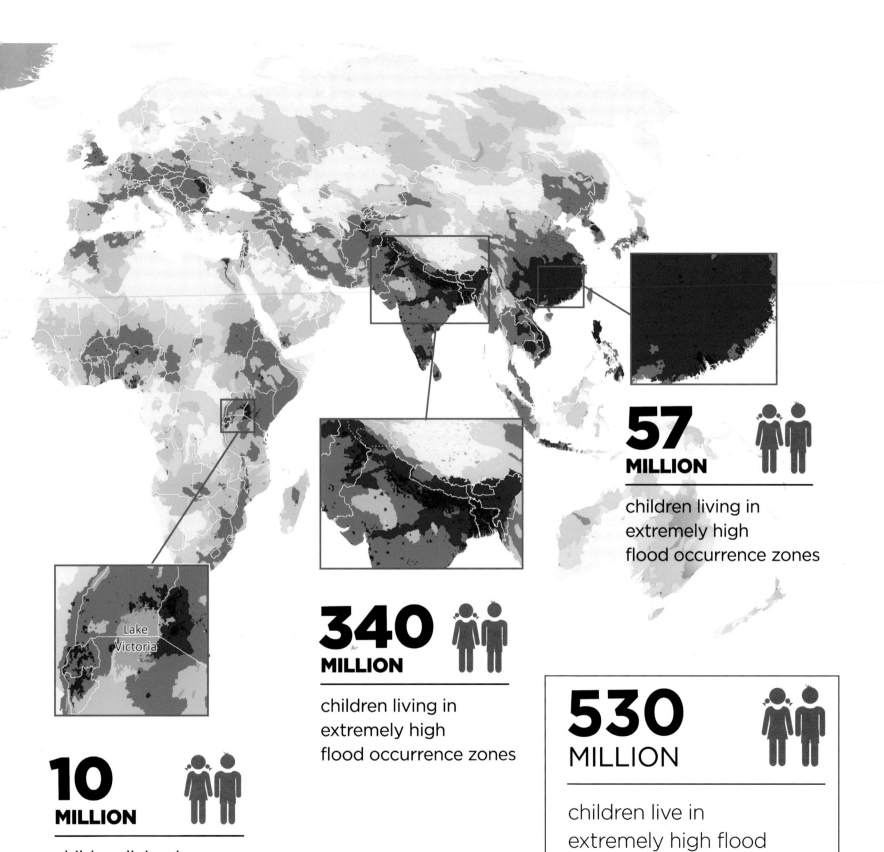

57 MILLION

children living in extremely high flood occurrence zones

340 MILLION

children living in extremely high flood occurrence zones

10 MILLION

children living in extremely high flood occurrence zones

530 MILLION

children live in extremely high flood occurrence zones

Lake Victoria

Crop Migration and Change for Corn, Soybeans, and Spring Wheat

US Department of Agriculture, National Agricultural Statistics Service (USDA/NASS)
Fairfax, Virginia, USA
By Avery Sandborn and Lee Ebinger

The purpose of this geospatial analysis was to identify patterns of crop migration and change in the North Central region of the United States for corn, soybeans, and spring wheat, from 2006 to 2015. The resulting analysis and accompanying graphics illustrate the crop footprint over the past ten years has continuously extended in the northwest and west directions. Possible change factors include crop rotation, higher crop prices, market-focused programs, improved seed traits, and minimum/no till practices. Identifying where the crop planting differences are occurring and changes to the land cover will help to inform agricultural best practices and improve crop estimations.

Contact

Lee Ebinger
Lee.Ebinger@nass.usda.gov

Software

ArcGIS for Desktop 10.3.1, ERDAS Imagine 2011

Data Source

USDA/NASS Cropland Data Layers 2006-2015

Courtesy of USDA/NASS.

Mean Centroids—Crop Migration, 2006-2015

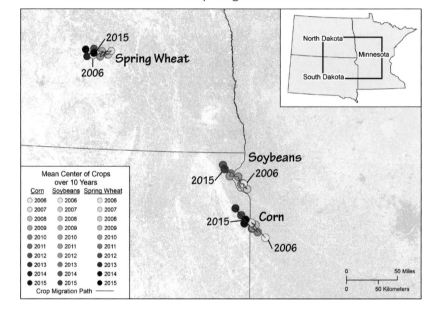

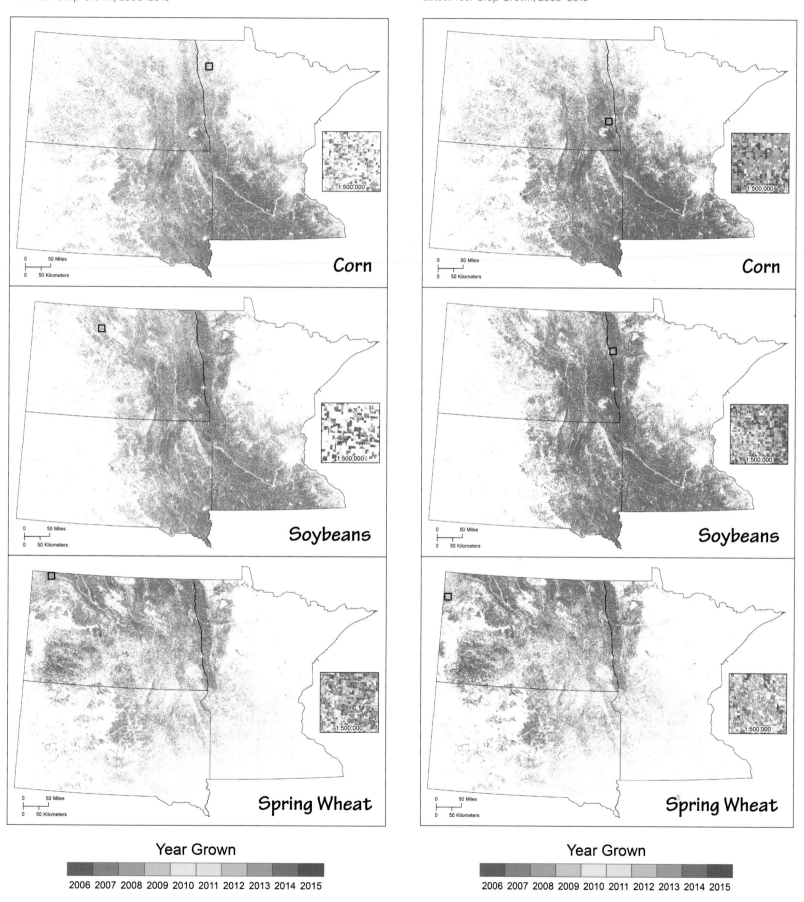

Corn

Corn

Soybeans

Soybeans

Spring Wheat

Spring Wheat

Year Grown

2006 2007 2008 2009 2010 2011 2012 2013 2014 2015

Year Grown

2006 2007 2008 2009 2010 2011 2012 2013 2014 2015

Assessment of a Killer Freeze on Winter Corn in Mexico

US Department of Agriculture, Foreign Agricultural
Service (USDA/FAS)
Washington, District of Columbia, USA
By Arnella Trent, Lisa Colson, and Christianna Townsend

This map is an assessment of a "killer" freeze on winter corn in Mexico. Using ArcGIS Desktop, satellite imagery, temperature data, area data on winter corn, and normalized difference vegetation index derived from imagery allowed USDA/FAS to locate the area of impact.

The FAS collects, analyzes, and disseminates information about global food supply and demand, trade trends, and market opportunities. FAS seeks improved market access for US products, administers export financing and market development programs, and carries out global food aid and technical assistance programs.

Contact

Arnella Trent
arnella.trent@fas.usda.gov

Software

ArcGIS Desktop

Data Sources

Landsat, World Meteorological Organization, Crop Explorer, Moderate Resolution Imaging Spectroradiometer, Mexico Agrifood and Fisheries Information Service, National Geospatial-Intelligence Agency, GeoCover-LC

Courtesy of USDA/FAS.

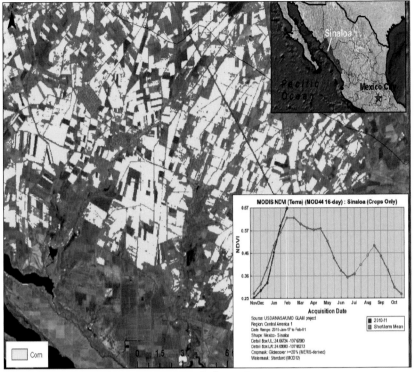

Corn Fields at Peak Vegetation in Culican District
Sinatoa, Mexica–Landsat Imagery 2, 2011

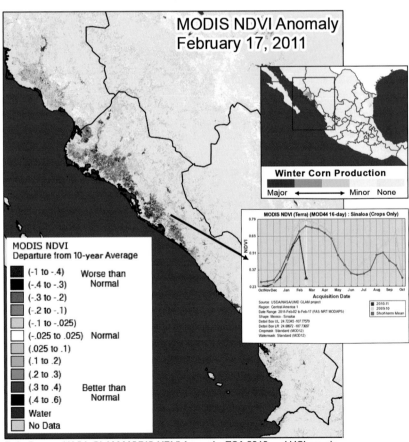

Data Source: NASA-GLAM MODIS NDVI Anomaly; ESA 2010 and UCLouvain, Globcover 2009 v2.3 (Crop Mask); Mexico SIAP/OEIDRUS, ESRI 2013

NDVI Anomaly in Freeze Affected Crop Areas: Sinaloa, Mexico

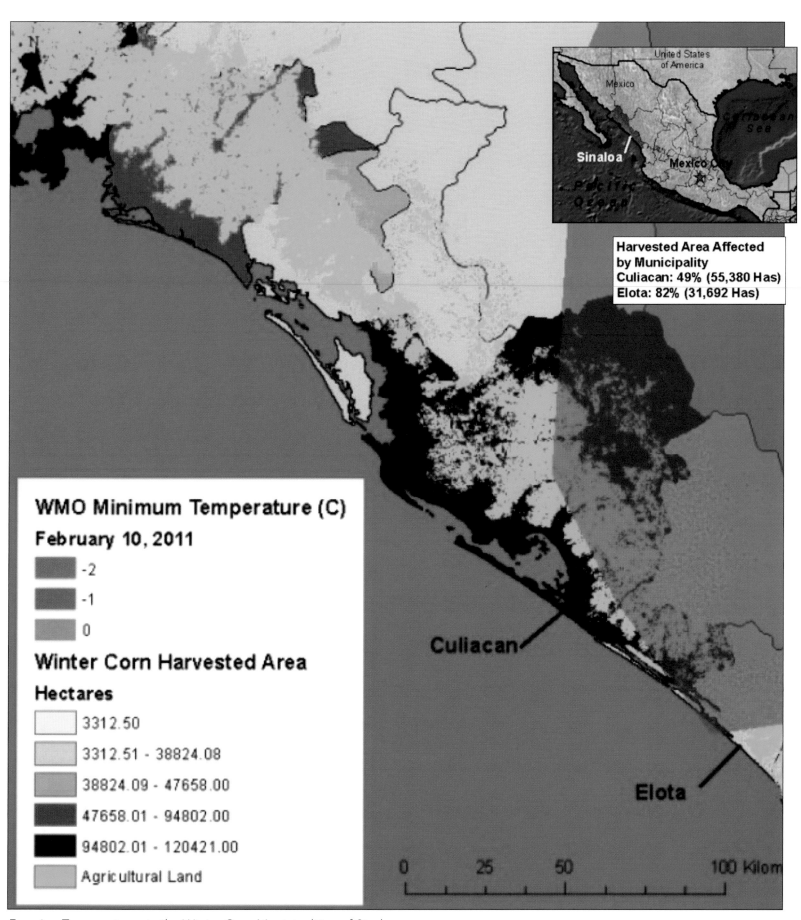

Freezing Temperatures in the Winter Corn Municipalities of Sinaloa

Hoover Wilderness Map

US Department of Agriculture (USDA) Forest Service
Ogden, Utah, USA
By Alfred Macias

Sharing a border with the Yosemite Wilderness along the Sierra Crest, the Hoover Wilderness is widely known for its extreme mountain terrain. The wilderness was first established as a "primitive area" in 1931 and was then protected as wilderness by the 1964 Wilderness Act. The Hoover has relatively little timber throughout much of its steep terrain. Its forests are composed of scattered groves of hemlock, pine, aspen, and cottonwood. Diverse wildflowers spread over the intermittent meadows found here, and black bears are common.

Contact

Alfred Macias
amacias@fs.fed.us

Software

ArcGIS for Desktop 10.3

Data Sources

FSTopo, US Geological Survey

Courtesy of Alfred Macias.

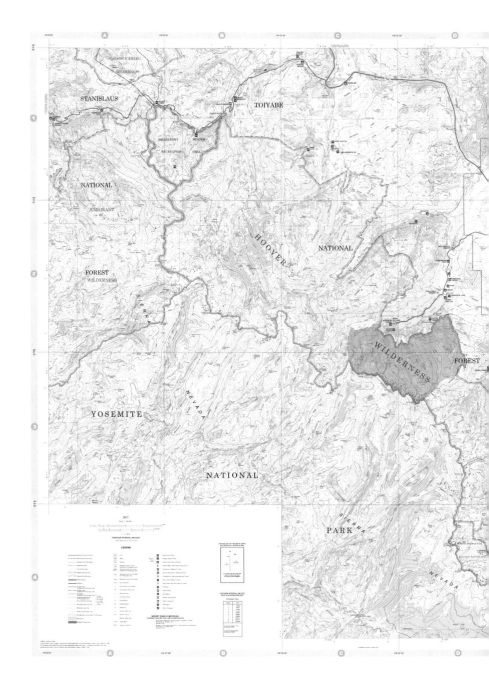

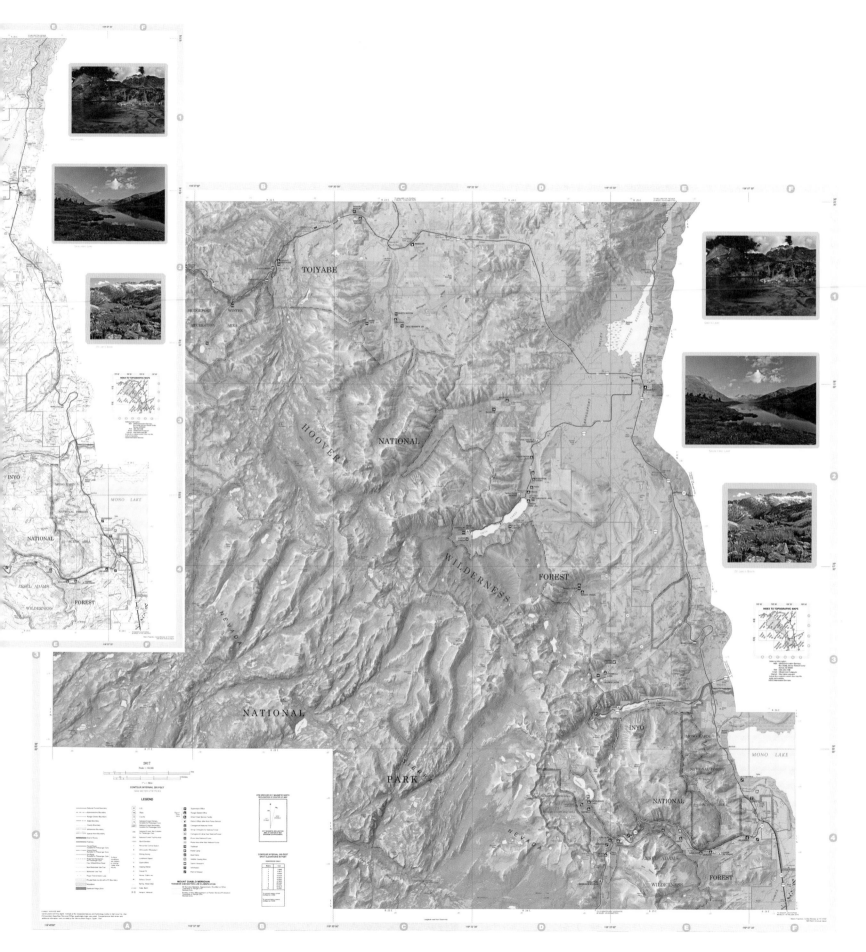

Displaying Electronic Navigational Chart Data in the MACHC

National Oceanic and Atmospheric Administration (NOAA)
Silver Spring, Maryland, USA
By John Nyberg (NOAA), Tom DePuyt (Esri)

The Meso-American and Caribbean Sea Hydrographic Commission (MACHC), with thirteen members and fourteen associate members, coordinates nautical charting, hydrographic activity, and marine spatial data infrastructure in the region. As part of the MACHC's effort to expand the use of nautical charts and associated data in support of the blue water economy and the region's marine economic infrastructure, it has employed ArcGIS for Maritime: Server to display electronic navigational charting data. Six member states currently contribute data to the open version of the MACHC service: Mexico, Brazil, Cuba, Netherlands, Colombia, and the United States.

Contact

Christie Ence
Christie.Ence@noaa.gov

Software

ArcGIS for Server 10.4, Adobe Illustrator

Data Source

NOAA

Courtesy of NOAA.

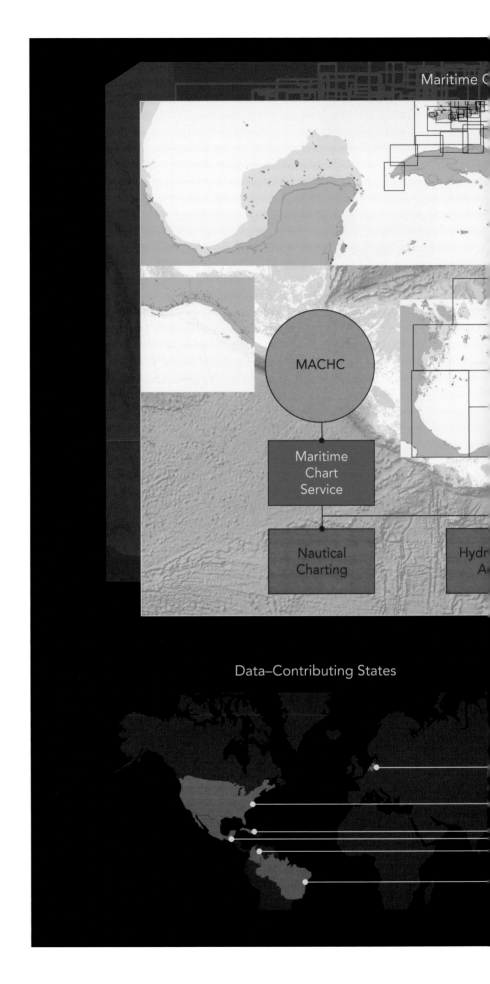

Service

Economic Development

Hydrographic Planning

Marine
Spatial Data
Infrastructure

MACHC Conference

Marine Spatial Data Infrastructure

Using GIS for Hydrotechnical Assessment of Riverine Dynamics and Floodplain Hazards

Golder Associates Inc.
Redmond, Washington, USA
By Benjamin Vang-Johnson, Andreas Kammereck, David Thurman, Scott Stoneman, and Adam Parkin

GIS software and geospatial data were used to perform hydrotechnical assessments of riverine conditions to characterize floodplain hazards along a dynamic portion of the North Fork Nooksack River in northwestern Washington state.

Hydrology of the project reach was assessed by delineating contributing basins, and correlating with US Geological Survey streamflow data (BASIN HYDROLOGY). Hydraulics of the project reach were assessed using a 2D hydraulic model to characterize flow conditions, predicted temporal and spatial flow patterns in the active river channel, and flow patterns in overbank floodplain areas (HYDRAULICS).

Historical aerial orthophotos from 1933 to 2015 (AERIAL) were used to identify, digitize, and assess channel fluvial geomorphic conditions and trends (GEOMORPHIC DATA). Historical channel trends and occupied channel areas were analyzed to predict channel morphology and changing riverine dynamics, and related erosion and scour hazards (AREA OCCUPIED ANALYSIS).

Contact

Benjamin Vang-Johnson
benjamin_vang-johnson@golder.com

Software

ArcGIS for Desktop 10.2.2, TUFLOW 2016-03, Adobe Photoshop, Adobe InDesign CC 2015.0

Data Sources

Whatcom County, US Department of Agriculture, Puget Sound LiDAR Consortium, Nooksack Indian Tribe, US Geological Survey, Golder Associates Inc.

Courtesy of Golder Associates Inc.

AERIAL

Historical aerial photographs were acquired from public sources from 1933 to 2015, totaling 21 individual aerial photos the example above is from 2015. Aerial photos were used to review and assess geomorphic trends at targeted reach scales.

GEOMORPHIC DATA

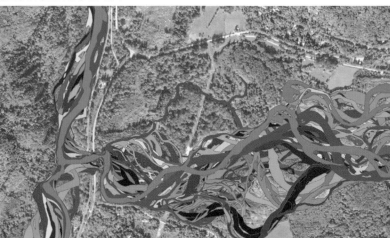

Active low-flow channels, high-flow overbank areas, and floodplain characteristics for each aerial photo series were reviewed and digitized and combined in a geospatial database to compare and assess fluvial geomorphic trends.

AREA OCCUPIED ANALYSIS

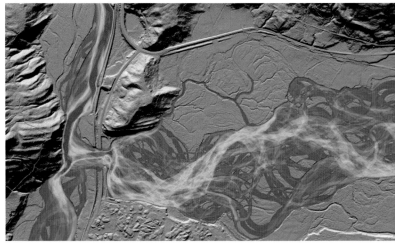

Geospatial database information (i.e. digitized channel results relative to modeled results) was rasterized and overlaied using GIS tools with Lidar data to analyze the relative frequency of occurrence of historical geomorphic

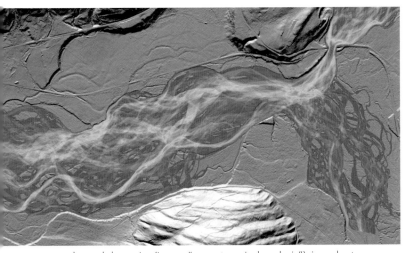

channel dynamics (i.e. an "area occupied analysis"), in order to assess and predict future channel changing trends and potential related erosion and scour hazards.

BASIN HYDROLOGY

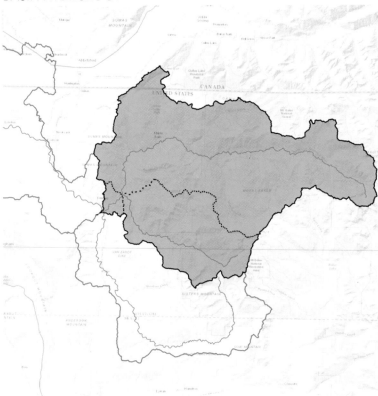

Contributing basin areas to the project area were delineated using digital elevation model data and ArcHydro tools, supplemented with available USGS flow data; and used to support hydrologic analysis of flows.

HYDRAULICS

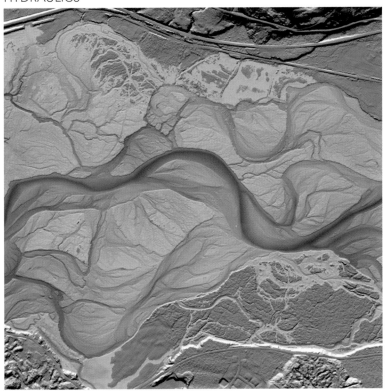

A two-dimensional hydraulic model was developed, incorporating the hydrologic results, to assess temporal and spatial inundation of the channel and floodplain areas.

Environmental Sampling at Palmer Station, Antarctica

Texas A&M University
College Station, Texas, USA
By Andrew Klein and Amanda Frazier

This map illustrates the concentrations of polycyclic aromatic hydrocarbons (PAHs) in marine sediments that are an indication of anthropogenic contamination. As shown on the map, PAHs from the wreckage of Bahía Paraíso, a transport ship that ran aground in Antarctica in 1989, were found in the sediments in the three years following the spill. PAHs were also detected in the sediments from a 2014 reoccupation of these sites. Additional research is required to determine if the current PAHs are consistent with the composition of diesel fuel discharged from the Bahía Paraíso or indicate another source of contamination.

Contact

Andrew Klein
klein@geog.tamu.edu

Software

ArcGIS for Desktop 10.3, Adobe Illustrator

Data Sources

Texas A&M University, DigitalGlobe, Inc.,
Polar Geospatial Center

Courtesy of Texas A&M University.

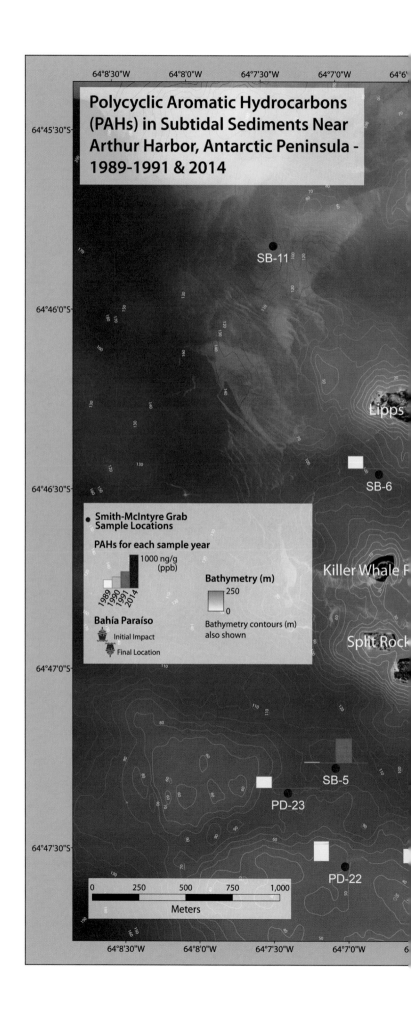

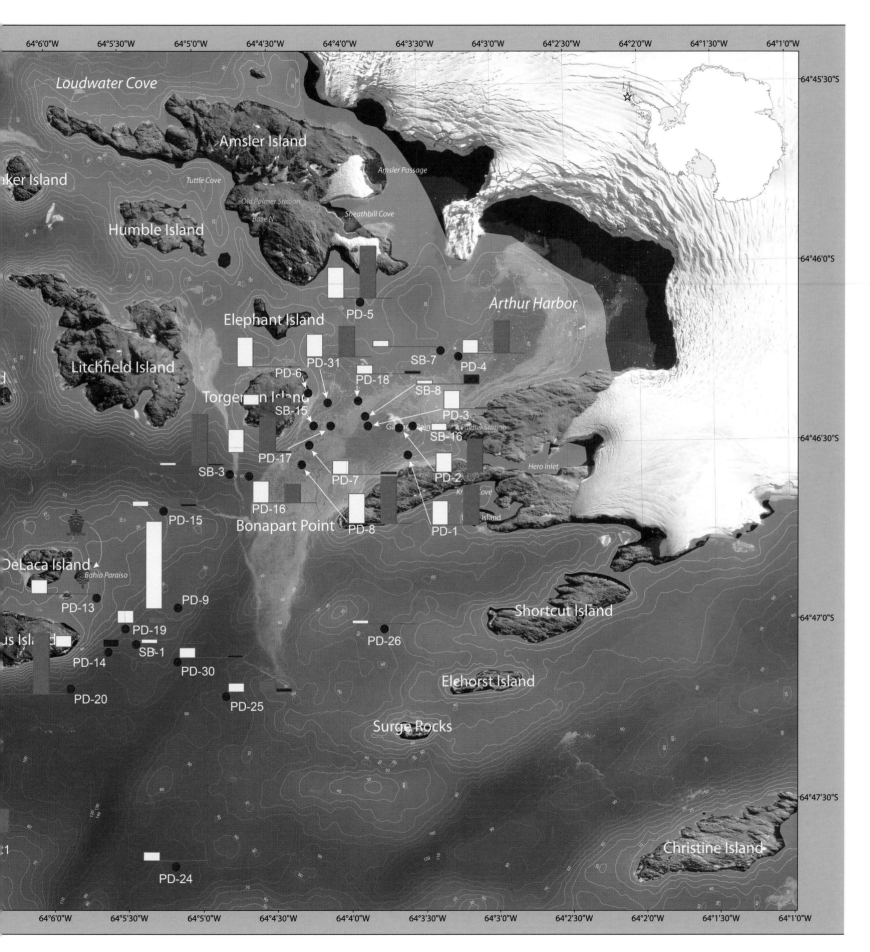

2016 Kumamoto Earthquake: Measuring Uplift and Depression Using Synthetic Aperture Radar

Japan Aerospace Exploration Agency (JAXA)
Tsukuba, Ibaraki, Japan
By Hiroto Nagai, Ryo Natsuaki, Mitsunori Ishihara, Takeo Tadono, Takeshi Motohka, and Shinichi Suzuki

Synthetic aperture radar (SAR) mounted on an earth observation satellite and operated by JAXA can observe horizontal and vertical earth surface movement comparing images obtained before and after the Kumamoto earthquake in April 2016. An Interference image was created by two images. There are several discontinuities in fringe pattern observed on the interferogram. Field observation was conducted, and it is suggested that there is a relationship between building or road damages and breakups on the image. By further developing this technique, it might become possible to estimate location of damage that is hidden by forest leaves and difficult to be found by aircraft and optical satellite observations.

Contacts

Hiroto Nagai
nagai.hiroto@jaxa.jp

Ryo Natsuaki
natsuaki@ee.t.u-tokyo.ac.jp

Software

ArcGIS Desktop

Data Sources

PALSAR-2 data by Japan Aerospace Exploration Agency, basic map information by Geospatial Information Authority of Japan

Courtesy of JAXA.

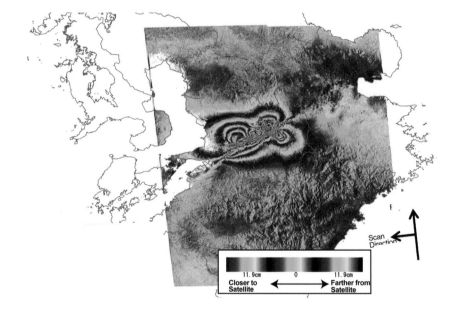

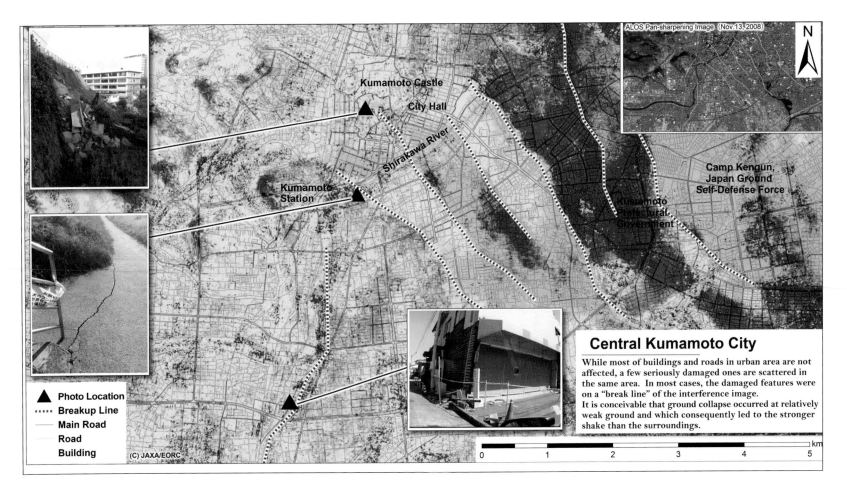

Central Kumamoto City

While most of buildings and roads in urban area are not affected, a few seriously damaged ones are scattered in the same area. In most cases, the damaged features were on a "break line" of the interference image.
It is conceivable that ground collapse occurred at relatively weak ground and which consequently led to the stronger shake than the surroundings.

ALOS Pan-sharpening Image (Nov. 13, 2008)

▲ Photo Location
••••• Breakup Line
— Main Road
— Road
  Building

(C) JAXA/EORC

km
0   1   2   3   4   5

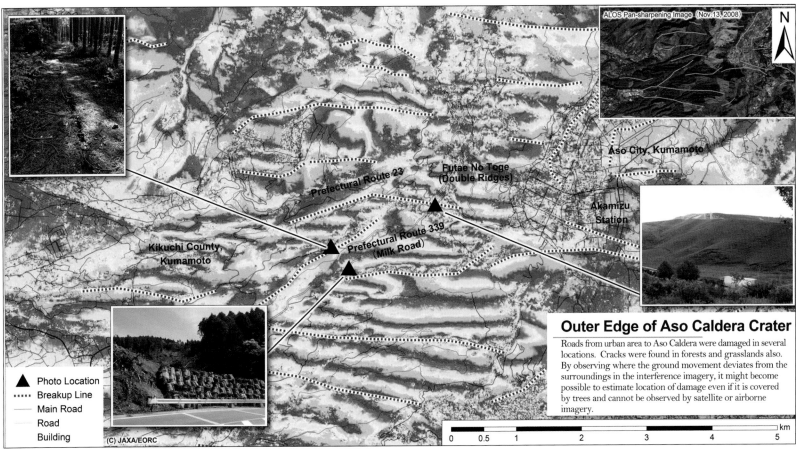

Outer Edge of Aso Caldera Crater

Roads from urban area to Aso Caldera were damaged in several locations. Cracks were found in forests and grasslands also. By observing where the ground movement deviates from the surroundings in the interference imagery, it might become possible to estimate location of damage even if it is covered by trees and cannot be observed by satellite or airborne imagery.

ALOS Pan-sharpening Image (Nov. 13, 2008)

▲ Photo Location
••••• Breakup Line
— Main Road
— Road
  Building

(C) JAXA/EORC

km
0   0.5   1   2   3   4   5

10-Year Posting Trend for Petroleum and Natural Gas Rights in Northern British Columbia

Ministry of Natural Gas Development
Victoria, British Columbia, Canada
By Mel Henze, Talitha Castillo, and Sara McPhail

For several decades, petroleum and natural gas (PNG) production in British Columbia, Canada, has been primarily from conventional resources where oil and gas flow easily without special technology. Within the past decade, however, the primary focus of PNG development has shifted to unconventional resources such as lower-quality reservoirs requiring special techniques for oil and gas to flow at economic rates.

Recent advances in horizontal drilling and completion techniques have enabled industry to target vast unconventional shale gas and tight gas resources in northeast British Columba within the Horn River Basin, Cordova Embayment, Liard Basin, and Montney.

Industry requests for the subsurface rights to explore and develop PNG resources are subject to a referral process involving First Nations, local governments, and other government agencies, resulting in some tenure requests not being disposed. This map represents annual posting requests for subsurface rights since 2006.

Contact

Nevis Antoniazzi
Nevis.Antoniazzi@gov.bc.ca

Software

ArcGIS for Desktop 10.2.2

Data Source

BC Geographic Warehouse

Courtesy of Ministry of Natural Gas Development.

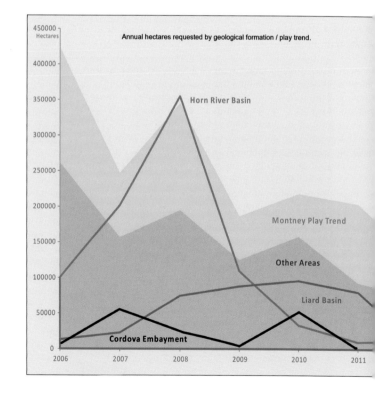

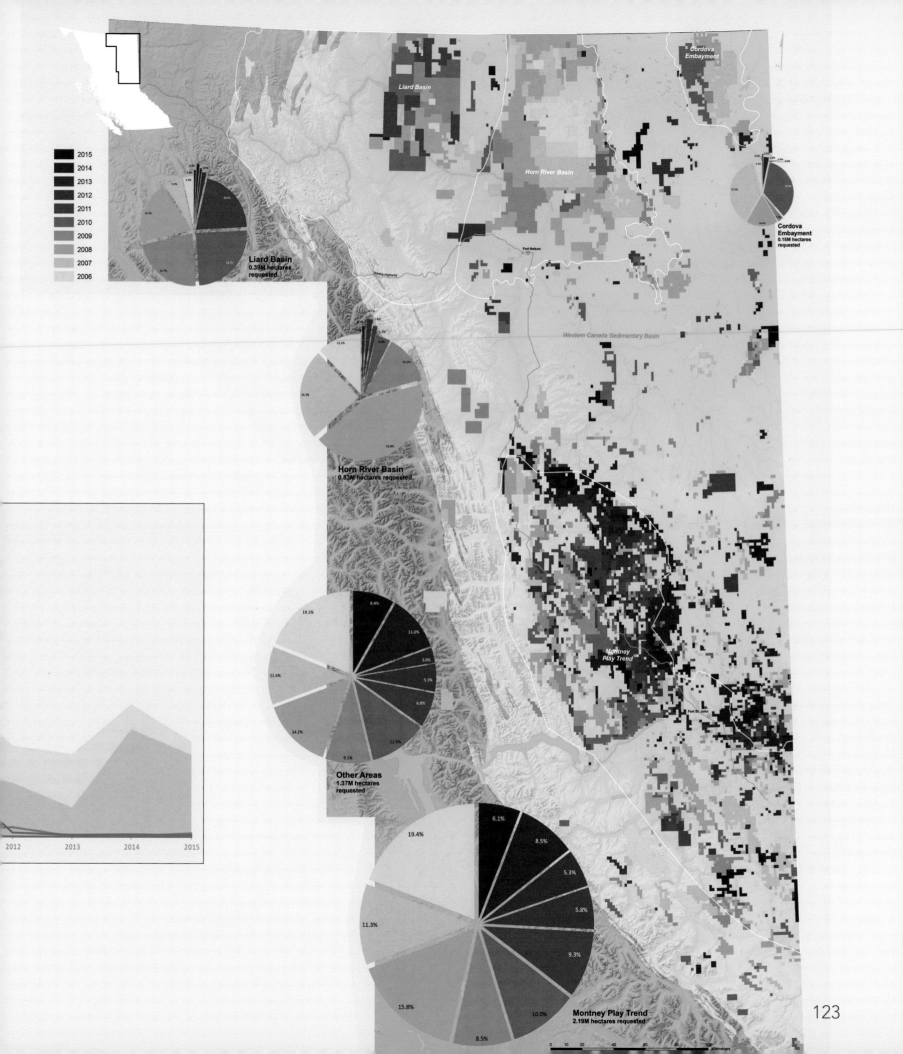

Liard Basin
0.39M hectares
requested

Cordova Embayment
0.15M hectares
requested

Horn River Basin
0.83M hectares requested

Other Areas
1.37M hectares
requested

Montney Play Trend
2.19M hectares requested

Liard Basin

Cordova Embayment

Horn River Basin

Montney Play Trend

Western Canada Sedimentary Basin

Fort Nelson

Fort St. John

2015
2014
2013
2012
2011
2010
2009
2008
2007
2006

2012   2013   2014   2015

123

Significant Sand Resource Areas in State and Federal Waters Offshore Monmouth County

New Jersey Department of Environmental Protection (NJDEP)

Trenton, New Jersey, USA

By Zehdreh Allen-Lafayette, Michael V. Castelli, Daniel Latini, Jane Uptegrove, Jeffrey S. Waldner, David W. Hall, and Andrea L. Friedman

The New Jersey Geological and Water Survey (NJGWS) maps the state's offshore geology and identifies offshore sand deposits by acquiring, analyzing, and interpreting marine geologic and geophysical data. NJGWS collected the seismic subbottom data used in this analysis in 2000 and 2001. The grid of subbottom profiles analyzed for this map extends from Sea Bright to just south of Manasquan Inlet.

This map identifies and quantifies the nearshore sand shoals offshore Monmouth County, New Jersey, located in both state and federal waters (within and beyond the 3-mile state/federal jurisdictional boundary) respectively. NJGWS delineated the base of sand, correlated to the vibracore lithology, for each of the sand shoals identified on this map to generate sand thickness data for all profiles that cross the feature. This map identifies fourteen additional shoal features. Sand volumes at these sites, with calculations based on a five-foot minimum thickness, range from 295,000 to 31,337,000 cubic yards.

Contact

Zehdreh Allen-Lafayette
zehdreh.allen-lafayette@dep.nj.gov

Software

ArcGIS Desktop, ArcInfo Workstation, Surfer, Microsoft Word, Microsoft® Excel, Adobe Illustrator, Adobe InDesign

Data Source

NJDEP

Courtesy of NJDEP.

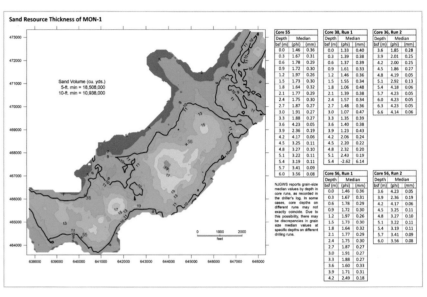

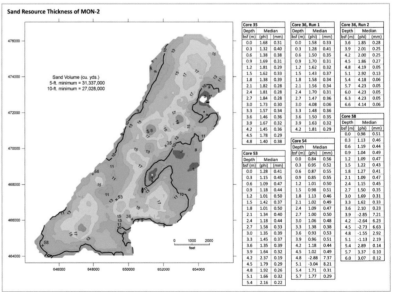

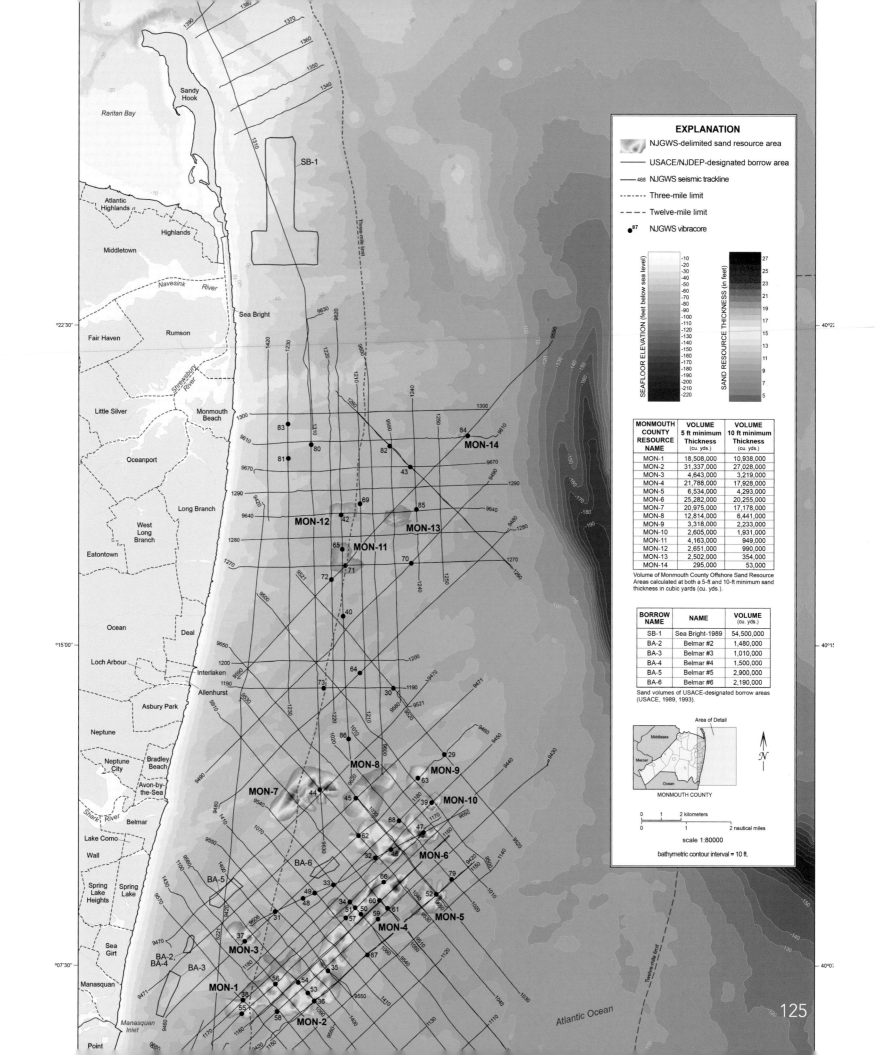

EXPLANATION

- NJGWS-delimited sand resource area
- —— USACE/NJDEP-designated borrow area
- —468— NJGWS seismic trackline
- —·—·— Three-mile limit
- —— — Twelve-mile limit
- ● 87 NJGWS vibracore

SEAFLOOR ELEVATION (feet below sea level)

| -10 |
| -20 |
| -30 |
| -40 |
| -50 |
| -60 |
| -70 |
| -80 |
| -90 |
| -100 |
| -110 |
| -120 |
| -130 |
| -140 |
| -150 |
| -160 |
| -170 |
| -180 |
| -190 |
| -200 |
| -210 |
| -220 |

SAND RESOURCE THICKNESS (in feet)

| 27 |
| 25 |
| 23 |
| 21 |
| 19 |
| 17 |
| 15 |
| 13 |
| 11 |
| 9 |
| 7 |
| 5 |

MONMOUTH COUNTY RESOURCE NAME	VOLUME 5 ft minimum Thickness (cu. yds.)	VOLUME 10 ft minimum Thickness (cu. yds.)
MON-1	18,508,000	10,938,000
MON-2	31,337,000	27,028,000
MON-3	4,643,000	3,219,000
MON-4	21,788,000	17,928,000
MON-5	6,534,000	4,293,000
MON-6	25,282,000	20,255,000
MON-7	20,975,000	17,178,000
MON-8	12,814,000	6,441,000
MON-9	3,318,000	2,233,000
MON-10	2,605,000	1,931,000
MON-11	4,163,000	949,000
MON-12	2,651,000	990,000
MON-13	2,502,000	354,000
MON-14	295,000	53,000

Volume of Monmouth County Offshore Sand Resource Areas calculated at both a 5-ft and 10-ft minimum sand thickness in cubic yards (cu. yds.).

BORROW NAME	NAME	VOLUME (cu. yds.)
SB-1	Sea Bright-1989	54,500,000
BA-2	Belmar #2	1,480,000
BA-3	Belmar #3	1,010,000
BA-4	Belmar #4	1,500,000
BA-5	Belmar #5	2,900,000
BA-6	Belmar #6	2,190,000

Sand volumes of USACE-designated borrow areas (USACE, 1989, 1993).

Area of Detail

MONMOUTH COUNTY

0   1   2 kilometers

0   1   2 nautical miles

scale 1:80000

bathymetric contour interval = 10 ft.

125

City of West Linn Street Tree Map

City of West Linn
West Linn, Oregon, USA
By Kathy Aha, GISP

This map was developed as part of the American Public Works Association accreditation process for the City of West Linn. The preliminary inventory was completed using aerial photography and on-site evaluation of each tree within the city's right-of-way. Each tree was verified in the field by staff interns, along with identifying tree species, size, and condition.

The map provides a display of street trees by tree classification and includes a map overlay of tree canopy developed by Portland Metro's Research Center. This inventory is intended to assist Public Works Street Department staff in identifying tree maintenance areas and tracking within their asset management system, but also provides city administrators an overview of West Linn's tree coverage.

Contact

Kathy Aha
kaha@westlinnoregon.gov

Software

ArcGIS for Desktop 10.3

Data Sources

City of West Linn, Clackamas County, Metro DRC

Courtesy of City of West Linn.

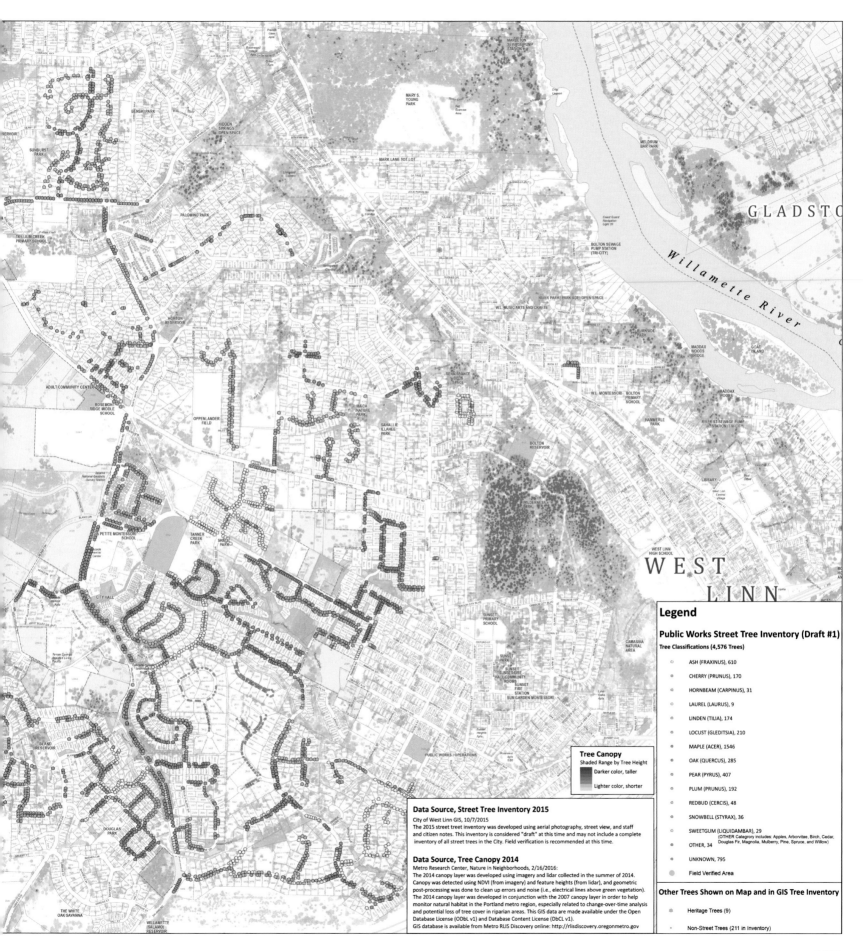

Legend

Public Works Street Tree Inventory (Draft #1)

Tree Classifications (4,576 Trees)

◌	ASH (FRAXINUS), 610
◌	CHERRY (PRUNUS), 170
◌	HORNBEAM (CARPINUS), 31
◌	LAUREL (LAURUS), 9
◌	LINDEN (TILIA), 174
◌	LOCUST (GLEDITSIA), 210
◌	MAPLE (ACER), 1546
◌	OAK (QUERCUS), 285
◌	PEAR (PYRUS), 407
◌	PLUM (PRUNUS), 192
◌	REDBUD (CERCIS), 48
◌	SNOWBELL (STYRAX), 36
◌	SWEETGUM (LIQUIDAMBAR), 29
◌	OTHER, 34 — (OTHER Category includes: Apples, Arborvitae, Birch, Cedar, Douglas Fir, Magnolia, Mulberry, Pine, Spruce, and Willow)
◌	UNKNOWN, 795
◌	Field Verified Area

Other Trees Shown on Map and in GIS Tree Inventory

◌	Heritage Trees (9)
◌	Non-Street Trees (211 in Inventory)

Tree Canopy
Shaded Range by Tree Height

■ Darker color, taller

□ Lighter color, shorter

Data Source, Street Tree Inventory 2015

City of West Linn GIS, 10/7/2015
The 2015 street treet inventory was developed using aerial photography, street view, and staff and citizen notes. This inventory is considered "draft" at this time and may not include a complete inventory of all street trees in the City. Field verification is recommended at this time.

Data Source, Tree Canopy 2014

Metro Research Center, Nature in Neighborhoods, 2/16/2016:
The 2014 canopy layer was developed using imagery and lidar collected in the summer of 2014. Canopy was detected using NDVI (from imagery) and feature heights (from lidar), and geometric post-processing was done to clean up errors and noise (i.e., electrical lines above green vegetation). The 2014 canopy layer was developed in conjunction with the 2007 canopy layer in order to help monitor natural habitat in the Portland metro region, especially related to change-over-time analysis and potential loss of tree cover in riparian areas. This GIS data are made available under the Open Database License (ODbL v1) and Database Content License (DbCL v1).
GIS database is available from Metro RLIS Discovery online: http://rlisdiscovery.oregonmetro.gov

Overhead to Underground: A 3D GIS Utility Relocation Rendering

CobbFendley
Houston, Texas, USA
By Larry Jahn

This 3D GIS map was used to market CobbFendley's overhead-to-underground utility relocation capabilities by presenting a visual before and after utility relocation representation. CobbFendley, a multidisciplined civil engineering firm, has been successfully designing and relocating utilities since 1980. Overhead utilities are relocated underground for beautification purposes, economic development, and damage prevention.

Relocating utilities underground creates an attractive streetscape, increases green space, and appeals to new development. Other important benefits of the relocation include securing and protecting the utilities from everyday environmental factors to ensure service continuity.

Contact

Larry Jahn
ljahn@cobbfendley.com

Software

ArcGIS for Desktop 10.2, ArcScene, SketchUp

Data Source

Cobb-Fendley

Courtesy of CobbzFendley

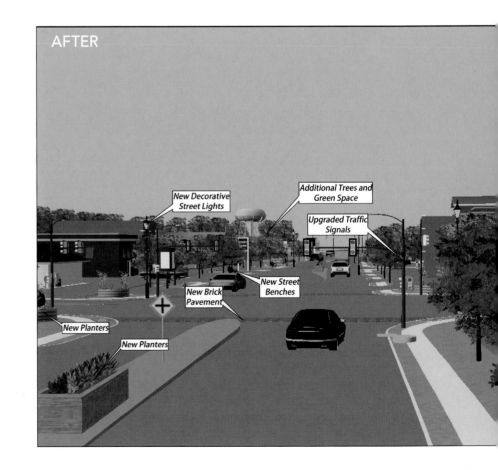

This image displays a cluttered, congested streetscape as a result of a multitude of above-ground utilities (e.g. aerial electric and aerial telephone).

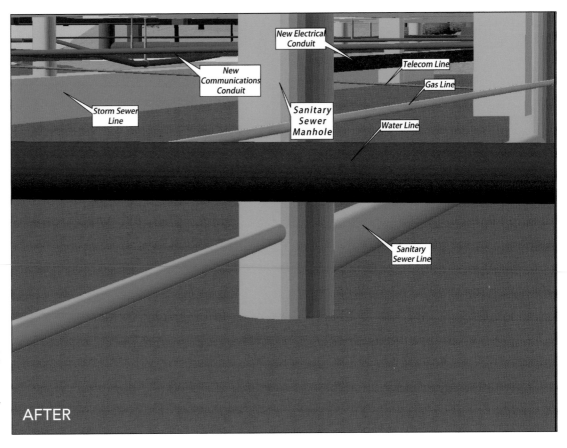

This image displays the complex networks of various utility infrastructures beneath the surface after the utility relocations have been completed.

This image displays a zoomed-in view of the enhanced streetscape. Most of the utilities were relocated from above ground to below ground, and aesthetic upgrades such as more trees, new pavement, and new light standards were installed to beautify the streetscape and create an attractive and renewed environment.

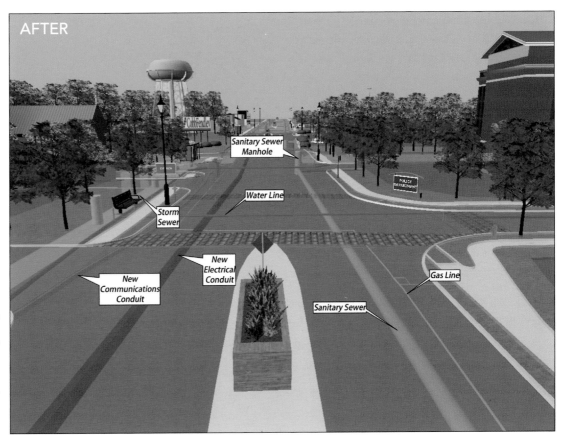

This image displays a zoomed-out view of the enhanced streetscape. The various utility infrastructure networks are visible underground. Utilities such as electrical and telecom previously cluttered the streetscape, but are now relocated beneath the surface.

Climate-Smart Cities: New York City

The Trust for Public Land
Santa Fe, New Mexico, USA
By Chris David, Holly Elwell, Carolyn Ives, Nick Viau (AllPoints GIS), and Lindsay Withers

The Trust for Public Land is working in partnership with researchers at Columbia and Drexel Universities to plan and implement green infrastructure improvements along vulnerable waterfront areas in New York City to address future threats and inform waterfront planning. The conservation agenda includes research on green infrastructure performance during Superstorm Sandy, GIS-based planning to identify priority conservation sites and on-the-ground projects to encourage wetland restoration and creatively designed resilient waterfront parks.

These maps are part of a suite of planning tools, including the trust's Climate-Smart™ Cities New York City online viewer, that allows officials and partners to weigh different scenarios, view results, and better plan for green infrastructure.

Contact

Chris David
Chris.David@tpl.org

Software

ArcGIS for Desktop 10.3, Configurable Map Viewer

Data Source

Esri, City of New York, Federal Emergency Management Agency, US Army Corps of Engineers, Drexel University, National Oceanic and Atmospheric Administration, University of South Carolina US Census Bureau, US Fish and Wildlife Service, US Geological Survey Regional Plan Association

Copyright © The Trust for Public Land. Information on these maps is provided for purposes of discussion and visualization only.

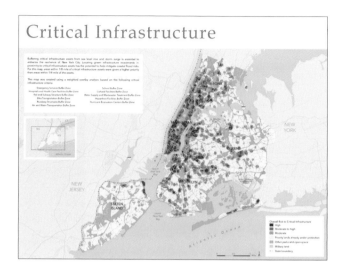

Critical Infrastructure

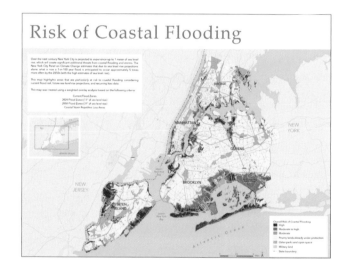

Risk of Coastal Flooding

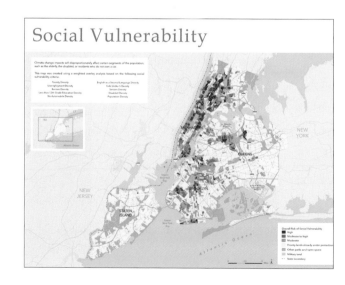

Social Vulnerability

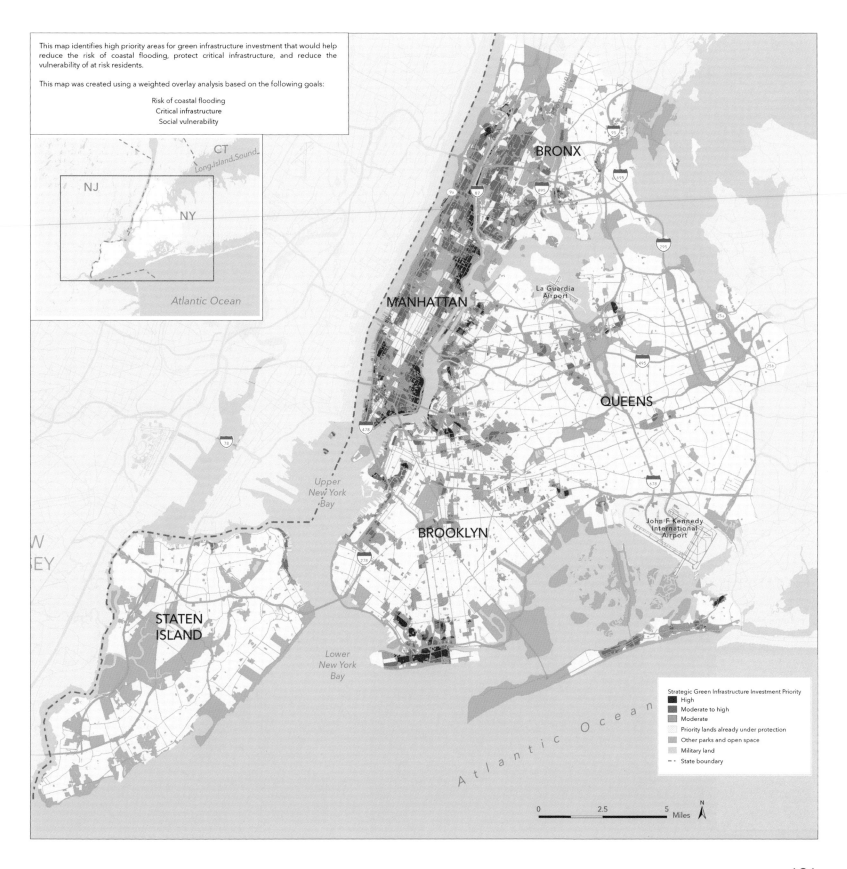

This map identifies high priority areas for green infrastructure investment that would help reduce the risk of coastal flooding, protect critical infrastructure, and reduce the vulnerability of at risk residents.

This map was created using a weighted overlay analysis based on the following goals:

Risk of coastal flooding
Critical infrastructure
Social vulnerability

CT

NJ

NY

Long Island Sound

Atlantic Ocean

BRONX

MANHATTAN

La Guardia Airport

QUEENS

Upper New York Bay

BROOKLYN

John F. Kennedy International Airport

STATEN ISLAND

Lower New York Bay

Atlantic Ocean

Strategic Green Infrastructure Investment Priority
- High
- Moderate to high
- Moderate
- Priority lands already under protection
- Other parks and open space
- Military land
- State boundary

0   2.5   5 Miles

N

131

Multiple Products, One Solution: Ancient Seas to Modern Charts

National Oceanic and Atmospheric Administration (NOAA), Office of Coast Survey
Silver Spring, Maryland, USA
By Megan Bartlett and Elise Athens

From the early nineteenth century, NOAA's nautical charts have employed a variety of acquisition techniques. Ferdinand Hassler's collection of scientific instruments to conduct the first surveys of New York Harbor are now museum pieces, making way for the ever-evolving technological advances in the science of hydrography. Historically, mariners used lead weighted lines to survey the seas. Today, NOAA uses sophisticated computer systems and equipment mounted to ships, planes, and autonomous underwater vehicles to create the modern nautical chart. Even with these advances and a suite of products covering roughly 3.4 million square nautical miles, less than 5 percent of the earth's oceans have been explored.

The Marine Chart Division's Nautical Information System stores chart-relevant data in an enterprise geodatabase that complies with the International Hydrographic Organization's S-57 standards for nautical content. Within this geodatabase, NOAA raster and electronic navigational chart products are produced using the ArcGIS for Maritime: Charting extension. This modernized approach and workflow allows NOAA to edit data once, and leverage the revisions within both navigational product suites in an efficient and timely manner. Using these tools, the cartographic finishing workload is greatly reduced, while still allowing for the time-honored duty of today's nautical cartographers to balance function and form in the creation of a quality nautical chart.

Contact

Megan Bartlett
megan.bartlett@noaa.gov

Software

ArcGIS® for Maritime: Charting 10.3.1

Data Source

NOAA

Courtesy of NOAA, Office of Coast Survey.

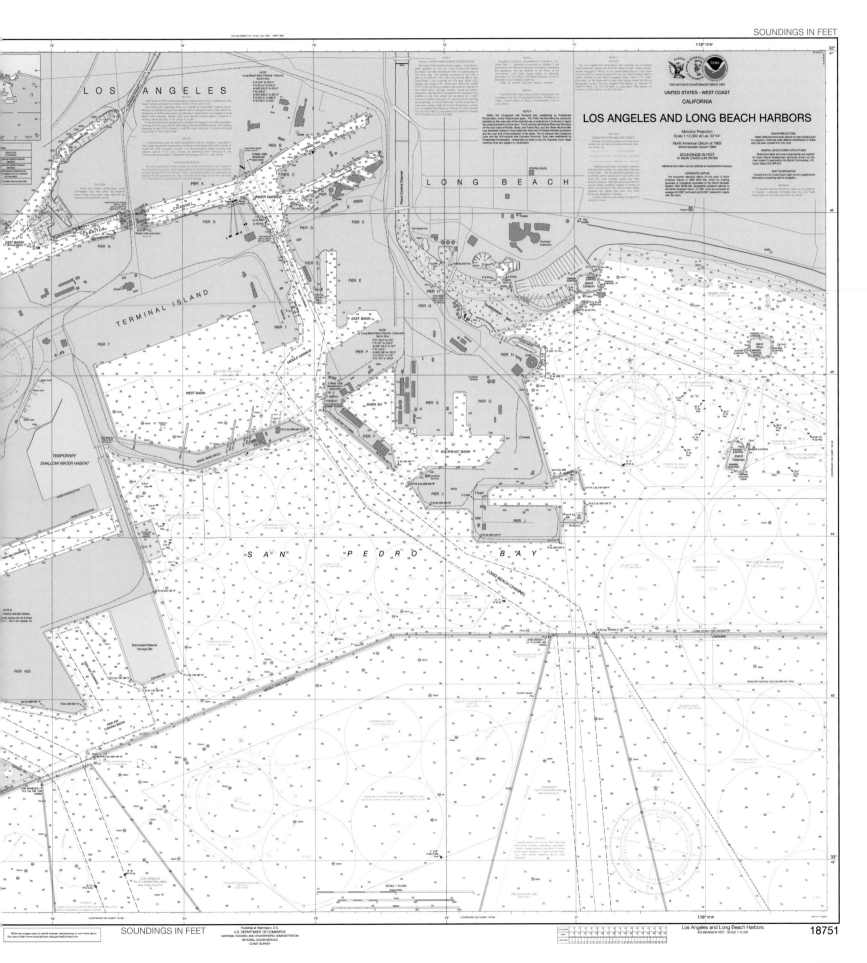

UNITED STATES - WEST COAST

CALIFORNIA

LOS ANGELES AND LONG BEACH HARBORS

Mercator Projection
Scale 1:12,000 at Lat. 33°44'
North American Datum of 1983
(World Geodetic System 1984)

SOUNDINGS IN FEET
AT MEAN LOWER LOW WATER

LOS ANGELES

LONG BEACH

TERMINAL ISLAND

SAN PEDRO BAY

SCALE 1:12,000

Published at Washington, D.C.
U.S. DEPARTMENT OF COMMERCE
NATIONAL OCEANIC AND ATMOSPHERIC ADMINISTRATION
NATIONAL OCEAN SERVICE
COAST SURVEY

SOUNDINGS IN FEET

Los Angeles and Long Beach Harbors
SOUNDINGS IN FEET · SCALE 1:12,000

18751

133

Air Operations Planning Map Series

University of Minnesota Polar Geospatial Center
Minneapolis, Minnesota, USA
By Michael Clementz

In the remote and vast continent of Antarctica, safety is of the utmost importance, especially during the winter months when darkness and frigid temperatures further complicate operations. These maps were developed by the Polar Geospatial Center (PGC) at the University of Minnesota as the US Antarctic Program's (USAP) contribution to a collaborative international project to produce air operations planning maps.

The objective of this series was to develop standardized maps for planning safe scientific research operations with coverage of priority areas in Antarctica. These maps are being delivered to the USAP to replace smaller, outdated maps that lack current and accurate datasets. In its entirety, this map series shows that international collaboration can produce an important operational resource for the Antarctic community; one that extends beyond the scope of each individual organization.

Contact

Michael Clementz
cleme399@umn.edu

Software

ArcGIS for Desktop 10.3

Data Sources

National Snow and Ice Data Center, Radarsat Antarctic Mapping Project, Scientific Committee on Antarctic Research, Antarctic Digital Database, US Antarctic Program, US Geological Survey Geographic Names Information System

Courtesy of Michael Clementz, Polar Geospatial Center.

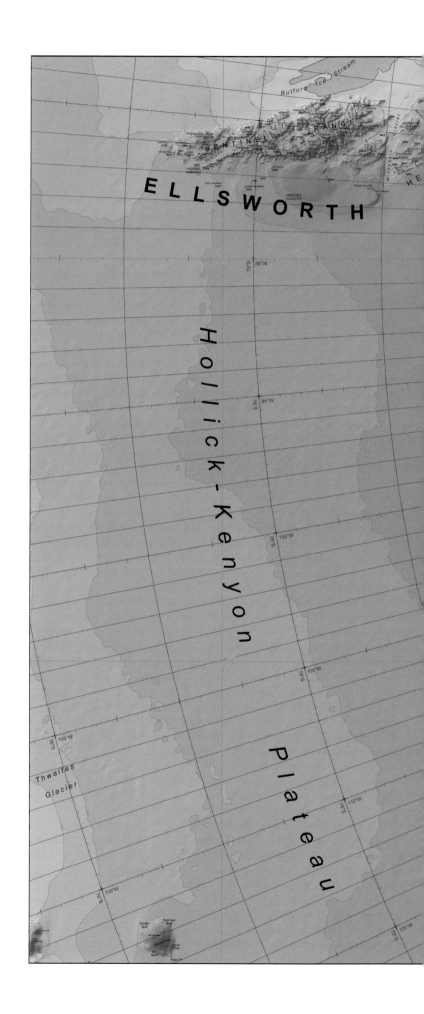

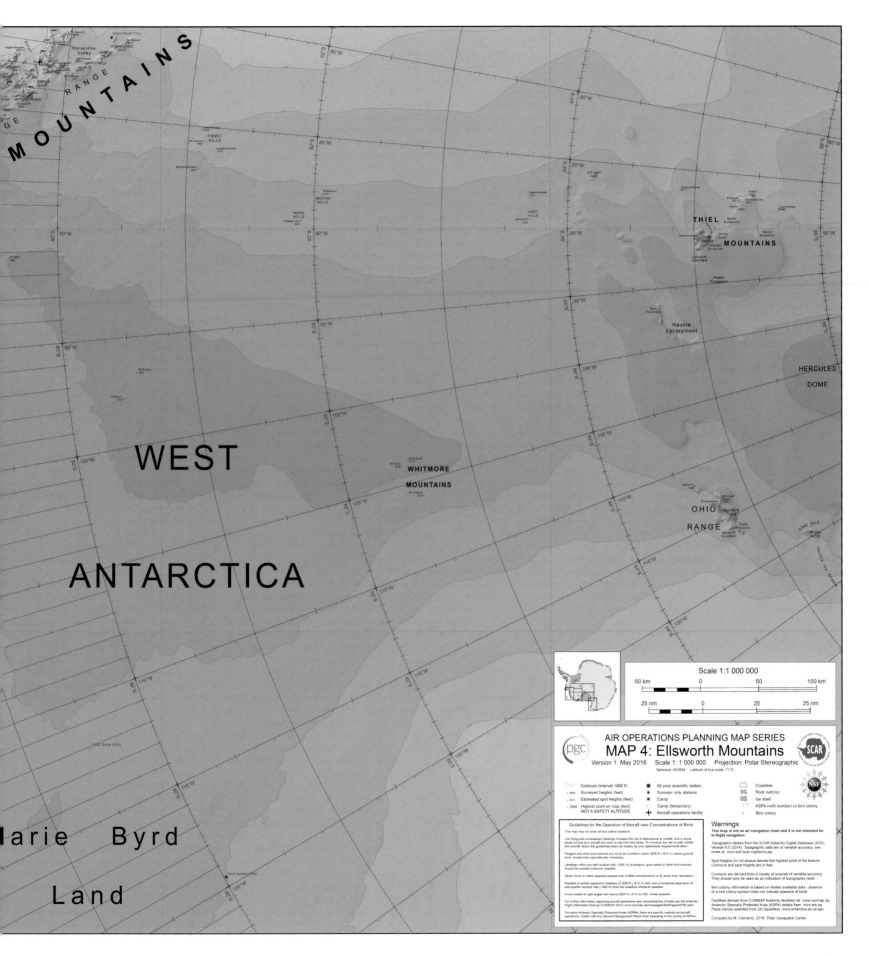

RANGE

MOUNTAINS

WEST

ANTARCTICA

Marie Byrd

Land

THIEL

MOUNTAINS

WHITMORE

MOUNTAINS

HERCULES

DOME

OHIO

RANGE

Havola
Escarpment

PIRRIT
HILLS

NASH
HILLS

MARTIN
HILLS

HART
HILLS

AIR OPERATIONS PLANNING MAP SERIES
MAP 4: Ellsworth Mountains
Version 1: May 2016   Scale 1: 1 000 000   Projection: Polar Stereographic
Spheroid: WGS84   Latitude of true scale: 71°S

pgc   SCAR   NSF

Contours (interval 1000 ft)
Surveyed heights (feet)
Estimated spot heights (feet)
Highest point on map (feet)
NOT A SAFETY ALTITUDE

All year scientific station
Summer only stations
Camp
Camp (temporary)
Aircraft operations facility

Coastline
Rock outcrop
Ice shelf
ASPA (with number) or bird colony
Bird colony

3D Building Massing Model for New York City

Applied Geographics Inc. (AppGeo)
Boston, Massachusetts, USA
By Mike Wiley

AppGeo developed a 3D massing model for the City of New York with varying degrees of detail for one million buildings in the city. All buildings were modeled according to Open Geospatial Consortium's CityGML specification. The massing model was delivered in three levels of detail (LOD), differentiated by roof, facade/walls, and ground plane factors.

AppGeo and the City of New York concluded that, with the exception of iconic buildings, a hybrid level of detail between LOD1 and LOD2 would be most appropriate for the city. AppGeo completed this project with data outputs of an Esri multipatch geodatabase and CityGML.

Contact

Thomas Harrington
tharr@appgeo.com

Software

ArcGIS® Pro

Data Sources

Esri, Applied Geographics Inc.

Courtesy of Applied Geographics Inc.

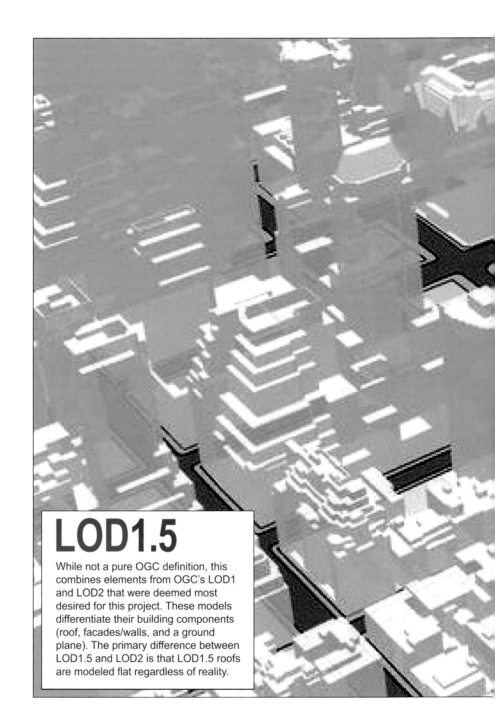

LOD1.5

While not a pure OGC definition, this combines elements from OGC's LOD1 and LOD2 that were deemed most desired for this project. These models differentiate their building components (roof, facades/walls, and a ground plane). The primary difference between LOD1.5 and LOD2 is that LOD1.5 roofs are modeled flat regardless of reality.

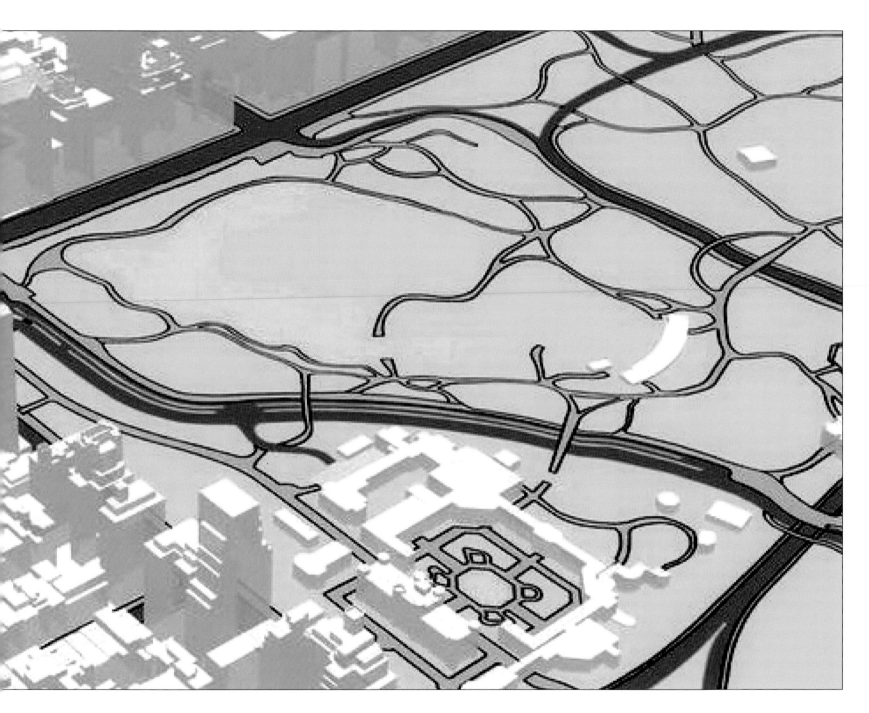

LOD2

Like LOD1.5, these models differentiate their building components such as roof, facades/walls, and a ground plane. In the case of these models, their roofs were modeled to support rendering of sloped roofs.

LOD3

These models are often referred to as architectural models where the roof modeling represents real object forms but not containing interior structures (reserved for LOD4). LOD3 denotes architectural models with detailed wall and roof structures potentially including doors and windows. In the case of the Statue of Liberty, the details of "roof", "walls" and the modeling of the windows/doors are what makes this an LOD3 model.

LASAN: Protecting Public Health and the Environment

City of Los Angeles, Bureau of Sanitation (LASAN)
Los Angeles, California, USA
By Jennifer-Ann R. Geronca, Oscar Figueroa, and Jose Lozano

This display of maps shows the wide range of services provided by LASAN and how GIS is used in operations. Among the services are scheduling of service, modeling sewers, planning stormwater capture projects, and tracking polluters. The Bureau of Sanitation is leveraging GIS to protect public health and the environment.

Contact

Jennifer-Ann R. Geronca
Jennifer.Geronca@lacity.org

Software

ArcGIS for Desktop 10.3.1

Data Source

Los Angeles City Public Works Department

Courtesy of LASAN.

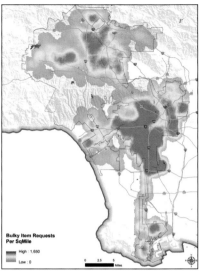

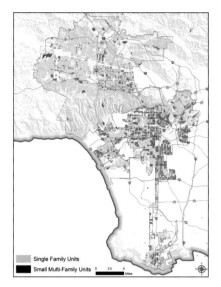

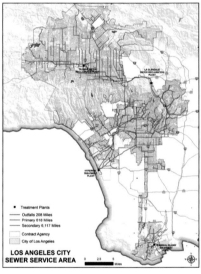

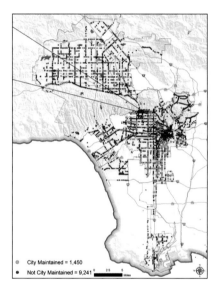

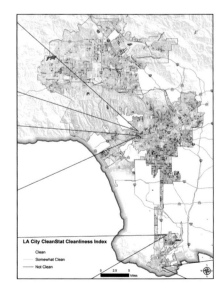

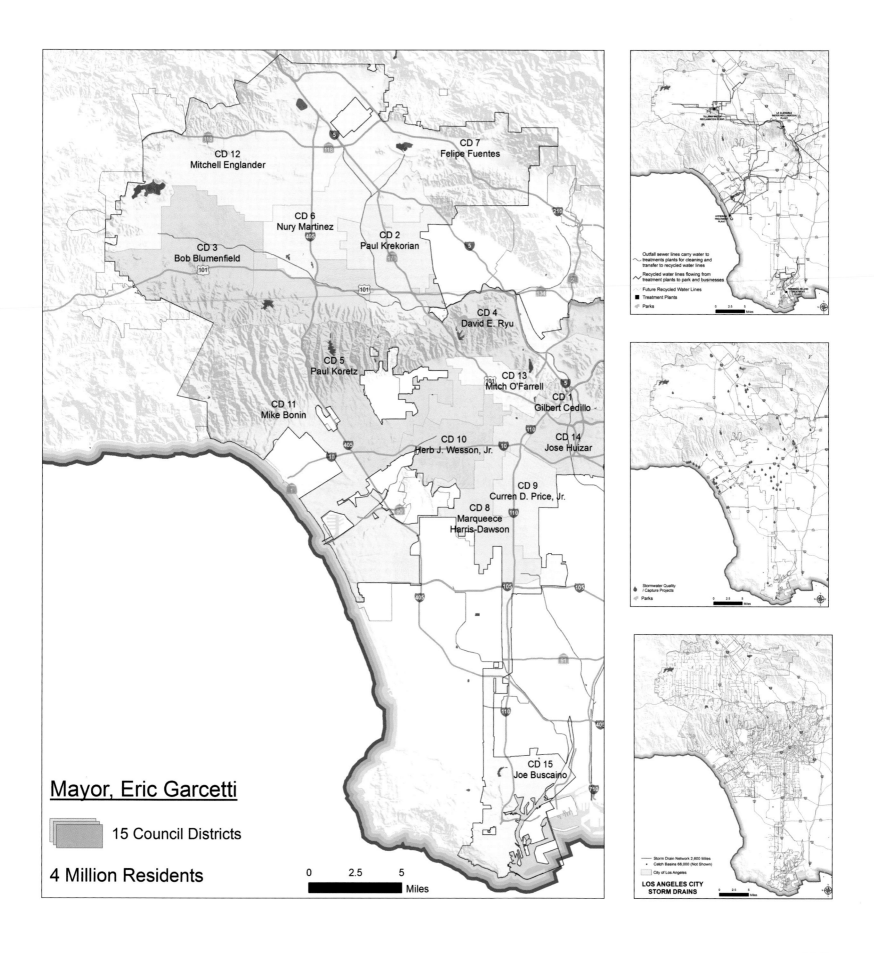

Mayor, Eric Garcetti

15 Council Districts

4 Million Residents

CD 12
Mitchell Englander

CD 7
Felipe Fuentes

CD 6
Nury Martinez

CD 3
Bob Blumenfield

CD 2
Paul Krekorian

CD 4
David E. Ryu

CD 5
Paul Koretz

CD 13
Mitch O'Farrell

CD 1
Gilbert Cedillo

CD 11
Mike Bonin

CD 10
Herb J. Wesson, Jr.

CD 14
Jose Huizar

CD 9
Curren D. Price, Jr.

CD 8
Marqueece
Harris-Dawson

CD 15
Joe Buscaino

0   2.5   5
Miles

Outfall sewer lines carry water to
treatments plants for cleaning and
transfer to recycled water lines

Recycled water lines flowing from
treatment plants to park and businesses

Future Recycled Water Lines

Treatment Plants

Parks

0   2.5   5
Miles

Stormwater Quality
/ Capture Projects

Parks

0   2.5   5
Miles

Storm Drain Network 2,800 Miles

Catch Basins 68,000 (Not Shown)

City of Los Angeles

LOS ANGELES CITY
STORM DRAINS

0   2.5   5
Miles

139

City of Scottsdale Hydrant Map

City of Scottsdale
Scottsdale, Arizona, USA
By Mele D. Koneya

The City of Scottsdale has close to 11,000 hydrants within its boundaries. The City of Scottsdale Fire Department is required to physically inspect and flush each of these hydrants annually because ensuring the working condition of the fire hydrants is critical. If any functional problems or damages are found, the city's water department is notified that a repair is needed. In 2016, a new program was developed in which the fire department would flush and inspect two thirds of the hydrants while the water department would perform preventive maintenance on the remaining one third. The hydrants to be inspected by the fire department will rotate over a three-year cycle.

Contact

Mele D. Koneya
mkoneya@scottsdaleaz.gov

Software

ArcGIS Desktop

Data Source

City of Scottsdale

Courtesy of City of Scottsdale.

Web AppBuilder for ArcGIS® (Developer Edition) 1.2 was used to build an application based around an ArcGIS Online web map consisting of internal ArcSDE feature classes. Custom code and custom widgets were implemented where needed to improve the process for field crews and fire department staff.

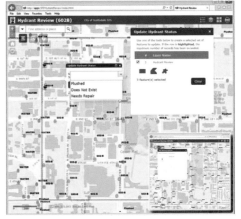

Fire department crews update the status attribute to show 'Flushed', 'Does Not Exist', or 'Needs Repair' using the Batch Attribute Editor widget. The Batch Attribute Editor widget was customized to populate the shift when a hydrant's status is updated. The edit widget allow crews to add hydrants found in the field that were not shown on the map.

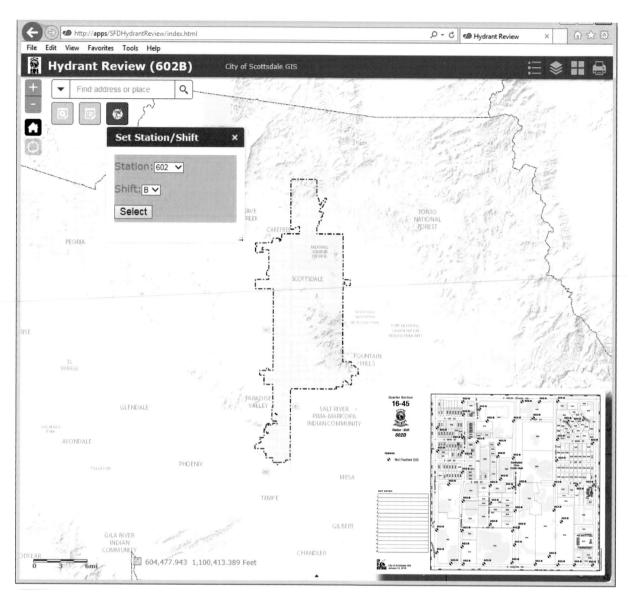

Quarter-section based maps were created using ArcMap Data Driven pages for SFD crews to view the hydrants assigned to them. As inspections are completed Fire department crews use the Web AppBuilder application to select their shift number and to update the status of the hydrants.

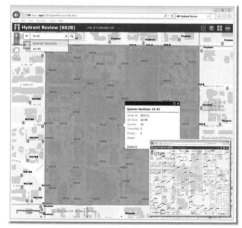

Using the built in search widget, field crews are able to find a given quarter section, zoom in, and view the status of hydrants assigned to their shift.

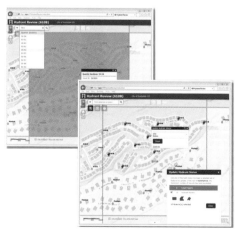

After an area has been identified that needs further inspection the crews can then zoom to an area using the search widget and update the status of the hydrants with the Batch Attribute Editor widget.

Standard table of contents and layer controls are available to show the status of the hydrants and to provide other layers to the crews, such as current aerials, for viewing the hydrant locations.

ADWEA Executive Dashboard

Abu Dhabi Water & Electricity Authority (ADWEA)
Abu Dhabi, United Arab Emirates
By Shaima Al Hammadi

The Executive Dashboard solution is a comprehensive GIS-based decision-support framework that includes maps and tools to facilitate a number of planning and operations management activities for ADWEA managers. This suite of solutions does not require any advanced GIS knowledge, while providing managers within the ADWEA group with GIS-based tools to explore the various aspects of the utility business.

An integrated reporting engine was developed to generate summary and statistical reporting at various levels and based on GIS map selections, both spatial and query-based. Additionally, targeted maps to visualize the water demand forecasts up to the year 2030 against forecast population growth have been created to leverage spatial analysis in optimizing the sources of production on the basis of capacity and predicted demand. Finally, the solution also includes a performance management and key performance indicator dashboard that displays GIS and non-GIS information and key performance indicators directly on the map or as gauges for enhanced decision-making.

Contact

Shaima Al Hammadi
shhammadi@adwea.ae

Software

ArcGIS for Server 10.2.1

Data Source

ADWEA

Courtesy of ADWEA.

ADWEA SAIDI & SAIFI KPIs

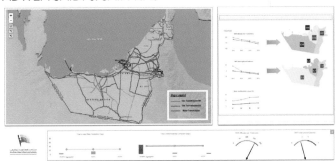

Population vs Demand Forcast

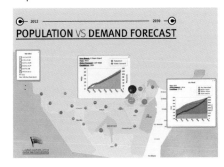

HR Dashboard

The solution is equipped with a dashboard consisting of several widgets that display the most important ADWEA network statistics based on TRANSCO's water and electricity transmission networks, as well as ADDC and AADC's water and electricity distribution networks.

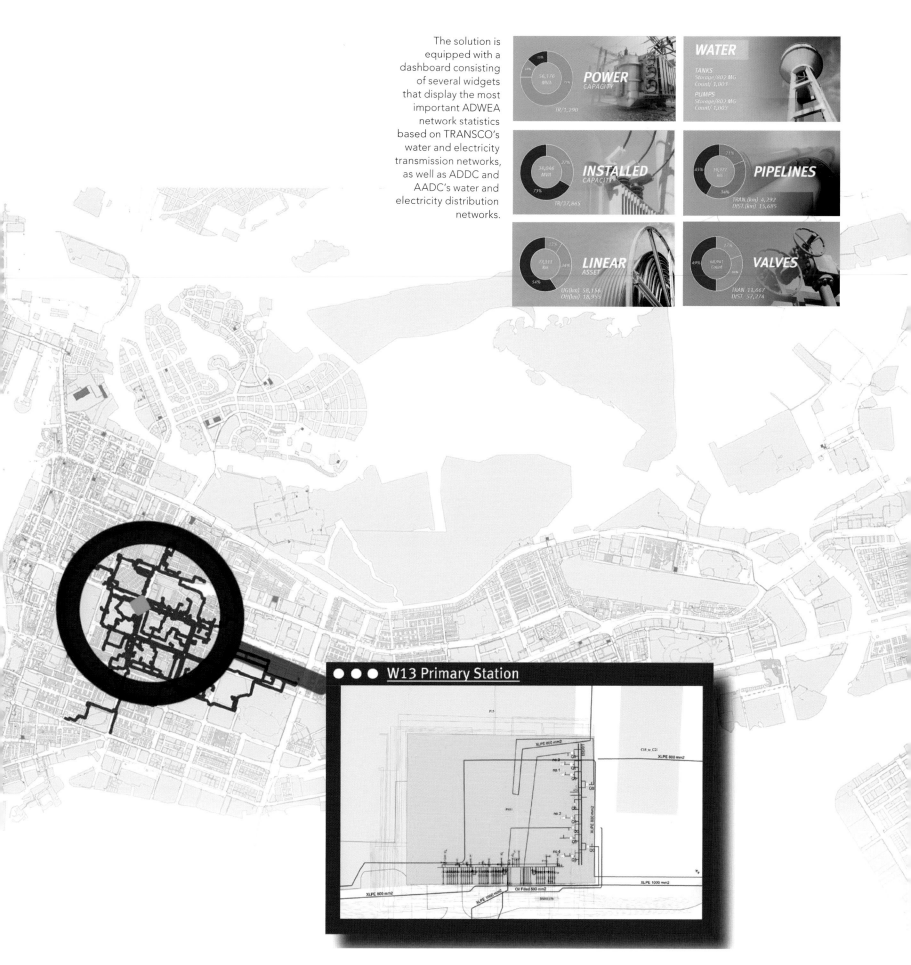

Sound Transit 3 Package and Climate Change

Sound Transit
Seattle, Washington, USA
By Mike Strong and Charlie Morton

Sound Transit is a regional transit agency that plans, builds, and operates express bus, light rail, and commuter train services for Seattle and surrounding counties. In 2012, Sound Transit asked the University of Washington's Climate Impact Group to evaluate the agency's long-term risks from the effects of climate change. The project identified potential climate change impacts on agency operations, assets, and long-term planning. Additionally, options were identified for strengthening the agency's resilience to these impacts and opportunities for integrating climate change considerations into agency decision-making processes.

In November 2016, voters approved a measure to add 62 miles of light rail, new bus rapid transit lines, as well as extend and expand an existing commuter train line. The work from the Climate Impacts Group study gave the agency a way to take a baseline look at possible climate change impacts, in conjunction with this expansion package.

Contact

Mike Strong
Mike.Strong@soundtransit.org

Software

ArcGIS for Desktop 10.2, Adobe InDesign

Data Sources

Sound Transit, King County, Pierce County, Snohomish County, Washington State Department of Transportation, OpenStreetMap

Courtesy of Sound Transit.

Map 13
1:48.000

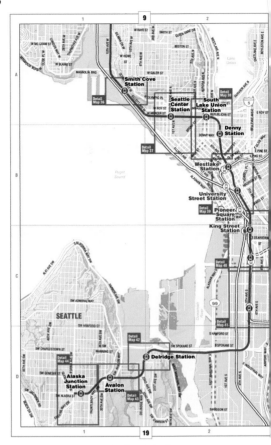

Sound Transit 3 Draft Plan - 6/2/16
The location of all proposed facilites is subject to change.

Map 1
1-16
1:48.000

1-4

Sound Transit 3 Draft Plan - 6/2/16
The location of all proposed facilites is subject to change.

Sino-Singapore Tianjin Eco-City

Beijing GISUNI Information Technology Co., Ltd.
By Xuedong Li, Eva Peng, Qingqing Zhao, and Yaxin Zhou

Sino-Singapore Tianjin Eco-city is a cooperative program between China and Singapore, which plays an important role in demonstrating how to build a society that conserves resources and is environmentally friendly. The concept of refined location management could enhance the city service level and urban governance significantly. A location-based services (LBS) platform was developed along with Sino-Singapore Eco-City, which served as the base platform of "Sino-Singapore Eco-City Spatial Information Cloud."

One of the key features of this LBS platform is that all the maps of the Eco-City, extending over 30 square kilometers, were displayed by campus mapping. The form of buildings, the texture of plants, mountains, rocks, and roads reflected the surface features in reality at a fine-grained level.

Contact

Cynthia Wu
wuchen@gisuni.com

Software

ArcGIS for Desktop 10.2

Data Sources

Emapgo, DigitalGlobe

Courtesy of Beijing GISUNI Information Technology Co., Ltd.

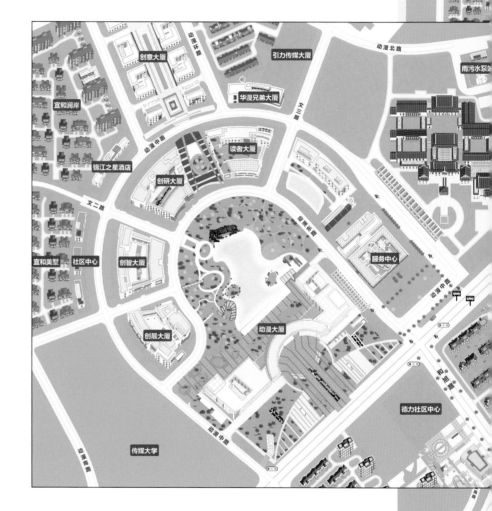

147

Prague Institute of Planning and Development Maps

Institut plánování a rozvoje hl. m. Prahy (Prague Institute of Planning and Development)
Prague, Czech Republic
By Jana Irová and Kateřina Hynková

Planning analytical materials are fundamental background information for development planning and decision-makers in Prague. It is a system of continuously updated spatial data describing all major aspects of the city, including natural conditions, built-up environment, land use, transportation, utilities, public services, demography, economy, and culture. Every two years the summary evaluation of the state of the city and its sustainable development is updated, giving important feedback and recommendations for further development policies.

Built-up structure is a key map for understanding spatial and morphological characteristics of the city form. The map describes typology of built up spaces (from low-density family houses to high-rise building areas), height levels, public spaces definition, and other important features. The built-up structure map is used as the background for zoning (development) plan updates as well as for decision-making on the spatial context and spatial impact of the new development proposals.

Property ownership conditions as essential development factors are visualized through the 3D city model. These 3D representations and visualization tools provide better orientation in the area, enabling easier reading of the map and faster understanding of the issue. Visualization shows the major ownership classes including state, municipality, universities, physical persons, and churches.

Contact

Jiří Čtyroký
ctyroky@ipr.praha.eu

Software

ArcGIS for Desktop 10.3.1, CityEngine 2016.1

Data Sources

Prague Institute of Planning and Development

Courtesy of Prague Institute of Planning and Development.

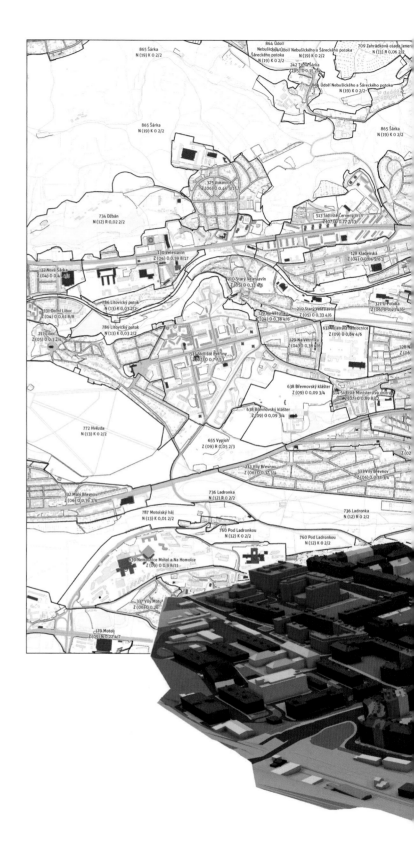

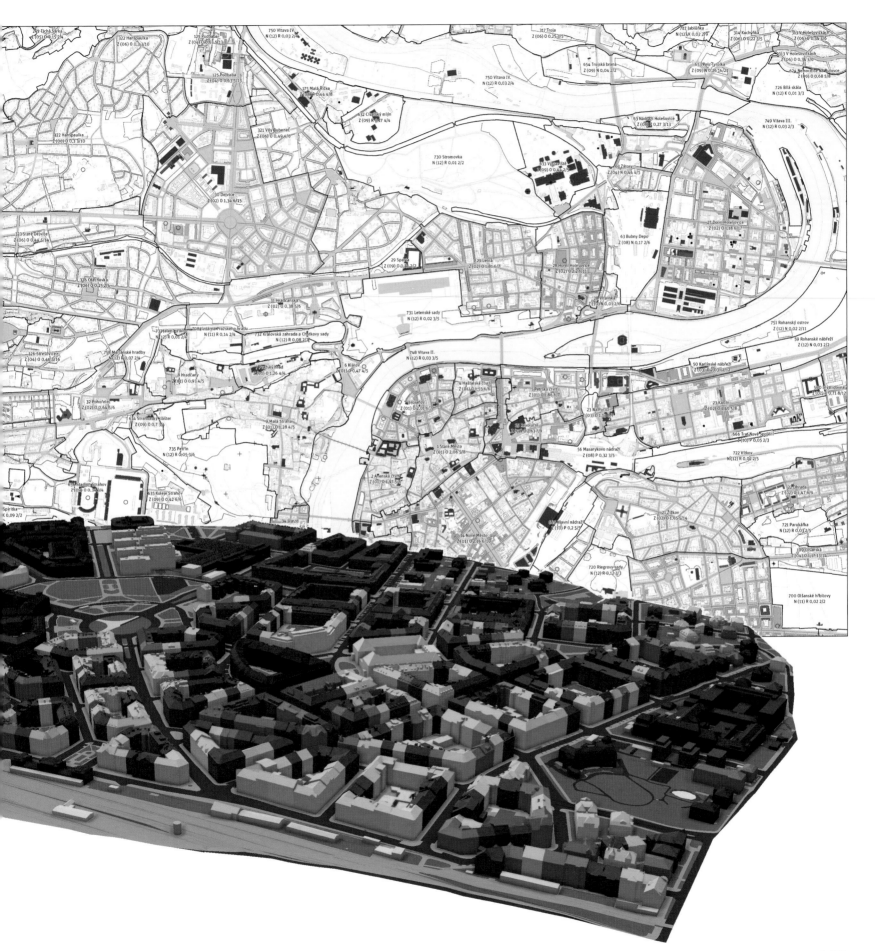

149

COVAGE Networks Maps

Les réseaux COVAGE (COVAGE Networks
Rueil-Malmaison, France
By Jean-Philippe Morisseau and Anne-Laure Fernet

COVAGE is a French telecommunications
company that operates fiber-optic networks
accessible to a variety of retail service providers.
More than two hundred operators use COVAGE
networks to serve their customers locally and
nationally. GIS plays an essential role at each
step of a network's life, from designing to
marketing. The main goals of the COVAGE GIS
team are to guarantee integrity and quality of the
cartographic repository, develop or maintain GIS
tools, and design cartographic products. These
maps show some of the products designed by
the GIS team.

Contact

Jean-Philippe Morisseau
be-sig.carto@covage.com

Software

ArcGIS for Desktop 10.3

Data Source

COVAGE Networks

Courtesy of COVAGE Networks.

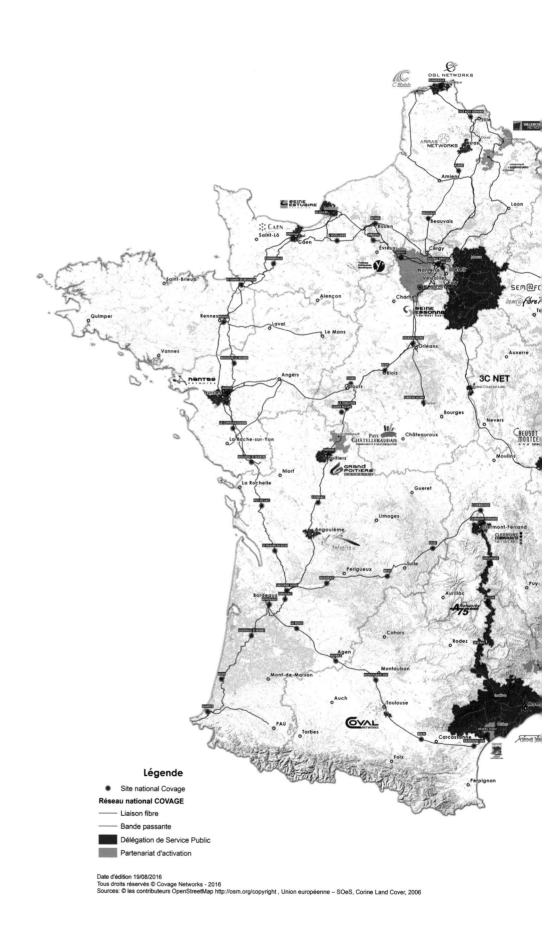

Légende

● Site national Covage

Réseau national COVAGE

——— Liaison fibre

——— Bande passante

■ Délégation de Service Public

■ Partenariat d'activation

Date d'édition 19/08/2016
Tous droits réservés © Covage Networks - 2016
Sources: © les contributeurs OpenStreetMap http://osm.org/copyright , Union européenne – SOeS, Corine Land Cover, 2006

septembre 5, 2016

Points Techniques

● Chambre + BPE

● Chambre

— Partenariat d'Activation

— Cables

— Infrastructures RTN

▬ Infrastructures

▬ Emprise chantier en cours

▬ Emprise chantier achevé

1:18 056

0   0,15   0,3   0,6 mi

0   0,25   0,5   1 km

Sources: Esri, HERE, DeLorme, Intermap, increment P Corp, GEBCO, USGS,
FAO, NPS, NRCAN, GeoBase, IGN, Kadaster NL, Ordnance Survey, Esri
Japan, METI, Esri China (Hong Kong), swisstopo, Mapmyindia, ©
OpenStreetMap contributors, and the GIS User Community

Covage
Copyright 2015

Légende

⊡ Chambre avec boîte de raccordement

— Réseau desserte ZA

······ Raccordement infrastructure existante

0   25 50   100   150   200
                                    Mètres

Oregon and Washington Coast Large Print Map

GM Johnson & Associates, Ltd.
Vancouver, British Columbia, Canada
By GM Johnson & Associates, Ltd.

This map is composed of three major segments. The main map comes from state maps of Washington and Oregon. The second component consists of a series of street map enlargements of cities along the coast from the GM Johnson City Map Series. The third component features write-ups on cities and spots all down the coast. The descriptive text of different areas turns the Washington and Oregon Coast Large Print Map into a guide of the area.

Contact

Guy Johnson
gjohnson@gmjohnsonmaps.com

Software

ArcGIS for Desktop 10.1, Adobe Illustrator, Dbase, FME, Label-ez, Microstation

Data Sources

Washington Department of Transportation, Oregon Department of Transportation, US Geological Survey, US Census Bureau, Skagit County, Jefferson County, Callam County, Grays Harbor County, Clatsop County, Lincoln County, and John Philip King.

2 WARRENTON (pop. 4,650, alt. 5 ft.) fronts the south shore of Youngs Bay. Clatsop Spit, the finger of land extending off to the northwest, includes Fort Stevens State Park, one of a trio of former military installations guarding the entrance to the Columbia. The park has historical military fortifications, beaches and miles of trails. Its Battery Russell was the only mainland fort bombed by the Japanese during World War II. Out on the beach you can still see the rusting, barnacle-encrusted remains of the four-masted British vessel Peter Iredale, foundered in a 1906 storm. South Jetty extends west from the tip of the spit. Together with its counterpart on the Washington bank, the jetties channel the flow of the Columbia, scouring its mouth of treacherous sand buildup.

LEWIS AND CLARK NATIONAL HISTORICAL PARK contains a full-scale replica of Fort Clatsop, the 1805-06 wintering site of the Lewis & Clark expedition. Their exploration helped solidify America's claim to the vast Oregon Country. The site includes a visitor center and interpretive trails, including the 6.5-mile Fort to Sea Trail leading west to Sunset Beach.

4 CANNON BEACH (pop. 1,600, alt. 100 ft.) is a picturesque resort community fronting a spectacular 3½-mile long white-sand beach. Steep, forested hills back the townsite and form bold headlands to the north and south. Photogenic rocks pierce the sea just offshore, including Haystack Rock, a 235-foot monolith, one of the coast's most photographed features. Wooden structures ranging in style from Cape Cod to Craftsman line the town's narrow, shady side streets. Flowers abound. Cannon Beach sports a variety of interesting shops and two-dozen art galleries. The active artist community has earned Cannon Beach the nickname "Oregon's Carmel." Ecola State Park tucks into the southern flanks of 1,136-foot Tillamook Head just north of Cannon Beach. The road ends at scenic Indian Beach - look for see sea lions on the offshore rocks. The ruins of a lighthouse, known as "Terrible Tilly," occupy the inhospitable redoubt of Tillamook Rock, two miles off its namesake headland.

5 MANZANITA (pop. 725, alt. 111 ft.) is a pleasant resort town on a 7-mile long beach near the base of 1,800-foot Neahkahnie Mountain. Local legend relates that survivors of the 1705 wreck of Spanish galleon buried their cargo of bullion somewhere on the slopes of Neahkahnie Mountain. Decades of treasure seekers have only unearthed chunks of beeswax bearing Latin religious markings. Just north of Manzanita, US-101 swings around the precipitous face of Neahkahnie Mountain, several hundred feet above the sea. In places the roadway has been carved into the mountainside. Viewpoints offer a sweeping panorama south along the coast, across Nehalem Bay to Cape Meares and distant Cape Lookout on the far horizon - one of the classic images of the Oregon Coast.

6 NEHALEM (pop. 240, alt. 28 ft.) lines the bank of its namesake river, just above the point where it empties into Nehalem Bay. Main Street shops are gaily painted and bedecked with flowerpots. The Nehalem River Valley is a major dairying district.

7 WHEELER (pop. 455, alt. 18 ft.) was once a fishing port and shingle milling center. Today Wheeler has a small resident artist colony and is sprucing up its weathered visage.

8 ROCKAWAY BEACH (pop. 1,375, alt. 16 ft.) has blocks of cottages, shops and eateries catering to tourists and summer residents. Look for the landmark Twin Rocks, two pinnacles in the sea just beyond the surf line.

9 GARIBALDI (pop. 895, alt. 10 ft.) is a fishing port built on the hilly north shore of Tillamook Bay. The ruins of a large lumber mill dominate the waterfront. Captain Gray spent two days in this area in 1788, cited by some historians as the first American landing on what is today Oregon. Lumberman's Park features an old Southern Pacific steam locomotive and is the terminus of the Oregon Coast Scenic, Railway, offering summer weekend excursion train trips between Garibaldi and Rockaway Beach.

15 DEPOE BAY (pop. 1,405, alt. 58 ft.) is a compact fishing and resort town perched on hillsides overlooking the Pacific. The seven-acre bay is billed as the world's smallest navigable saltwater harbor. The Highway 101 bridge over the bay and is a great spot to watch commercial and sportfishing boats navigate the narrow channel entrance. The rocky shoreline here makes for outstanding wave watching, especially during winter storms.

16 Between Depoe Bay and Newport US-101 climbs the shoulder of CAPE FOULWEATHER in long, well-engineered grades. The parallel old highway (signed "Scenic Loop") twists through thick rain forest. Both roads top out at Otter Crest Viewpoint, 500 feet above the ocean. In clear weather a grand panorama stretches

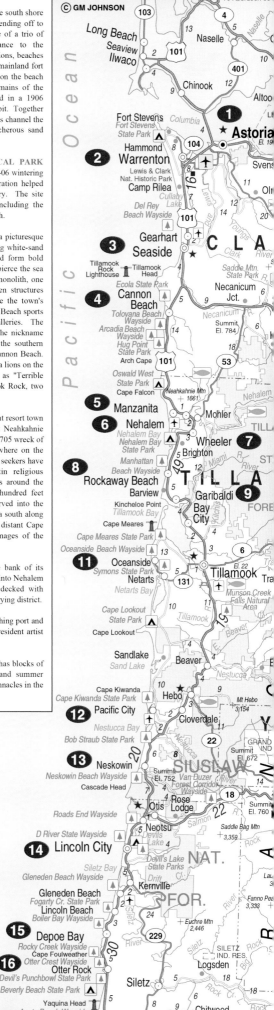

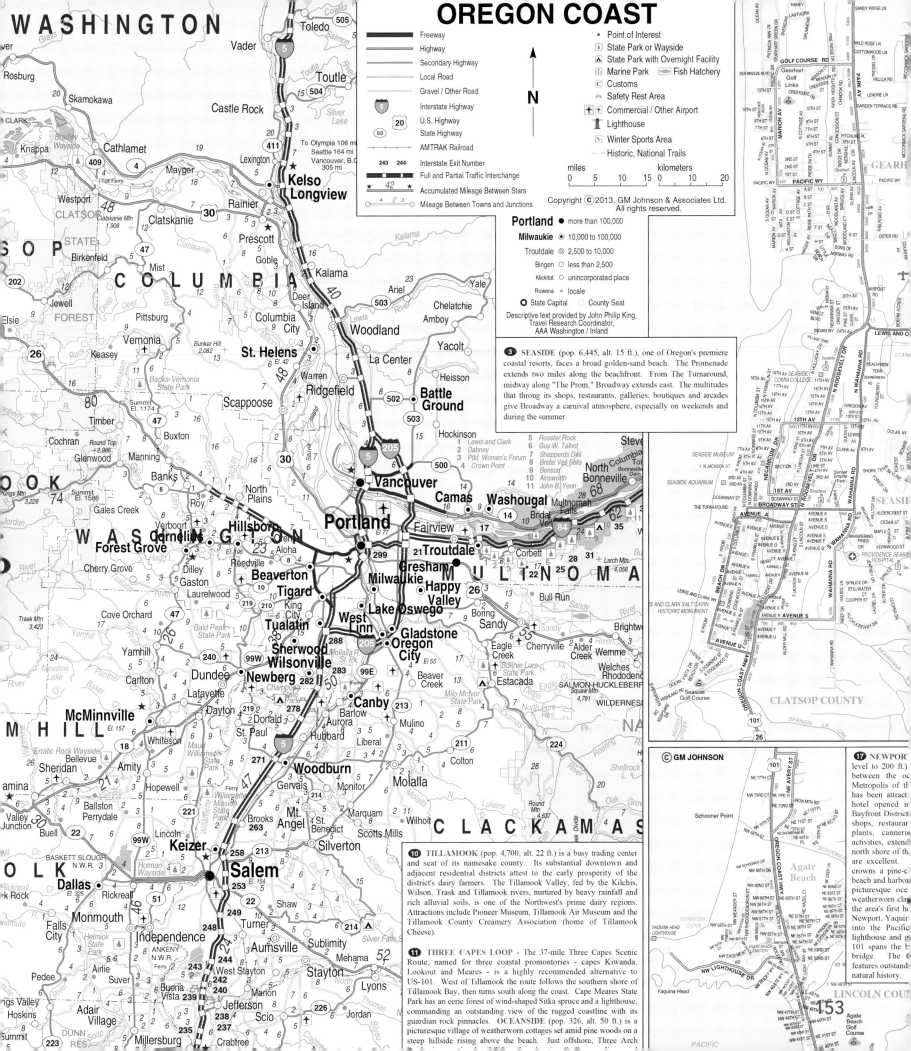

Columbus Metro Bike Map

Mid-Ohio Regional Planning Commission
Columbus, Ohio, USA
By Cheri Mansperger

This map was created as a reference tool for bicyclists in the greater Columbus, Ohio, area. Along with existing bike facilities, roadways were color-coded to help cyclists determine which routes may be best suited for their level of riding experience. This "level of comfort" coding, for non-rush-hour traffic, uses green as "easy," yellow as "moderate," and red as "difficult." Colors were assigned on the basis of roadway attributes (speed, traffic volume, width, shoulder, existing bike facility, etc.) and local bicyclist community input.

Central Ohio Greenway trails are highlighted as they are off-road, nonmotorized multiuse trails that are heavily traveled and provide excellent access to downtown and other destinations in Columbus. Fifty thousand maps were printed to coordinate with National Bike to Work Week. They were distributed to local bike shops, libraries, and city offices to encourage people to get on their bikes to exercise and discover how easy it is to get out of their cars and ride bikes for commuting or making short trips.

Contact

Cheri Mansperger
cmansperger@morpc.org

Software

ArcGIS for Desktop 10.3.1

Data Sources

Mid-Ohio Regional Planning Commission,
Local Government Agencies

Courtesy of Mid-Ohio Regional Planning Commission.

LEVEL OF COMFORT

GOOD
Road suitable for bicyclists with basic skills.

MODERATE
Road suitable for bicyclists with intermediate skills.

POOR
Road suitable for bicyclists with advanced skills. Extreme caution should be used.

RESIDENTIAL
Low speed residential road suitable for bicyclists with basic skills.

MULTI-USE PATH
Path separate from roadway, on which bicyclists and other non-motorized users are permitted.

BIKE LANE OR BIKE BOULEVARD
Section of roadway designated for bicyclists by paint markings.

CENTRAL OHIO GREENWAY TRAIL

Trailhead
Park and Pedal at Trailhead
COTA Park & Ride
Library
Middle/High School
Park
River
Stream
Railroad
County Boundary

Desolation Wilderness Trip Planning

US Department of Agriculture (USDA) Forest Service, Eldorado National Forest
Placerville, California, USA
By Debra Tatman, Melanie Rossi, Diana Erickson, Mario Chocooj, and Jon Erickson

Desolation Wilderness Area (Eldorado National Forest and Lake Tahoe Basin Management Unit) is one of the most heavily visited wilderness areas for its size (63,960 acres) in the United States. To protect its unique beauty and wilderness character, visitor use is actively managed. The Eldorado National Forest designed a series of signs for seven Desolation Wilderness trailheads, as well as Forest Service offices to assist visitors with trip planning.

Each sign includes information about the specific location, what visitors need to know before embarking on their adventure, the wilderness permit system in place for using the trails, where a visitor is allowed to stay overnight, and particulars about individual trails including distance, difficulty, and which wilderness management zone the trail is contained in. These zones designate a maximum number of dispersed campsites each night to minimize recreation impacts. Understanding where these zones are in relation to the trail system is critical to visitor safety and resource protection.

Contact
Debra Tatman
dtatman@fs.fed.us

Software
ArcGIS for Desktop 10.2, Adobe Illustrator

Data Source
USDA Forest Service

Courtesy of USDA Forest Service.

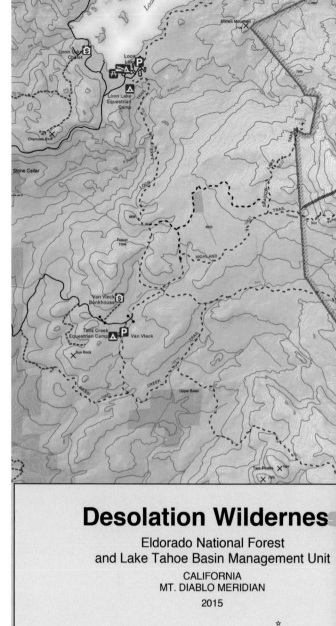

Desolation Wildernes

Eldorado National Forest
and Lake Tahoe Basin Management Unit
CALIFORNIA
MT. DIABLO MERIDIAN
2015

Scale 1:45,292

0.5   0   0.5   1
Miles

14.11 DEGREES
252 MILS

2010 Magnetic North
Declination at Center of Sheet

Contour Interval 40'

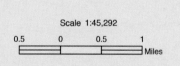

——— Primary Highway	🅰 Campground
——— Secondary and Tertiary Roads	🅿 Picnic Area, Da
▪▪▪▪▪▪ Unimproved Road	🆂 Boat Ramp
- - - - Maintained Trail	🅿 Pack Station
- - - - Primitive Trail	❓ Visitor Informa
17E01 Forest Trail	🅿 Interpretive or
//// Wilderness Boundary	🆂 Forest Service
Private Land	🅿 Trailhead Park
State Park	🅿 Parking
Camping Restricted 500 Feet from Lake	🅰 Lookout
//// Wilderness Management Zones	↦ Locked Gate
	⊂ Boat Dock

Map created by Eldorado National Forest Geospatial Services Group

Wrangell Forest Visitor Map

US Department of Agriculture (USDA) Forest Service
Juneau, Alaska, USA
By Robert Francis, Dustin Wittwer, Andrew Keske, and
Carol Teitzel

This map highlights the recreational opportunities
of the Wrangell Ranger District that encompasses
1.5 million acres in the temperate rain forest-covered
islands of the Alexander Archipelago and the
glaciated Coastal Mountains of southeast Alaska.
The heart of the area is the Stikine River, the fastest
flowing navigable river in North America and home
of the Wrangell Tlingit people, the Shtax'héen Kwáan
(named for the Stikine River). Their origin, stories,
and archaeological manifestations predate European
arrival by thousands of years.

The map used a hybrid hillshade that balances the
macro features with micro details. The Forest Service
used the traditional, coarse 30-meter hillshade derived
from the National Elevation Dataset to illustrate the
macro landscape, but blended a 5-meter hillshade
derived from an InSAR digital surface model, to
highlight the surface details. Contour lines are also
derived from 5-meter interferometric synthetic
aperture radar, but are from the digital terrain model
representing the ground.

Contact

Robert Francis
rlfrancis@fs.fed.us

Software

ArcGIS for Desktop 10.2.2, Adobe InDesign

Data Source

USDA Forest Service

Courtesy of USDA Forest Service.

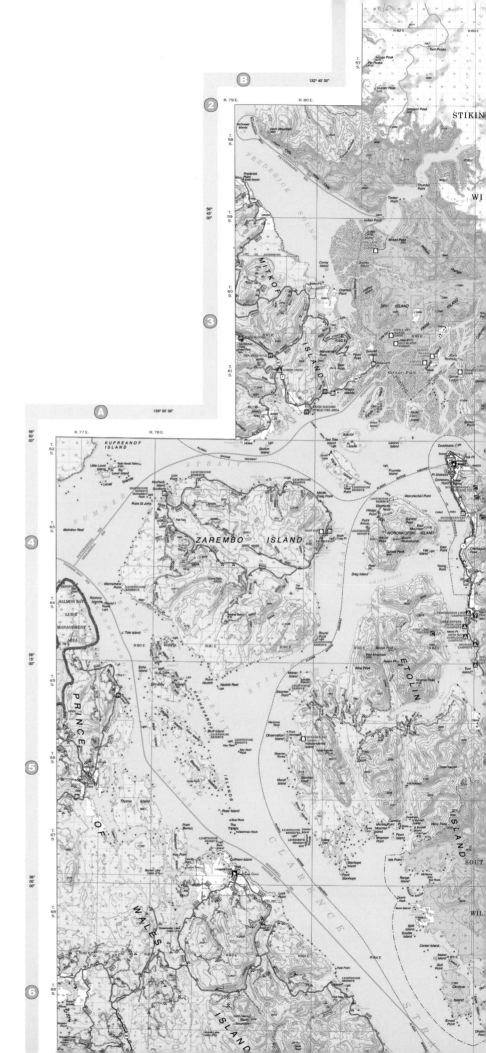

159

City of Bellingham Bike Map

City of Bellingham
Bellingham, Washington, USA
By Chris Behee

This bike map was developed after the City of Bellingham adopted its Bicycle Master Plan in 2014. The tabs of the story map highlight the existing bicycle network, recently completed projects, areas where green paint bike markings are used, Interstate 5 crossings, and the complete network recommended in the master plan. Additional graphics and videos on each tab provide educational information explaining what specific markings mean and how to navigate the various types of routes. Links to images provide on-the-ground views of specific locations such as the Interstate 5 crossings.

Contact

Chris Behee
cbehee@cob.org

Software

ArcGIS Online

Data Sources

City of Bellingham GIS, Esri

Courtesy of City of Bellingham.

Palestine Tourist City Maps

Good Shepherd Engineering (GSE), Palestine Mapping Center (PalMap)
Beit Jala, West Bank, Palestine
By Michael and Hanna Younan

These detailed maps of Palestinian cities allow tourists and locals to mobilize. They were created to help direct users to tourist sites and assist them with on-site maneuvering. Map data was gathered from the field and entered into the ArcGIS for Desktop geodatabase with cartographic production created for public distribution.

Contact

Michael Younan
gse@gsecc.com

Software

ArcGIS for Desktop 10.4

Data Sources

GSE/PalMap, Ministry of Tourism Palestine

Courtesy of GSE/PalMap and Ministry of Tourism Palestine

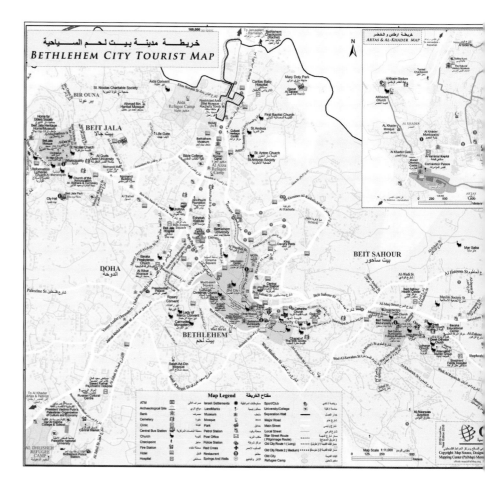

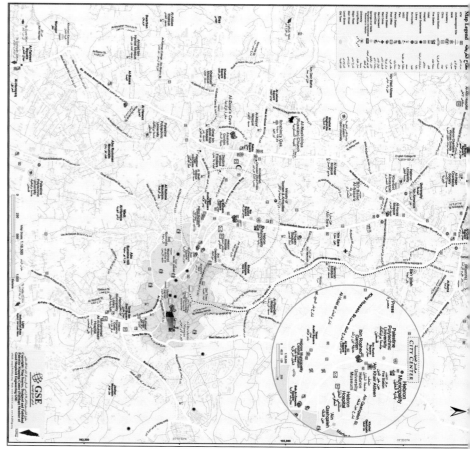

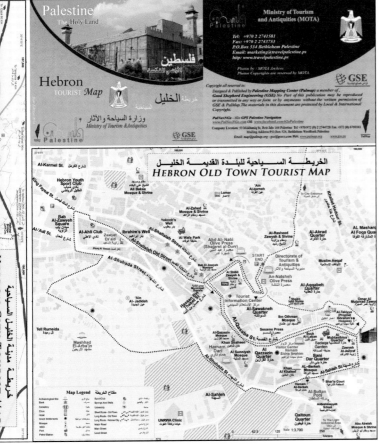

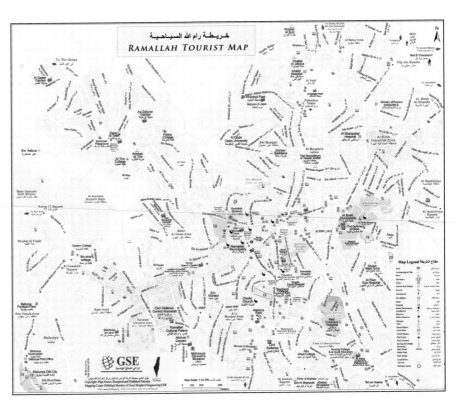

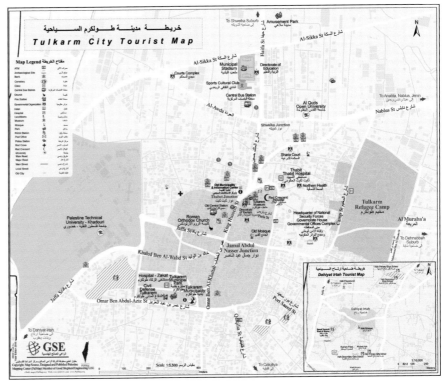

Visualization of Origin-Destination Flow

Southern California Association of Governments (SCAG)
Los Angeles,California, USA
By Paige Montojo, Tyler J. Lindberg, Tom Vo, and Jung Seo

Analyzing the origin-destination (OD) commuter flow is important for understanding workers' commuting patterns, particularly from regional planning perspectives. SCAG, the nation's largest Metropolitan Planning Organization (MPO) representing six counties and 191 cities, has conducted an OD flow analysis and visualization for all jurisdictions in the region.

To analyze and visualize the OD flows, SCAG staff has developed the automated workflow using ArcGIS, Python scripting, statistical analysis software (SAS), and LEHD (Longitudinal Employment and Household Dynamics) Origin-Destination Employment Statistics (LODES) data. The maps depict the commuter flows between home and workplace throughout the region and help jurisdictions, business communities, and residents visually understand where workers are employed and where workers live.

Contact

Jung Seo
seo@scag.ca.gov

Software

ArcGIS for Desktop 10.3

Data Sources

US Census, Longitudinal Employer-Household Dynamics Program

Courtesy of SCAG.

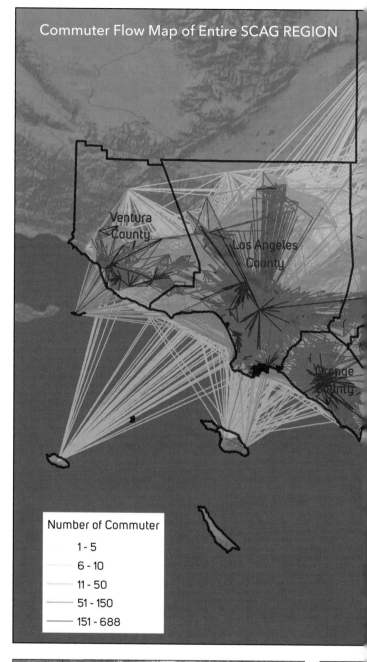

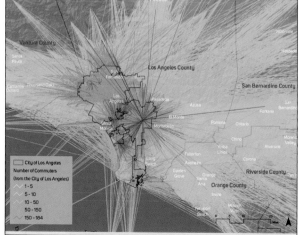

The City of Los Angeles

City Commuter Flow Maps

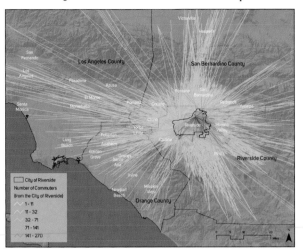

The City of Riverside

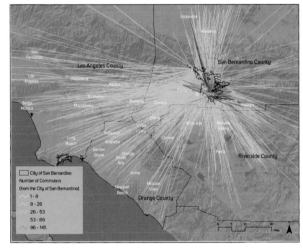

The City of San Bernardino

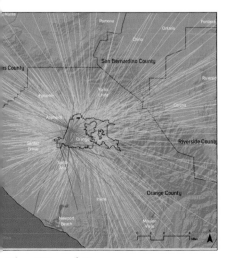

The City of Orange

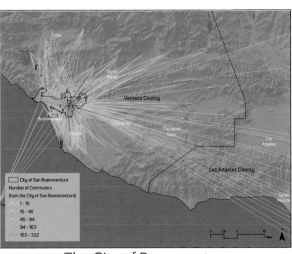

The City of Buenaventura

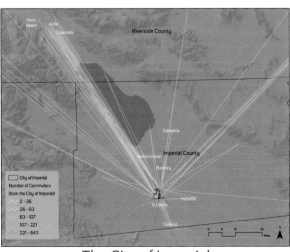

The City of Imperial

Roads of Texas Basemap

81 West Cartography LLC
Oviedo, Florida, USA
By Shawn M. Baldwin

This comprehensive basemap of the roads of Texas is the foundation for a variety of map and atlas applications, both digital and paper-based. Using a common-core geodatabase, this basemap can be applied to "on-demand" thematic maps at different scales as well as stock maps for a wide variety of users, purposes, and themes.

One such user of this map is a billboard company in Texas. With their proprietary data added to the map, executives can make decisions about resources, operations, and sales strategies by enabling them to understand spatial relationships between locations of their billboards and the field service staff and sales force. This, in turn, allows the leadership to focus on more efficient billboard servicing and more effective market research activities.

In addition to the road and street network, this map features hydrography, populated areas, and selected points and areas of interest for reference. Insets of major population centers provide greater detail. Further, the cartographic styling presented here has been replicated across other state maps, resulting in a uniform nationwide product.

Contact

Shawn M. Baldwin
81westcarto@gmail.com

Software

ArcGIS for Desktop 10.4

Data Sources

US Census Bureau TIGER/Line, US Department of Transportation Bureau of Transportation Statistics, US Geological Survey National Hydrography Dataset

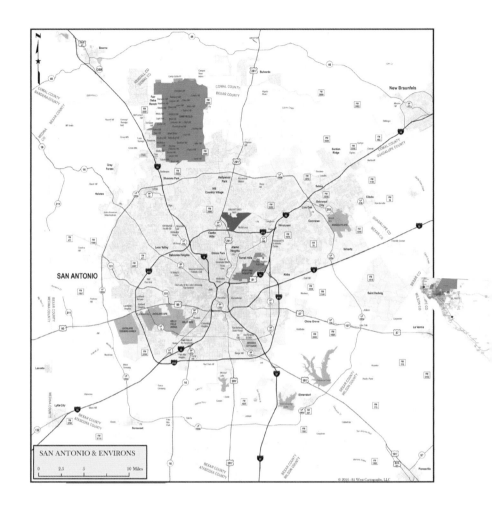

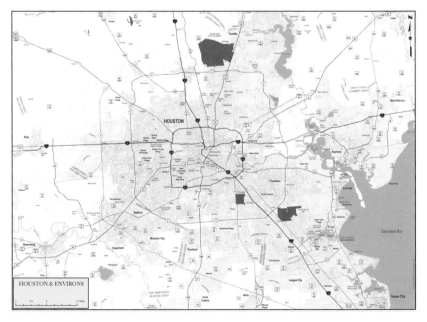

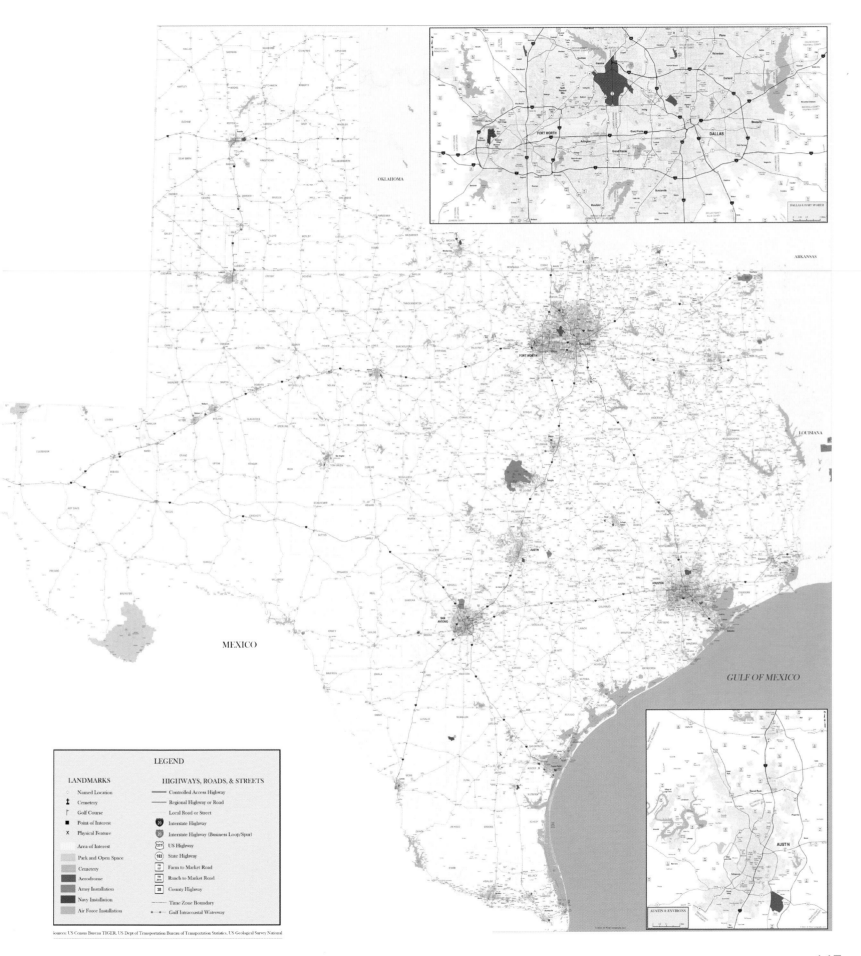

LANDMARKS

- ○ Named Location
- ✝ Cemetery
- ⚑ Golf Course
- ■ Point of Interest
- X Physical Feature

Area of Interest
Park and Open Space
Cemetery
Aerodrome
Army Installation
Navy Installation
Air Force Installation

LEGEND

HIGHWAYS, ROADS, & STREETS

- ━━━ Controlled Access Highway
- ──── Regional Highway or Road
- ──── Local Road or Street
- Interstate Highway
- Interstate Highway (Business Loop/Spur)
- US Highway
- State Highway
- Farm to Market Road
- Ranch to Market Road
- County Highway
- ┄┄┄ Time Zone Boundary
- •─•─ Gulf Intracoastal Waterway

OKLAHOMA

ARKANSAS

MEXICO

LOUISIANA

GULF OF MEXICO

DALLAS

FORT WORTH

AUSTIN

HOUSTON

SAN ANTONIO

DALLAS & FORT WORTH

AUSTIN & ENVIRONS

Sources: US Census Bureau TIGER, US Dept of Transportation Bureau of Transportation Statistics, US Geological Survey National

Aviation in the United States

Kansas Department of Transportation (KDOT)
Topeka, Kansas, USA
By Kyle Gonterwitz

This map started with some analysis for the Kansas Secretary of Transportation about aviation in Kansas, looking at the location relationships of registered aircraft, active pilots, flight operations, and public airports in the state. The analysis included a map showing the percentage of pilots representing the adult population compared with aviation across the country. As the author, a private pilot and aviation enthusiast, became more familiar with data sources available from the FAA, the analysis expanded into an overview of air transportation in the United States depicted in this map.

Contact

Kyle Gonterwitz
kyleg@ksdot.org

Software

ArcGIS Pro, Adobe InDeisgn, ArcGIS Desktop, Microsoft Excel, IBM Watson

Data Source

Federal Aviation Administration

Courtesy of KDOT.

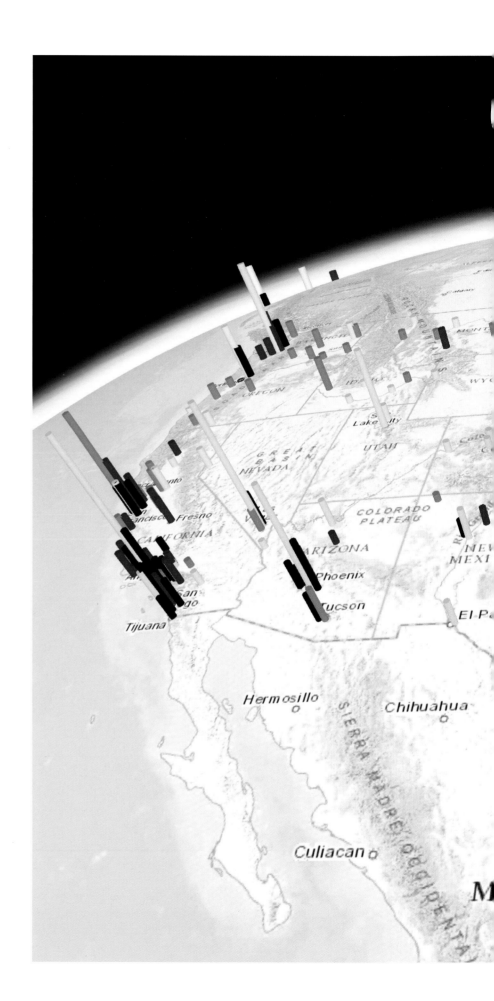

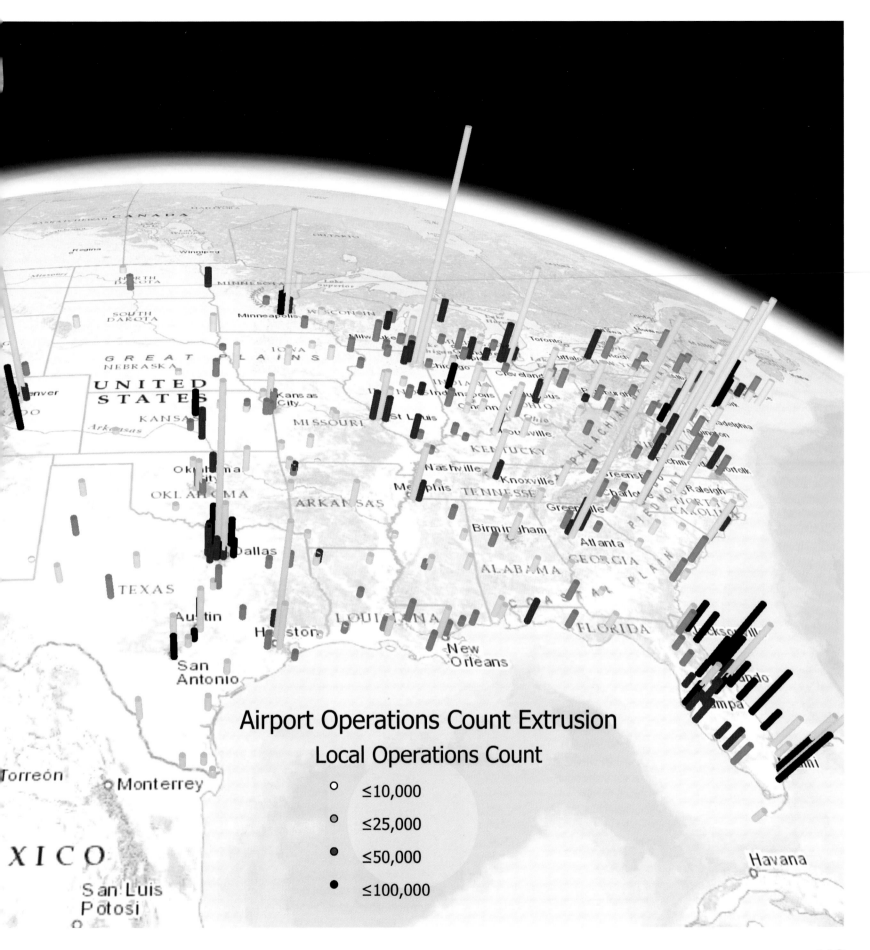

Airport Operations Count Extrusion
Local Operations Count

○ ≤10,000
○ ≤25,000
● ≤50,000
● ≤100,000

GIS-Based Investment Management Systems

General Directorate of Highways
Ankara, Cankaya, Turkey
By General Directorate of Highways

The General Directorate of Highways is a state agency in charge of the construction and maintenance of all public roadways outside of cities and towns in Turkey. A web- and mobile-based GIS application for the General Directorate of Highways integrates existing GIS datasets with bidding data and project information that includes engineering structures such as bridges, viaducts, tunnels, and roads, and surveying information derived from highway management sources.

Contact

Özgenç Uslu
ouslu@kgm.gov.tr

Software

ArcGIS for Desktop 10.3

Data Source

General Directorate of Highways

Courtesy of General Directorate of Highways.

Web Map Services

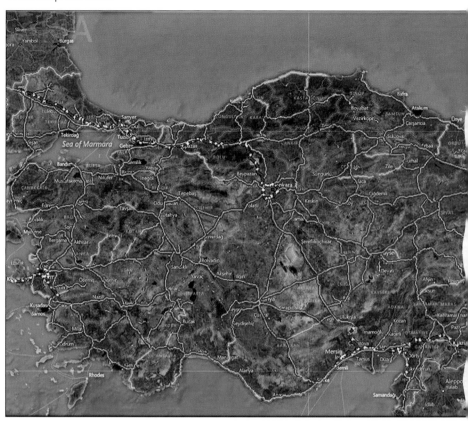

Results

While the visual tracking of the projects, which are under the investment program, is being carried out with classical procedures, online presentation of these projects via support of the visual map is realized by developed web and mobile based solutions.

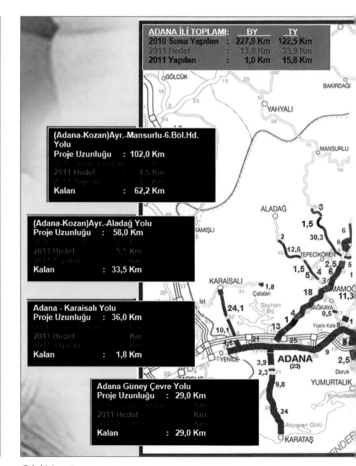

Old Version

Web Application

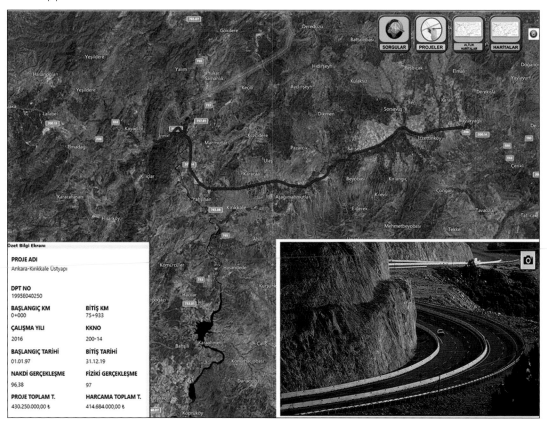

Özet Bilgi Ekranı

PROJE ADI
Ankara-Kırıkkale Üstyapı

DPT NO
1995E040250

BAŞLANGIÇ KM	**BİTİŞ KM**
0+000	75+933
ÇALIŞMA YILI	**KKNO**
2016	200-14
BAŞLANGIÇ TARİHİ	**BİTİŞ TARİHİ**
01.01.97	31.12.19
NAKDİ GERÇEKLEŞME	**FİZİKİ GERÇEKLEŞME**
96,38	97
PROJE TOPLAM T.	**HARCAMA TOPLAM T.**
430.250.000,00 ₺	414.684.000,00 ₺

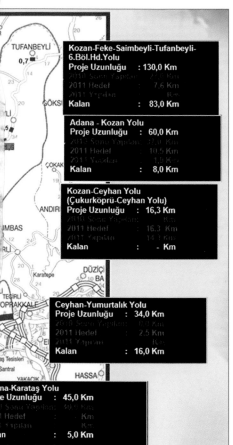

Kozan-Feke-Saimbeyli-Tufanbeyli-6.Böl.Hd.Yolu
Proje Uzunluğu : 130,0 Km
2011 Hedef : 7,6 Km
Kalan : 83,0 Km

Adana - Kozan Yolu
Proje Uzunluğu : 60,0 Km
2011 Hedef : 10,5 Km
Kalan : 8,0 Km

Kozan-Ceyhan Yolu
(Çukurköprü-Ceyhan Yolu)
Proje Uzunluğu : 16,3 Km
2011 Hedef : 16,3 Km
Kalan : - Km

Ceyhan-Yumurtalık Yolu
Proje Uzunluğu : 34,0 Km
2011 Hedef : 2,5 Km
Kalan : 16,0 Km

...na-Karataş Yolu
...e Uzunluğu : 45,0 Km
...Hedef : Km
: 5,0 Km

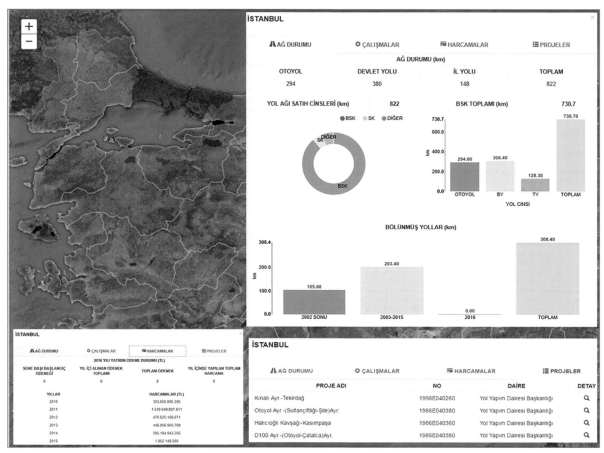

İSTANBUL

🏛 AĞ DURUMU   ⚙ ÇALIŞMALAR   🖩 HARCAMALAR   ☰ PROJELER

AĞ DURUMU (km)

OTOYOL	DEVLET YOLU	İL YOLU	TOPLAM
294	380	148	822

YOL AĞI SATIH CİNSLERİ (km)   822   BSK TOPLAMI (km)   730.7

BÖLÜNMÜŞ YOLLAR (km)

İSTANBUL

🏛 AĞ DURUMU   ⚙ ÇALIŞMALAR   🖩 HARCAMALAR   ☰ PROJELER

2016 YILI YATIRIM ÖDEME DURUMU (TL)

SENE BAŞI BAŞLANGIÇ ÖDENEĞİ	YIL İÇİ ALINAN ÖDENEK TOPLAMI	TOPLAM ÖDENEK	YIL İÇİNDE YAPILAN TOPLAM HARCAMA
0	0	0	0

YILLAR	HARCAMALAR (TL)
2010	303.650.895.206
2011	1.519.649.837.611
2012	470.025.168.071
2013	446.056.900.769
2014	585.184.943.266
2015	1.052.148.500

İSTANBUL

🏛 AĞ DURUMU   ⚙ ÇALIŞMALAR   🖩 HARCAMALAR   ☰ PROJELER

PROJE ADI	NO	DAİRE	DETAY
Kınalı Ayr.-Tekirdağ	1998E040260	Yol Yapım Dairesi Başkanlığı	🔍
Otoyol Ayr.-(Sultançiftliği-Şile)Ayr.	1986E040380	Yol Yapım Dairesi Başkanlığı	🔍
Halıcıoğlu Kavşağı-Kasımpaşa	1986E040360	Yol Yapım Dairesi Başkanlığı	🔍
D100 Ayr.-(Otoyol-Çatalca)Ayr.	1986E040380	Yol Yapım Dairesi Başkanlığı	🔍

New Version

VTrans Bicycle Corridor Priority

Vermont Agency of Transportation (VTrans)
Montpelier, Vermont, USA
By Johnathan Croft

This map was developed in phase I of the Vermont State Highway On-Road Bicycle Plan. The plan will help VTrans incorporate improvements into highway projects in a strategic, cost- effective manner where there is the most demand for on-road bicycle use. The map represents current and potential bicycle use on the state highway system. Use is based on proximity to certain types of land use, comments from over 2,000 members of the public gathered through a crowd-sourced Wikimap and using bicycle trip data from over 10,000 users, of Strava in Vermont, a smartphone application used by bicyclists to track their rides. The culmination of this analysis is the Bicycle Corridor Priorities data layer, which provides direct input to the decision-making process for highway improvements, maintenance activities, and other projects.

Contact

Johnathan Croft
johnathan.croft@vermont.gov

Software

ArcGIS for Desktop 10.3.1

Data Sources

VTrans, Vermont Center for Geographic Information, VTrans Contractors

Courtesy of VTrans.

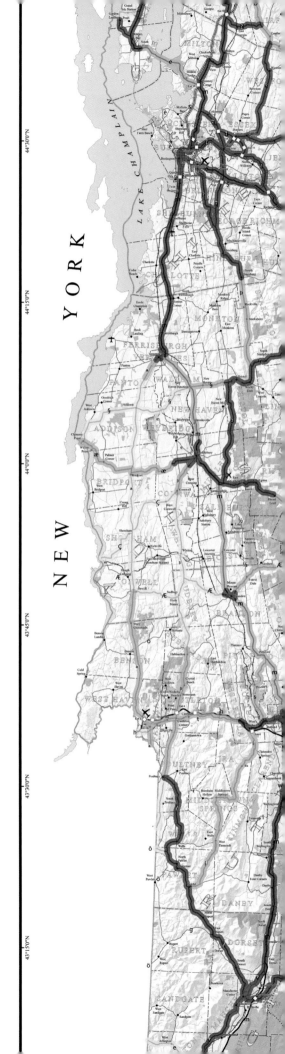

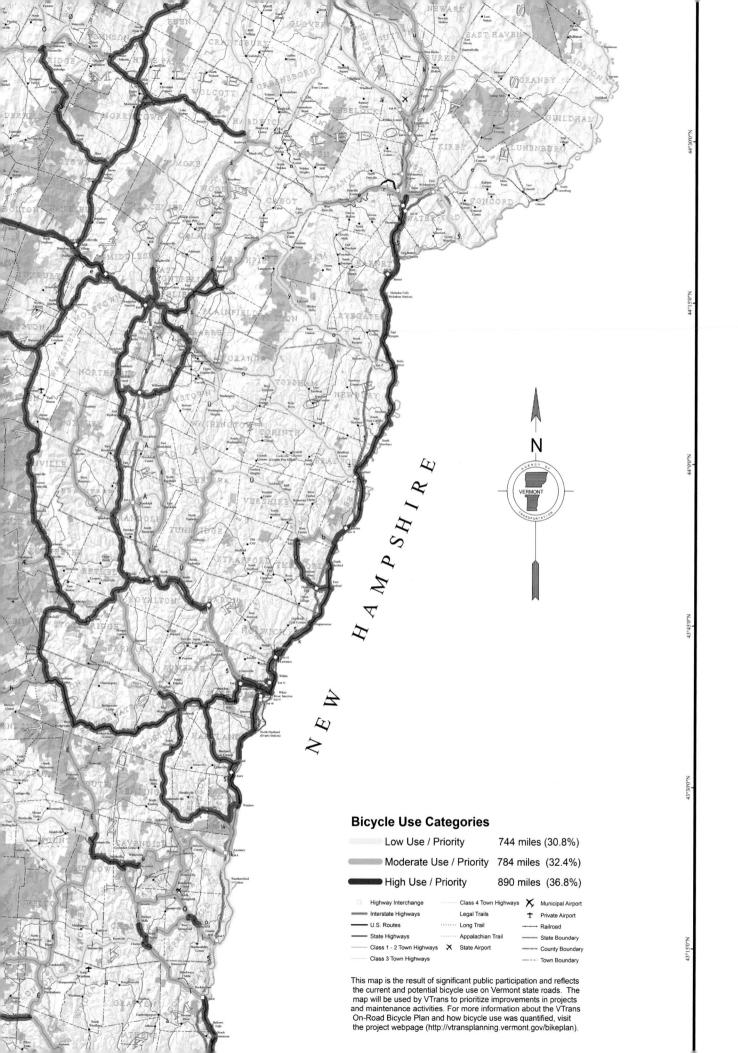

Bicycle Use Categories

Low Use / Priority	744 miles	(30.8%)
Moderate Use / Priority	784 miles	(32.4%)
High Use / Priority	890 miles	(36.8%)

☐ Highway Interchange	Class 4 Town Highways	✗ Municipal Airport
Interstate Highways	Legal Trails	✝ Private Airport
U.S. Routes	Long Trail	Railroad
State Highways	Appalachian Trail	State Boundary
Class 1 - 2 Town Highways	✗ State Airport	County Boundary
Class 3 Town Highways		Town Boundary

This map is the result of significant public participation and reflects the current and potential bicycle use on Vermont state roads. The map will be used by VTrans to prioritize improvements in projects and maintenance activities. For more information about the VTrans On-Road Bicycle Plan and how bicycle use was quantified, visit the project webpage (http://vtransplanning.vermont.gov/bikeplan).

San Francisco International Airport Basemap

San Francisco International Airport (SFO) GIS
San Franscisco, California, USA
By Jason Hill, Guy Michael, Agie Gilmore, and James Kong

This basemap consists of the core airport infrastructure including all major roadways, runways, taxiways, pavement markings, fences, gates, boundaries, buildings, structures, and terminals. Created and maintained by the SFO GIS team, the basemap has more than twenty feature classes housed within the GIS enterprise database and is used for planning purposes, referencing locations, design preparation, and cartographic aesthetics within the different airport departments.

The basemap is one of the most commonly requested GIS maps and services from the airport departments and personnel internally as well as airlines, tenants, and consultants. It is constantly being disseminated electronically, contained as a background for online and mobile web mapping apps, displayed within the terminals and offices throughout the entire airport.

Contact

Jason Hill
jason.hill@flysfo.com

Software

ArcGIS for Desktop 10.4

Data Source

SFO

Courtesy of Jason Hill and Guy Michael, SFO GIS.

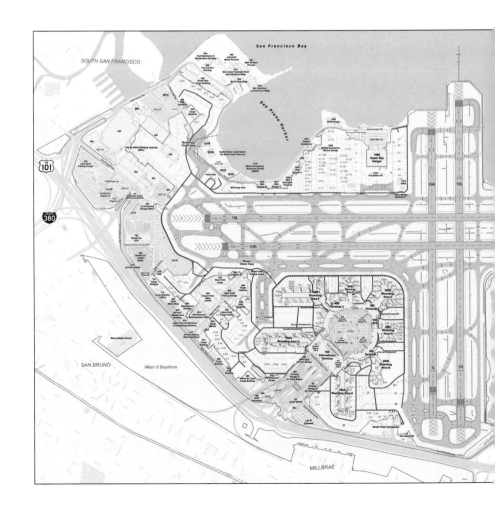

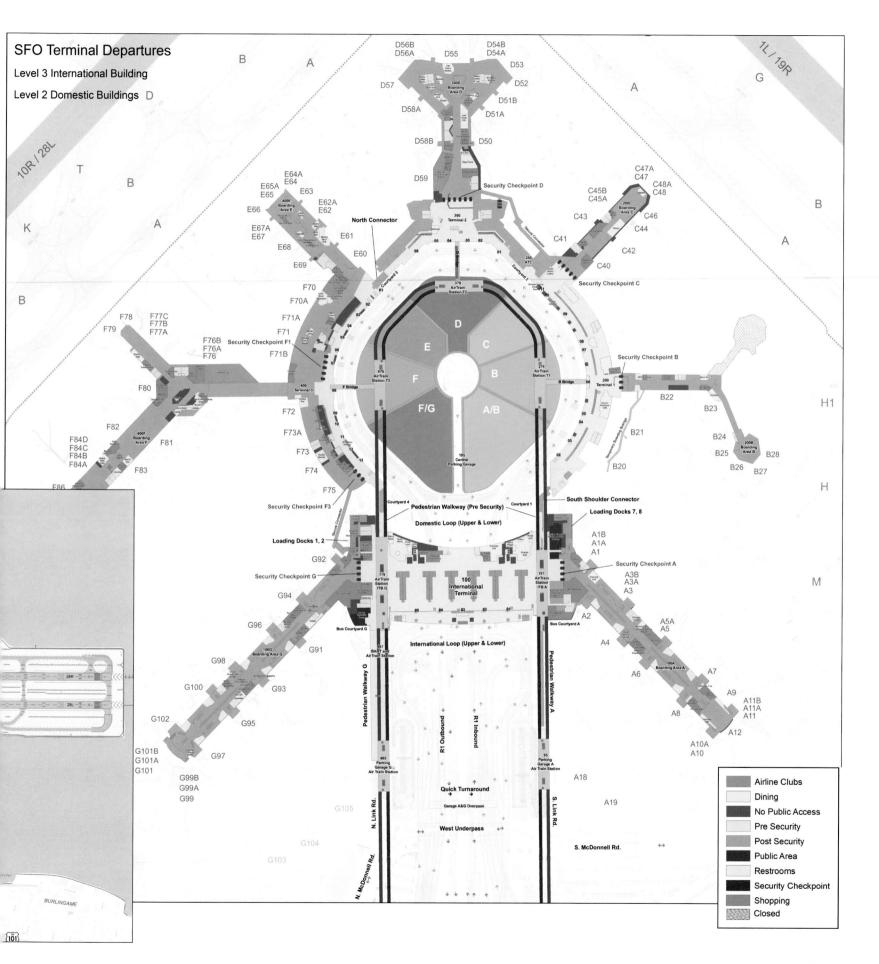

SFO Terminal Departures

Level 3 International Building

Level 2 Domestic Buildings D

Digitized Power Networks and the Road Ahead

Electricity Authority of Cyprus
Lefkosia, Cyprus
By Electricity Authority of Cyprus

These maps emphasize the increasing role of GIS in preparing the infrastructure to cope with the challenges of evolving electric distribution systems. The incorporation of network data and connections into the GIS, building of the network topology, matching location with network connectivity, and building enhanced algorithms provide the necessary prerequisites for network analysis and operation.

GIS serves as a platform on which the evolution of the networks of the future, as envisioned by power systems researchers, becomes feasible. Many network management solutions will rely on the power of GIS to attain the necessary information intelligence to complete tasks.

Contact

Yiannakis Ioannou
yioannou@eac.com.cy

Software

ArcGIS Desktop, ArcFM, DIgSILENT PowerFactory

Data Sources

Electricity Authority of Cyprus

Courtesy of Electricity Authority of Cyprus.

Transmission System of Cyprus

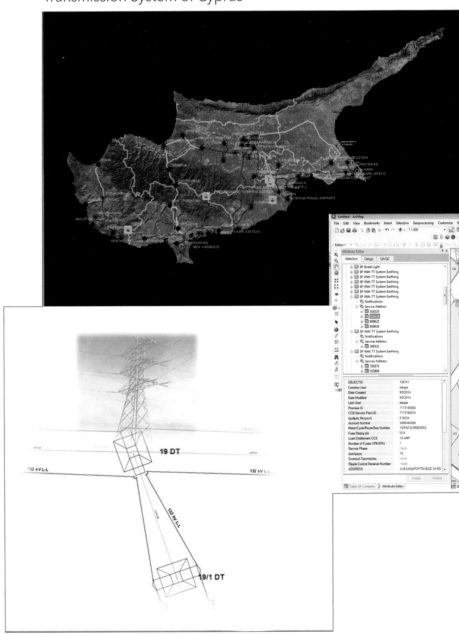

Transmission Tower

Distribution of Photovoltaic Systems

MV Distribution Network Urban/Rural Region

Spatially Enable Enchanced
Network Topology

Accumulation of Network Connections in an LV Feeder

Project NOKOGI: A New Conception of GIS

Pražská plynárenská distribuce (Prague Gas Distribution)
Prague, Czech Republic
By Daniel Souček and Jana Součková

The Pražská Plynárenská Distribuce (PPD) is the big natural gas provider in the Czech Republic and has used the ArcGIS platform since 2006. In 2015, PPD started an upgrade of GIS technology to improve its workflows through a project called NOKOGI.

The concept of NOKOGI (a Czech acronym for new GIS concept) was to employ standard ArcGIS technology to open up the system and bring the majority of users to the web. Developers weren't bound by the former technology, and they focused on replacing overcomplicated functions with much simpler ones. Using Web AppBuilder for ArcGIS, they created one app that contained various web maps of the utility network, and with AppStudio for ArcGIS, they built a corresponding mobile app.

PPD determined that, from there, the company's GIS administrators could use these app builders to customize and adjust the tools—as well as build new apps and update old ones—since neither requires any coding. With its underlying HTML5 technology, the app can be used in web browsers on various devices. This cultivates a unified user experience among office employees and field workers.

Contact

Daniel Souček
daniel.soucek@ppdistribuce.cz

Software

ArcGIS Desktop 10.2.1, ArcGIS for Server 10.3.1, Portal for ArcGIS® 10.3.1

Data Sources

Pražská plynárenská distribuce (Prague Gas Distribution), Ceský úrad zememerický a katastrální (Consultation of the Cadastre); Institut plánování a rozvoje hl. m. Prahy (Institute of Planning and Development, Prague); ARCDATA Prague.

Courtesy of Pražská Plynárenská Distribuce.

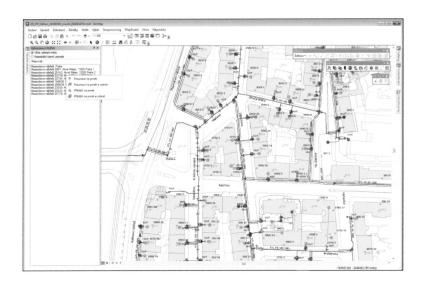

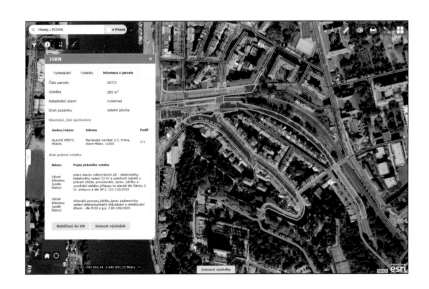

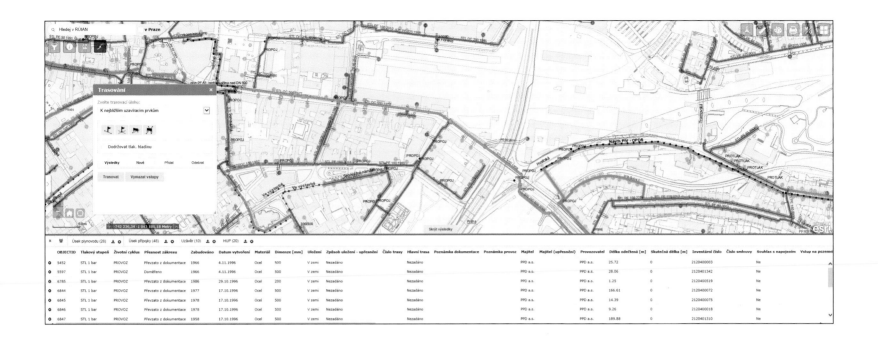

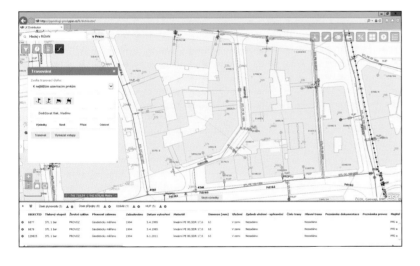

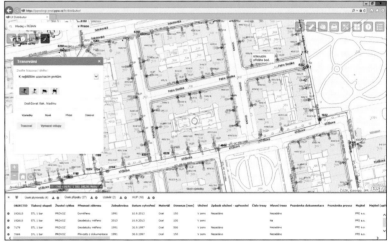

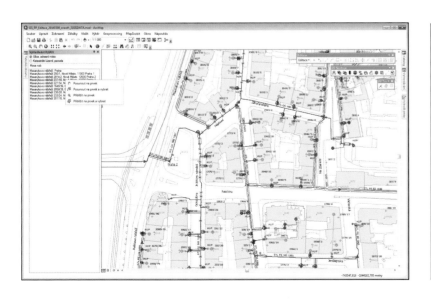

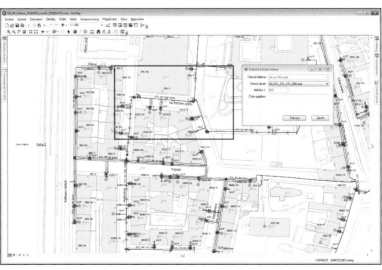

Modeling Overland Flow in a Landscape with Forest Roads

City of Seattle
North Bend, Washington, USA
By Mark Joselyn

Cedar River Municipal Watershed covers 96,000 acres, and the City of Seattle must meet regulatory requirements in managing its land, forests, and infrastructure to minimize threats to public resources. Lidar data provides a detailed representation of the ground surface. This ground model accurately captures depressions and subtle landforms, such as catch basins and ditches along roads, but does not detect such underground drainage structures as culverts and cross drains.

The approach described on these maps relies on the location of these drainage structures to modify the ground model using a moving window to derive a local minimum and create "sinks" to capture the effect drainage structures have in influencing actual drainage patterns. When combined with annual precipitation estimates, this data supports modeling culvert locations to determine the appropriate size of drainage structures on the basis of modeled flow accumulation and estimated precipitation. This information is important to road engineers, hydrologists, and others tasked with proper design and maintenance of the city's forested road network and related infrastructure.

Contact

Mark Joselyn
mark.joselyn@seattle.gov

Software

ArcGIS for Desktop 10.3

Data Source

City of Seattle

Courtesy of Mark Joselyn, Watershed Management Division, Seattle Public Utilities.

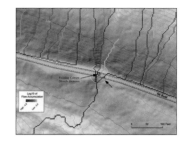

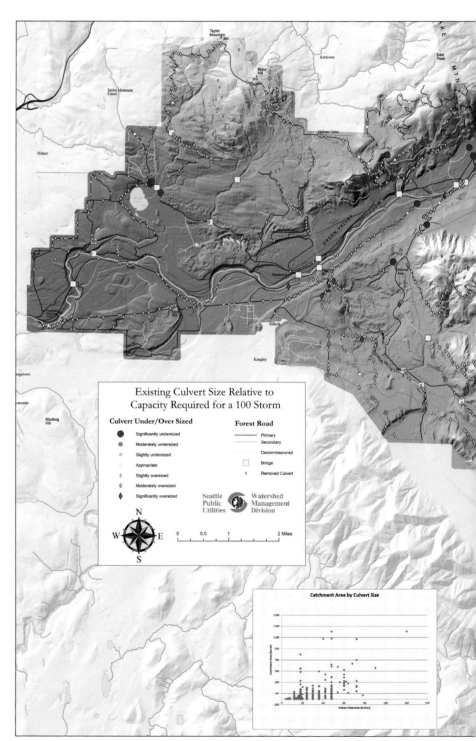

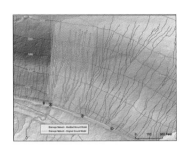

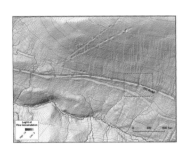

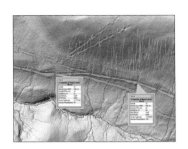

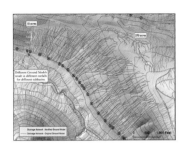

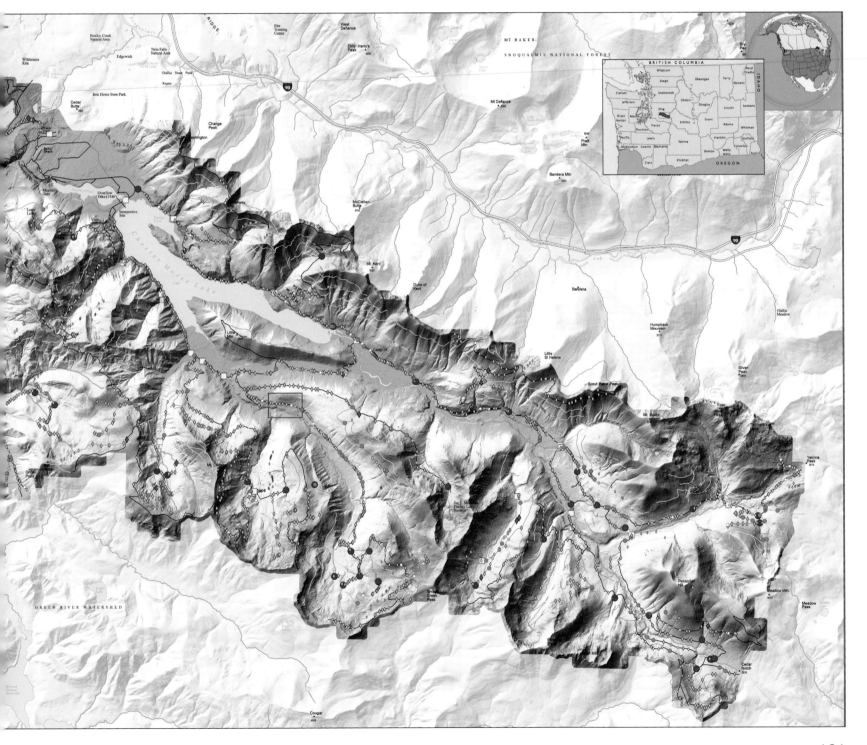

181

El Segundo Scalable Water Atlas Project

City of El Segundo
El Segundo, California, USA
By Michael McDaniel and Sumaiyah Umarji

The City of El Segundo's Water Division is responsible for designing, building, and maintaining the distribution system that includes pipes, valves, pumps, meters, and fire hydrants. This scalable water atlas project is designed to be used by all water division staff responsible for proper operation of the system. The project consists of the atlas, wall map, and ArcReader map file.

The atlas displays the various components of the city's water system, annotated with unique valve identifications on the basis of atlas page numbers, and other information relating to active pipes. The ninety-seven-page book is used by technicians in the field.

The wall map displays information relating to the active mains throughout the city. Designed to help engineers and supervisors locate plans for pipes by their location, the map is annotated with information relating to the pipes such as the plan number, year built, and pipe size.

The ArcReader map file has been set at nine scales, allowing users to drill down on an area of interest to inspect the water system at whatever scale is required. Each scale contains corresponding annotation files, and as the user zooms in, the water system is displayed in more detail while maintaining context like street names.

Contact

Michael McDaniel
mmcdaniel@elsegundo.org

Software

ArcGIS for Desktop 10.3.1

Data Source

City of El Segundo GIS

Courtesy of City of El Segundo.

Scale: 2,000

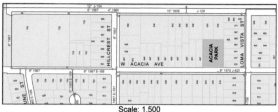

Scale: 1,500

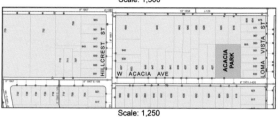

Scale: 1,250

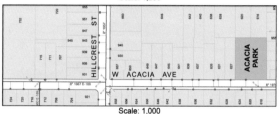

Scale: 1,000

Scale: 800

Scale: 500

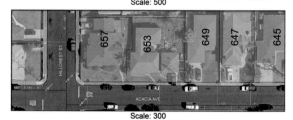

Scale: 300

Scale: 200

City of El Segundo Water Distribution System

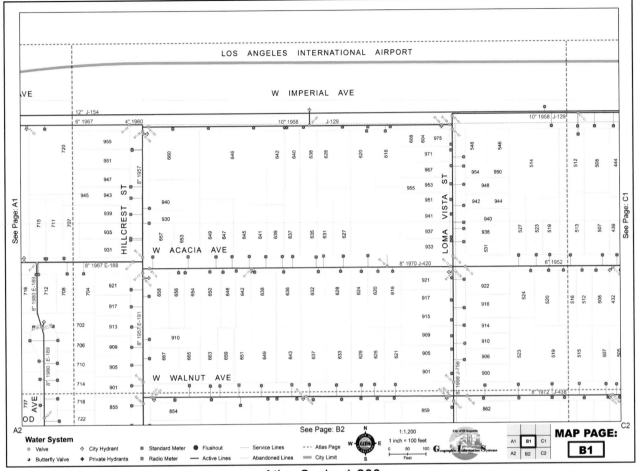

Atlas Scale: 1,200

City of El Segundo Water Distribution System Wall Map

Wall Map Scale: 4,800

Using GIS to Assist Sewer Authority Infrastructure Management

Greater New Haven Water Pollution Control Authority
(GNHWPCA)
New Haven, Connecticut, USA
By Ricardo Ceballos

Sewer infrastructure mapping plays a key role at the
GNHWPCA. The authority uses the ArcGIS suite to
create many different types of maps and analysis on
its sewer networks such as maps to identify and track
"hotspots" where sewer backups and bypasses had
occurred. GNHWPCA also uses GIS to maintain and
make adjustments to the existing sewer network as well
as update and maintain a database of all construction
projects in GNHWPCA's service area that require a
connection to the sewer system.

GNHWPCA uses a GIS-based system to automate
the call-before-you-dig ticket screening process. The
system provides an assessment of the assets potentially
at risk with a detailed GIS-based map of the sewer
facilities in the area.

Contact

Ricardo Ceballos
rceballos@gnhwpca.com

Software

ArcGIS for Desktop 10.3

Data Source

GNHWPCA

Courtesy of GNHWPCA.

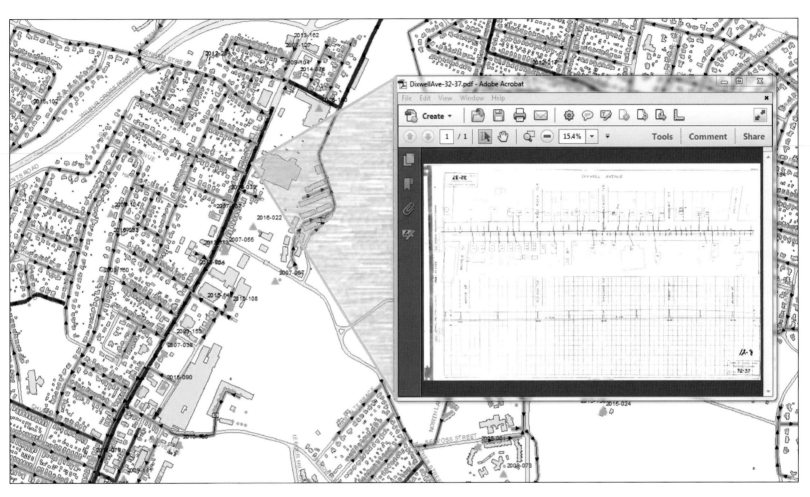

DixwellAve-32-37.pdf - Adobe Acrobat

File   Edit   View   Window   Help

Create ▾

1 / 1   15.4%

Tools | Comment | Share

DIXWELL AVENUE

32-37

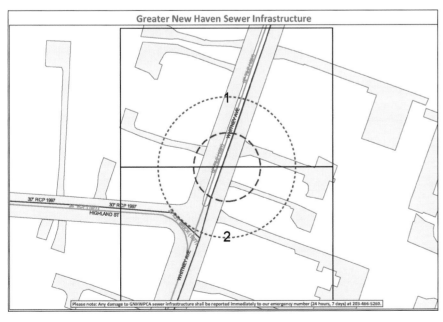

Greater New Haven Sewer Infrastructure

1

2

30" RCP 1997   30" RCP 1997

HIGHLAND ST

Please note: Any damage to GNHWPCA sewer infrastructure shall be reported immediately to our emergency number (24 hours, 7 days) at 203-466-5260.

UTILITIES—WATER AND WASTEWATER

Major Water, Sewer, and Reclaim Water Facilities for St. Johns County Utilities

St. Johns County Utilities
Saint Augustine, Florida, USA
By Erika Kinchen, Tom Tibbitts, and Karri Thomas

St. Johns County Utilities provides water, reuse, and sewer services through twenty treatment facilities, along with over 367 booster, master, and pump stations, and 1,248.9 miles of mains. Displaying the major facilities and infrastructure counts from GIS provides an operational awareness of the overall utility and the subsystems within it. Operational awareness is also served through GIS-centric tools including asset management, emergency response, hydraulic modeling, compliance, and mobile workflows.

Contact

Tom Tibbitts
ttibbitts@sjcfl.us

Software

ArcGIS for Desktop 10.3.1, Adobe Photoshop, Microsoft® Publisher

Data Source

St. Johns County Utilities

Courtesy of St. Johns County Utilities.

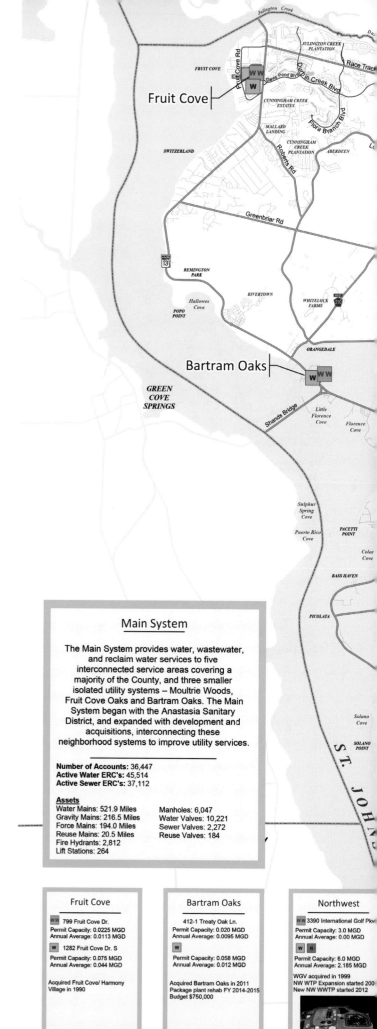

Main System

The Main System provides water, wastewater, and reclaim water services to five interconnected service areas covering a majority of the County, and three smaller isolated utility systems — Moultrie Woods, Fruit Cove Oaks and Bartram Oaks. The Main System began with the Anastasia Sanitary District, and expanded with development and acquisitions, interconnecting these neighborhood systems to improve utility services.

Number of Accounts: 36,447
Active Water ERC's: 45,514
Active Sewer ERC's: 37,112

Assets
Water Mains: 521.9 Miles
Gravity Mains: 216.5 Miles
Force Mains: 194.0 Miles
Reuse Mains: 20.5 Miles
Fire Hydrants: 2,812
Lift Stations: 264
Manholes: 6,047
Water Valves: 10,221
Sewer Valves: 2,272
Reuse Valves: 184

Fruit Cove

799 Fruit Cove Dr.
Permit Capacity: 0.0225 MGD
Annual Average: 0.0113 MGD

1282 Fruit Cove Dr. S
Permit Capacity: 0.075 MGD
Annual Average: 0.044 MGD

Acquired Fruit Cove/ Harmony Village in 1990

Bartram Oaks

412-1 Treaty Oak Ln.
Permit Capacity: 0.020 MGD
Annual Average: 0.0095 MGD

Permit Capacity: 0.058 MGD
Annual Average: 0.012 MGD

Acquired Bartram Oaks in 2011
Package plant rehab FY 2014-2015
Budget $750,000

Northwest

3390 International Golf Pkw
Permit Capacity: 3.0 MGD
Annual Average: 0.00 MGD

Permit Capacity: 6.0 MGD
Annual Average: 2.185 MGD

WGV acquired in 1999
NW WTP Expansion started 200
New NW WWTP started 2012

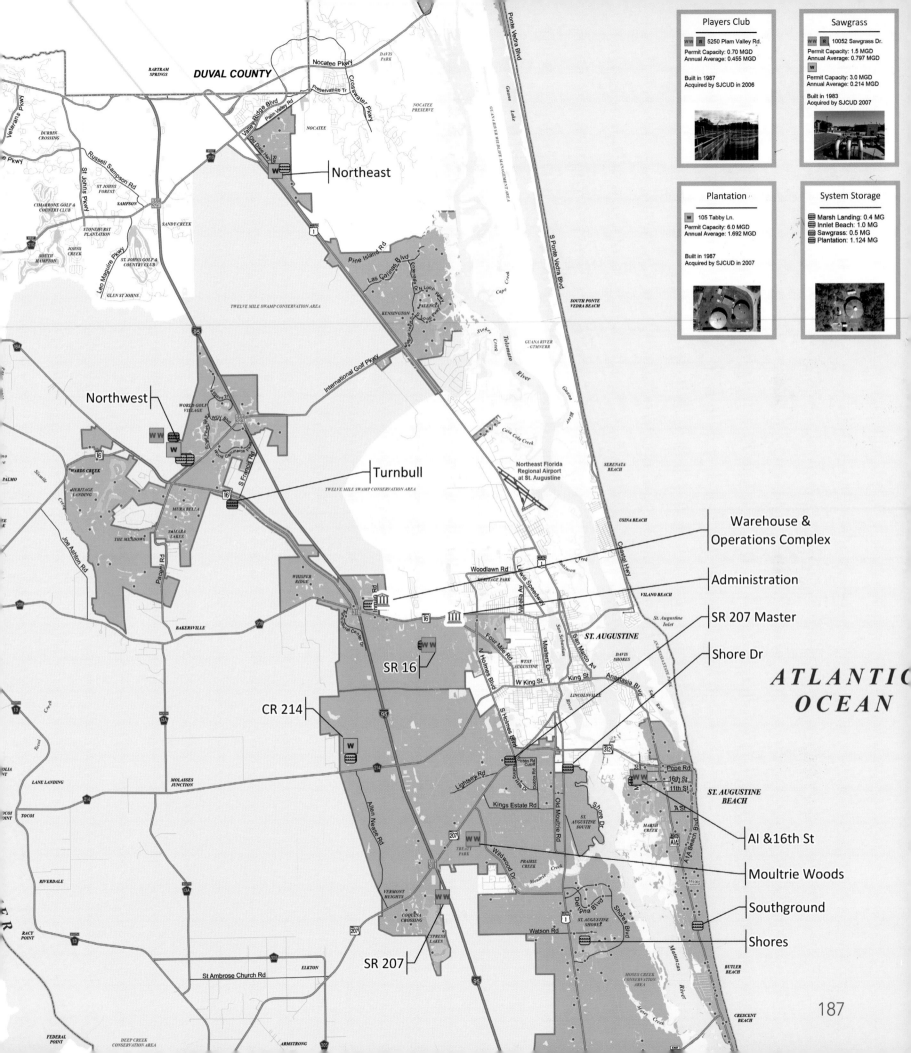

Players Club
WW R 5250 Plam Valley Rd.
Permit Capacity: 0.70 MGD
Annual Average: 0.455 MGD

Built in 1987
Acquired by SJCUD in 2006

Sawgrass
WW R 10052 Sawgrass Dr.
Permit Capacity: 1.5 MGD
Annual Average: 0.797 MGD

W
Permit Capacity: 3.0 MGD
Annual Average: 0.214 MGD

Built in 1983
Acquired by SJCUD 2007

Plantation
W 105 Tabby Ln.
Permit Capacity: 6.0 MGD
Annual Average: 1.692 MGD

Built in 1987
Acquired by SJCUD in 2007

System Storage
Marsh Landing: 0.4 MG
Inlet Beach: 1.0 MG
Sawgrass: 0.5 MG
Plantation: 1.124 MG

Northeast

Northwest

Turnbull

Warehouse &
Operations Complex

Administration

SR 207 Master

Shore Dr

SR 16

CR 214

A1 &16th St

Moultrie Woods

Southground

Shores

SR 207

ATLANTIC OCEAN

187

Wellhead Protection in Mesa

City of Mesa
Mesa, Arizona, USA
By Jarrod Celuch

This map shows Mesa's current city wells and 100-year capture zones. It also includes results of water sampling in current wells, old abandoned wells, and existing contaminated soils due to man-made pollution or subsidence. Besides groundwater from the thirty-eight city wells, the City of Mesa relies on other sources for its water supply: Salt River and Verde River water from Salt River Project, Colorado River water from the Central Arizona Project, and reclaimed water from city reclamation facilities.

Contact

Jarrod Celuch
jceluch@yahoo.com

Software

ArcGIS for Desktop 10.3

Data Sources

City of Mesa GIS, Arizona Department of Environmental Quality, Arizona Department of Water Resources

Courtesy of City of Mesa.

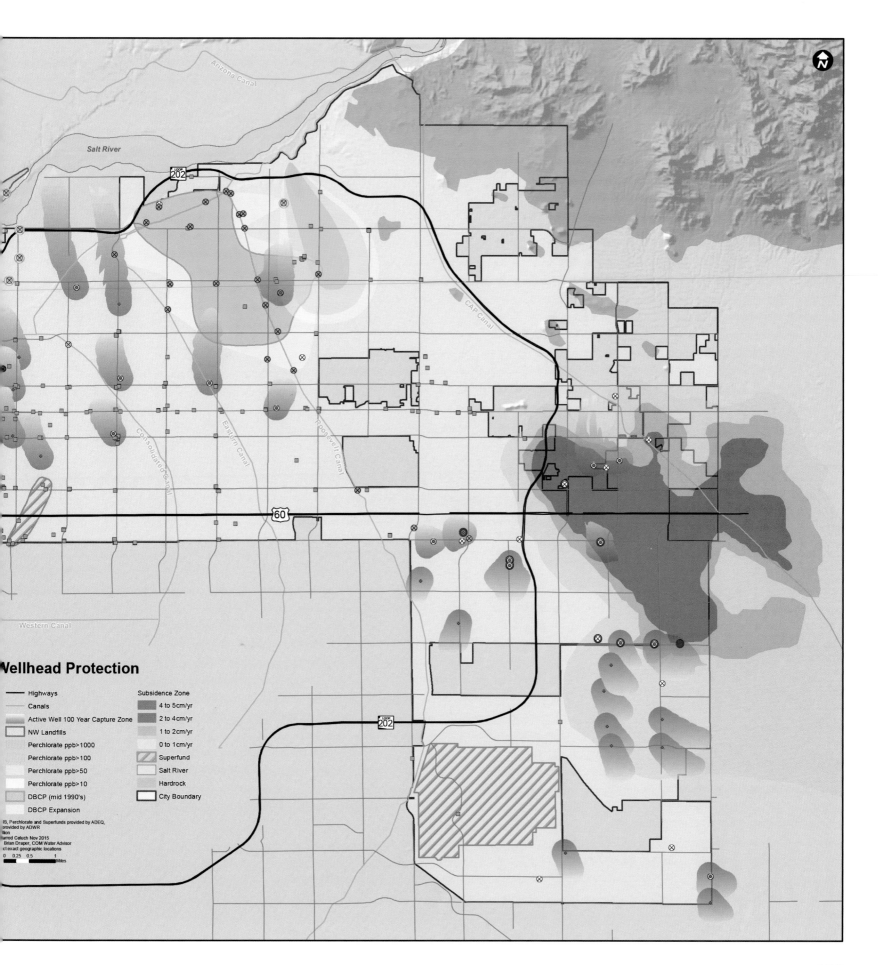

Wellhead Protection

— Highways	
— Canals	
▨ Active Well 100 Year Capture Zone	
☐ NW Landfills	
☐ Perchlorate ppb>1000	
☐ Perchlorate ppb>100	
☐ Perchlorate ppb>50	
☐ Perchlorate ppb>10	
☐ DBCP (mid 1990's)	
☐ DBCP Expansion	

Subsidence Zone
- ☐ 4 to 5cm/yr
- ☐ 2 to 4cm/yr
- ☐ 1 to 2cm/yr
- ☐ 0 to 1cm/yr
- ▨ Superfund
- ☐ Salt River
- ☐ Hardrock
- ☐ City Boundary

IS, Perchlorate and Superfunds provided by ADEQ,
provided by ADWR
llon
arrod Celuch Nov 2015
Brian Draper, COM Water Advisor
ct exact geographic locations

0   0.25 0.5   1
Miles

Salt River
LOOP 202
Arizona Canal
CAP Canal
Consolidated Canal
Eastern Canal
Roosevelt Canal
Western Canal
60
LOOP 202

Joint Outfall System Sewer Analysis

Sanitation Districts of Los Angeles County
Whittier, California, USA
By Peter W. Wilt

Formed in 1923, Sanitation Districts of Los Angeles County manages wastewater and solid waste on a regional scale and consists of twenty-four independent special districts serving about 5.6 million people. Seventeen sanitation districts signed an agreement that provides a regional, interconnected system of facilities known as the Joint Outfall System (JOS). The service area of JOS provides sewage treatment, reuse, and disposal for residential, commercial, and industrial users in seventy-three cities and unincorporated territory, including some areas within the city of Los Angeles.

Flow values for this map were compiled from the Sanitation Districts' flow monitoring program, which includes over 2,600 gauging locations throughout the sewer network. These locations are monitored for one to two weeks every three to four years, depending on the potential for growth within a tributary area of the sewer. Peak dry-weather flow is measured at representative manholes in each trunk and JOS Outfall sewer.

Contact

Peter W. Wilt
pwilt@lacsd.org

Software

ArcGIS for Desktop 10.1

Data Source

Sanitation Districts of Los Angeles County

Courtesy of Sanitation Districts of Los Angeles County.

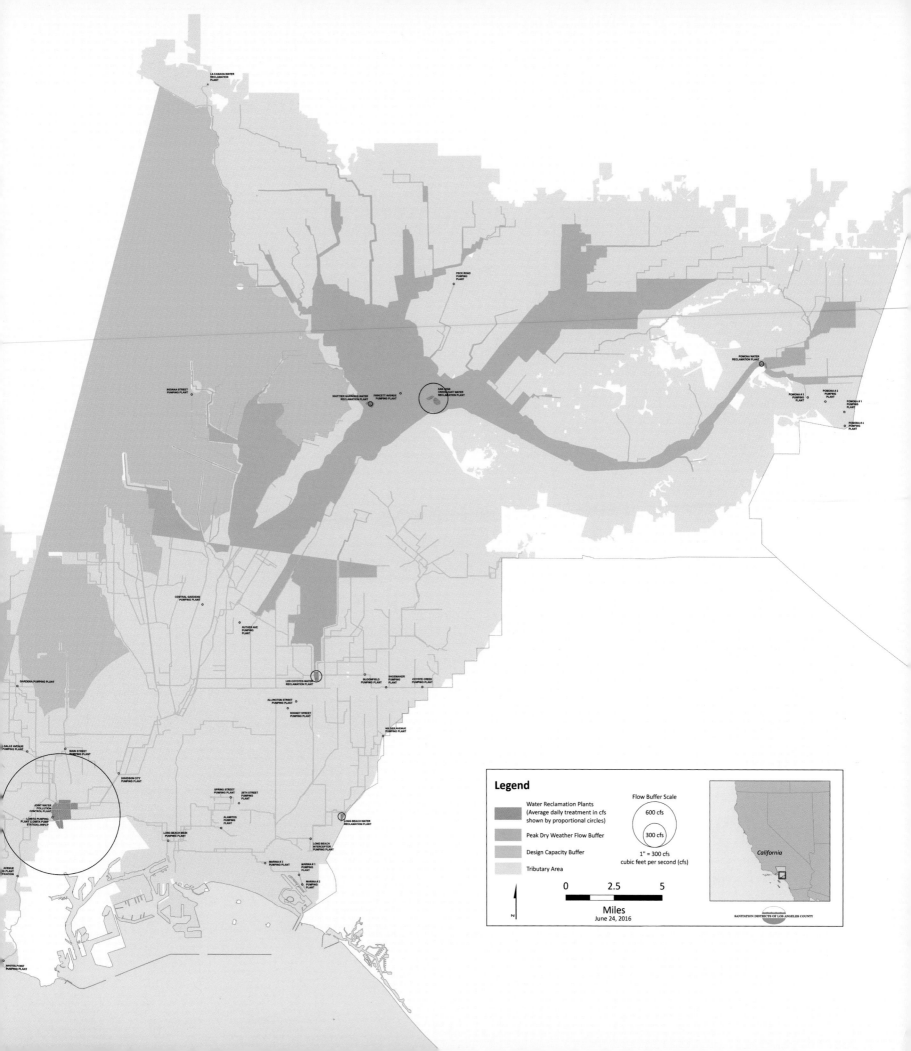

Legend

Water Reclamation Plants
(Average daily treatment in cfs
shown by proportional circles)

Peak Dry Weather Flow Buffer

Design Capacity Buffer

Tributary Area

Flow Buffer Scale

600 cfs

300 cfs

1" = 300 cfs
cubic feet per second (cfs)

California

0   2.5   5
Miles
June 24, 2016

SANITATION DISTRICTS OF LOS ANGELES COUNTY

INDEX BY ORGANIZATION

Agence française de la biodiversit (The French Agency for Biodiversity), Parc naturel marin d'Iroise (Iroise Marine Natural Park) – 36

Abu Dhabi Water and Electricity Authority (ADWEA) – 142

Applied Geographics, Inc. (AppGeo) – 136

Asia Air Survey Co., Ltd. – 20

Austin Community College – 4

Beijing GISUNI Information Technology Co., Ltd. – 146

Blue Raster, LLC – 106

Brigham Young University (BYU) – 34

Centers for Disease Control and Prevention (CDC) – 52

Center for International Earth Science Information Network (CIESIN) Columbia University – 74

City of Bellingham – 26, 160

City of El Segundo – 182

City of Los Angeles Bureau of Sanitation – 138

City of Mesa – 188

City of Oxnard – 82

City of Scottsdale – 140

City of Seattle – 180

City of West Jordan – 72

City of West Linn – 126

CobbFendley – 128

Coleman Group, Inc. – 100

County of Maui – 84

Electricity Authority of Cyprus–Distribution System Operator – 176

Environment and Climate Change Canada – 30

Federal Office of Topography (swisstopo) – 12

General Directorate of Highways – 170

GeoBC – 64

Geofutures, Ltd. – 102

GeoTech Center – 8

GM Johnson & Associates, Ltd. – 16, 152

Golder Associates, Inc. – 116

Good Shepherd Engineering (GSE), Palestine Mapping Center (PalMap) – 162

Greater New Haven Water Pollution Control Authority (GNHWPCA) – 184

HDR, Inc. – 54

Institut plánování a rozvoje hl. m. Prahy (Prague Institute of Planning and Development) – 148

InterDev – 80

Jacksonville Transportation Authority (JTA) – 40, 70

Japan Aerospace Exploration Agency (JAXA) – 120

Kansas Department of Transportation (KDOT) – 168

Kansas Geological Survey – 10

KAYA Associates – 104

Kokusai Kogyo Co., Ltd. – 6

Las Vegas Metropolitan Police Department – 56

Les réseaux COVAGE (COVAGE Networks) – 150

Los Angeles County Department of Mental Health – 92

Los Angeles County Office of the Assessor – 76

Long Island University – 14

Michael Baker International – 58, 60

Mid-Ohio Regional Planning Commission – 154

Ministry of Natural Gas Development – 122

National Land Service under the Ministry of Agriculture of the Republic of Lithuania – 86

National Oceanic and Atmospheric Administration (NOAA) Office of Coast Survey – 114, 132

New Jersey Department of Environmental Protection (NJDEP) – 124

North Carolina State Center for Health Statistics – 90

Planning and Development Services of Kenton County (PDS), LINK-GIS – 28

Pražská plynárenská distribuce (Prague Gas Distribution) – 178

Property & Liability Resource Bureau (PLRB) – 68

Sacramento County – 62

Sanitation Districts of Los Angeles County – 190

Science Office, Loudoun County Public Schools – 44, 48

San Francisco International Airport (SFO) GIS – 174

Sound Transit – 144

Southern California Association of Governments (SCAG) – 22, 94, 164

St. Johns County – 78

St. Johns County Utilities – 186

Texas A&M University – 118

Texas Workforce Commission – 98

The Nature Conservancy (TNC) – 18

The Times of London – 88

The Trust for Public Land – 32, 96, 130

University of California, San Diego, California Sea Grant Extension – 50

University of Maryland – 42

University of Minnesota Twin Cities – 38

University of Minnesota Polar Geospatial Center – 134

US Department of Agriculture Foreign Agricultural Service (USDA/FAS) – 110

US Department of Agriculture (USDA) Forest Service – 66, 112, 158

US Department of Agriculture National Agricultural Statistics Service (USDA/NASS) – 108

US Department of Agriculture (USDA) Forest Service, Eldorado National Forest – 156

Vermont Agency of Transportation (VTrans) – 172

Yale University – 24

81 West Cartography, LLC – 166